AF621583

MEASURING JUSTICE

Measuring Justice explores the ways in which South African court and managerial prosecutors deal with the quantification of social phenomena – such as justice, professional work or accountability – and address the radical simplifications of their inherent complexities, misrepresentations and editing as a consequence. While various studies show the concern of professionals about the damaging effects these quantitative forms of accountability have on the creativity, freedom and collaborative nature of expert systems, Mugler shows that the reactions and attitudes of these legal professionals differ substantially. Through careful scrutiny of the everyday work of prosecutors and how they reflect on the relationship between accountability, quantification and law, this book argues that actors who work daily with quantitative accountability measures develop a numerical reflexivity about the process.

JOHANNA MUGLER joined the Department for Social Anthropology at the University of Bern, Switzerland, as a Lecturer and Researcher in 2012. She holds a PhD in Social Anthropology from the Martin Luther University Halle-Wittenberg and was a PhD Candidate at the Max Planck Institute for Social Anthropology in Halle/Saale. Her primary research goals are directed at understanding how people and institutions are accomplishing social phenomena like accountability, justice, equality and redistribution. In her postdoctoral research 'Sharing Global Corporate Profits' she explores the fiscal accountabilities of global taxpayers and the negotiation and making of international tax norms within the 'G20 OECD Base Erosion and Profit Shifting' initiative.

CAMBRIDGE STUDIES IN LAW AND SOCIETY

Founded in 1997, Cambridge Studies in Law and Society is a hub for leading scholarship in socio-legal studies. Located at the intersection of law, the humanities, and the social sciences, it publishes empirically innovative and theoretically sophisticated work on law's manifestations in everyday life: from discourses to practices, and from institutions to cultures. The series editors have longstanding expertise in the interdisciplinary study of law, and welcome contributions that place legal phenomena in national, comparative, or international perspectives. Series authors come from a range of disciplines, including anthropology, history, law, literature, political science and sociology.

Series Editors

Mark Fathi Massoud, *University of California, Santa Cruz*

Jens Meierhenrich, *London School of Economics and Political Science*

Rachel E. Stern, *University of California, Berkeley*

A list of books in the series can be found at the back of this book.

MEASURING JUSTICE

Quantitative Accountability and the National Prosecuting Authority in South Africa

Johanna Mugler

Universität Bern

CAMBRIDGE
UNIVERSITY PRESS

CAMBRIDGE
UNIVERSITY PRESS

Shaftesbury Road, Cambridge CB2 8EA, United Kingdom

One Liberty Plaza, 20th Floor, New York, NY 10006, USA

477 Williamstown Road, Port Melbourne, VIC 3207, Australia

314–321, 3rd Floor, Plot 3, Splendor Forum, Jasola District Centre, New Delhi – 110025, India

103 Penang Road, #05–06/07, Visioncrest Commercial, Singapore 238467

Cambridge University Press is part of Cambridge University Press & Assessment, a department of the University of Cambridge.

We share the University's mission to contribute to society through the pursuit of education, learning and research at the highest international levels of excellence.

www.cambridge.org
Information on this title: www.cambridge.org/9781108465885

DOI: 10.1017/9781108566254

© Johanna Mugler 2019

This publication is in copyright. Subject to statutory exception and to the provisions of relevant collective licensing agreements, no reproduction of any part may take place without the written permission of Cambridge University Press & Assessment.

First published 2019
First paperback edition 2026

A catalogue record for this publication is available from the British Library

Library of Congress Cataloging-in-Publication data
Names: Mugler, Johanna, 1979– author.
Title: Measuring justice : quantitative accountability and the National Prosecuting Authority in South Africa / Johanna Mugler, Universitat Bern.
Description: Cambridge, United Kingdom ; New York, NY, USA : Cambridge University Press, 2018. | Series: Cambridge studies in law and society | Based on author's doctoral thesis, Martin-Luther-University Halle-Wittenberg, 2015 issued under title: By their own account : an ethnography of (quantitative) accountability and the National Prosecuting Authority in South Africa. | Includes bibliographical references.
Identifiers: LCCN 2018042764 | ISBN 9781108475112
Subjects: LCSH: National Prosecuting Authority of South Africa. | Public prosecutors – South Africa. | Prosecution – South Africa – Statistics.
Classification: LCC KTL1615 .M84 2018 | DDC 345.68/05042–dc23
LC record available at https://lccn.loc.gov/2018042764

ISBN 978-1-108-47511-2 Hardback
ISBN 978-1-108-46588-5 Paperback

Cambridge University Press & Assessment has no responsibility for the persistence or accuracy of URLs for external or third-party internet websites referred to in this publication and does not guarantee that any content on such websites is, or will remain, accurate or appropriate.

To Kenneth, Philippa and Edgar

CONTENTS

Acknowledgements *page* viii
List of Abbreviations xii
Legislation – Statutes xiii

Introduction 1

I From Apartheid Administrators to Lawyers of the People: A History of Accountability Inside the South African Prosecution Authority (1948–2018) 21

II Ethnographic Research in a Multi-Local Organisation: Access, Challenges and Methods 50

III 'Stats Talk' and Alternative Expressions of Accountability: NPA Lower Court Prosecutors at Work 73

IV No Fear of Numbers: Reactivity and the Political Economy of NPA Performance Measurement 92

V At the Top of the NPA: Managing with Numbers and Numerical Reflexivity 117

VI Lies, Damned Lies and Statistics: Making Sense of Misleading or Imperfect NPA Conviction Rates 140

Concluding Remarks 165

Bibliography 174
Index 192

ACKNOWLEDGEMENTS

Quantitative accountability might be considered an utterly dry topic for anthropological research. I have nevertheless derived much pleasure from researching and writing this book. This has not only to do with the fact that the concept of accountability is central to our understanding of how humans, institutions and organisations work and relate to each other, but also to do with a number of people who made my work possible. It is these individuals who I would like to mention and thank.

How the South African criminal justice systems work was a question which first galvanized during my time at the University of Cape Town and my previous research on private crime prevention and security strategies of ordinary people in South Africa. Witnessing how victims of crimes had to fight for justice or how they entirely gave up on justice because they felt the system was a 'complete failure' was deeply disturbing. It was these people's experiences, stories and perceptions, which they shared so openly and graciously with me between 2003 and 2005, that lead me to explore the working worlds of South African prosecutors. Thank you!

Soon after I put my first foot into a South African court in 2007, assisted by a South African policeman who took me under his wing and helped me to navigate the formal and informal rules of courts, I met 'my' first prosecutor who was so kind to trust me and to introduce me to her boss: a very respected, well connected and experienced senior prosecutor. Her energy levels, dedication, people skills, fast mind and busy schedule never failed to amaze me. I learned so much from her in the initial phase of my research where she permitted me to sit in her office, follow her around and speed around the highways of the greater city. She graciously introduced me to a number of important and indispensable contacts.

I owe an incredible thanks to her and all the prosecutors, control prosecutors, senior public prosecutors, chief prosecutors, deputy directors of public prosecutions, directors of public prosecution and other justice role players who so generously shared their experiences and views with me and allowed me to understand central aspects of their working lives, values and norms. This despite their busy working schedules, stressful family lives and their initial distrust of this strange German anthropologist knocking at their doors asking endless questions. This book would not have been made possible without all of you!

I want to especially thank one control prosecutor, whose patience with me and my work was beyond words throughout the entire phase of my research. His hope and passion for justice and a more equal and non-racial South Africa, despite the slow pace of change, was extremely inspiring. My wise friend, I trust he will know who he is when he reads this.

My exceptional supervisors were also crucial in conducting this research and completing this book. I am indebted to their intellectual and personal generosity and their professional support for me. Richard Rottenburg's strength of mind, incredible witty spirit and his capacity to listen and abstract and to be human were a constant source of inspiration and insight for me. I also thank him together with the participants of his LOST colloquium for all the stimulating debates we enjoyed around the topics of Law, Organization and Science and Technology. I also benefited from the input of various guests to the LOST colloquium. I want to name here especially Ellen Hertz who commented on my work shortly after I came back from the field and Vinh-Kim Nguyen whose academic and strategic life advice was much welcomed, being then new to academia.

I am also deeply indebted to my second supervisor Keebet von Benda-Beckmann. I profited enormously from her famous 'writing-up seminars' at the Max Planck Institute for Social Anthropology in Halle. I cherished them because they were 'Hart to Hart' and her sharp eye for detail taught me to be more specific and assisted me tremendously in pinning down and focusing my thoughts. I also want to specially thank her and her husband, the late Franz von Benda-Beckmann, who to our great sorrow passed away unexpectedly in 2013, for their personal and intellectual commitment to the International Max Planck Research School on Retaliation, Mediation and Punishment (IMPRS-REMEP), of which I had the privilege to be a member. Without Keebet's and Franz's sense of justice it would have not been the special and stimulating work environment it was.

Thanks a lot also to the REMEP coordinators Carolin Hillemanns and especially Bertram Turner who made it possible that an extraordinary group of twenty-five international doctoral students based at four Max Planck institutes scattered throughout Germany developed lasting friendship and fruitful discussions across the disciplines of International Law, Criminal Law, Legal History and Social Anthropology. Thank you Csaba Györy, Ab Drent, Severin Lenart, Friederike Stahlmann, Ghefari Elsayed, Lejla Vujinović, Shakira Bedoya Sánchez and Carolijn Terwindt for making our collective endeavour such productive fun.

I am especially grateful to the administrative staff of the Max Planck Institute for Social Anthropology in Halle where I was based for four years and who very generously financed my research. Bettina Mann and Kathrin

Niehaus and their respective teams have a seemingly endless capacity to make our work possible. This form of administrative support was invaluable!

I also want to thank John Comaroff. During several breakfasts at his favourite cafe in Cape Town he would provide me with precise intellectual, emotional and pragmatic support which was invaluable with challenging moments in the field. For instance, he was a great help when I was recovering from a physical attack and robbery and was forced to accept that being 'streetwise' is not enough to avoid becoming a victim of crime in South Africa and being at the wrong place at the wrong time is unavoidable; and at times when I had to accommodate myself to the slow pace of justice and the meaning and purpose of NPA performance statistics.

I also want to thank all the participants of the Workshop 'A World of Indicators. Knowledge Technologies of Regulation, Domination, Experimentation and Critique in an Interconnected Worlds' which I organised together with Sung-Joon Park at the Max Planck Institute for Social Anthropology in Halle in 2011. I felt extremely privileged and encouraged to have had the chance to work with such highly distinguished 'quantification' scholars such as Wendy Espeland, Theodore Porter and Sally Engle Merry during the workshop. Additionally, exchanges with financial and economic scholars like Barbara Grimpe, William Davies and Andrew Farlow contributed a lot to bringing my thinking forward.

Sally Engle Merry's input into my work during the workshop, but also during the course of the volume we edited together with Sung-Joon Park and Richard Rottenburg, was priceless. The final arguments benefited tremendously from her systematic way of giving feedback and her capacity to demand clearness, preciseness, but also a larger vision. Her openness to share some of her experiences with academia and motherhood with me were also extremely useful when I was getting used to the fact that one loses large parts of control over one's life when having children.

I am extremely thankful for the stimulating environment at the Institute for Anthropology at the University of Bern in Switzerland where a considerable portion of this book has been written. I want to thank especially Julia Eckert, for providing the financial, intellectual and emotional support for making the completion of this book possible. Her incredibly fast decision-making skills, deep and true academic spirit – her 'Freigeist' – and the frankness and intimacy of her colloquium never stopped to surprise and lift me. The same applies to her thoughtful guidance on how to successfully combine a happy family life with the demands of academia. I and the book could not have had a better mentor.

At Cambridge University Press I thank Finola O'Sullivan and Tom Randall and their assistants and reviewers for their incredibly thoughtful and numerous supports. Thank you for your confidence in the book and assisting me to improve it.

I am also very fortunate to have as colleagues and friends Larissa Vetters, Olaf Zenker, Jan Schenk, Songi Park, Luisa Piart, Anna-Lena Wolf, Laura Affolter, Sibylle Lustenberger, David Loher and Angela Lindt, and I thank them each for their invaluable and continuous contributions to my work. I want to especially thank my friends Emma Murray, Agnieszka Pasieka and Andrew Porter for their extraordinary help and support with the last version of the manuscript.

I also want to thank the Busse-Richters, de la Harpes, Deriazes, Gauger-Sörgels, Graemers, Hales, Beatrice Hesse, the Higgo-Browns, Vusi Malema, the Meissner-Dietrichs, Mittermeyer-Eberts, Murray-Baerts, Pasieka-Petrucellis, Porters, Robsons, Schwabes, Spencer-Hurfords, Sutter-Röhls, Watzingers, Sapho Yengana and the Zenkers. Laughing and talking to you was with no doubt fundamental for getting me through this project. You never fail to hearten me!

I owe my family an enormous debt of gratitude. I wish to thank my parents, Elisabeth and Jens-Jörg Mugler, who have always encouraged me to pursue my curiosity despite being strangers to the discipline and at home in much more established and conventional professions. Without their generosity, support and unconditional love I would not have had the strength to cope with the constant feeling of out-of-placeness that comes with being an Anthropologist. I also thank my father for showing me what it means to work hard and my mother for what it means to be critical. I am very grateful to my brother, Maximilian Mugler, who always makes this world through his presence as an older brother a better place for me.

Lastly, I feel deep gratitude to my husband Kenneth Brown for his countless contributions to this book. Right from the beginning of this project to its end he has been an enormous pillar of strength for me. He is my hardest critic but his loving faith in me never fails to make the difference. His legal expertise, trained eye for detail, adversarial spirit and experience as an Advocate of the Cape Bar was invaluable for the completion of this book as well as his fearless dedication to fatherhood. Philippa and Edgar, our daughter and son born in the middle of my writing this book, have enriched our lives beyond words. While they turned, with their joy of and zest for life but also their dependence and sensitivity, everything we knew upside down, they gave me the necessary creativity, energy and will to complete this project. So I dedicate it to you, Kenneth, Philippa and Eddie.

ABBREVIATIONS

(ADRM) Alternative Dispute Resolution Mechanism
(ANC) African National Congress
(Assault GBH) Assault with Intent to Cause Grievous Bodily Harm
(CBD) Central Business District
(CPP) Chief Public Prosecutor
(CC) Constitutional Court
(DA) Democratic Alliance
(DDPP) Deputy Director of Public Prosecution
(DOJCD) Department of Justice and Constitutional Development
(DPP) Director of Public Prosecution
(EFF) Economic Freedom Fighters
(NDPP) National Director of Public Prosecution
(NPA) National Prosecuting Authority
(PFMA) Public Finance Management Act
(SPP) Senior Public Prosecutor
(SAPS) South African Police Service
(SALC) South African Law Commission

LEGISLATION – STATUTES

- Certification of the Constitution of the Republic of South Africa, 1996
- Constitution of the Republic of South Africa, 1996 (Act 108 of 1996)
- Criminal Procedure Act, 1977 (Act 51 of 1997)
- Employment Equity Act, 1998 (Act 55 of 1998)
- General Law Amendment Act, 1961 (Act 39 of 1961)
- General Law Amendment Act, 1963 (Act 37 of 1963)
- Group Areas Act, 1950 (Act 41 of 1950)
- Immorality Amendment Act, 1950 (Act 21 of 1950)
- National Prosecuting Authority Act, 1998 (Act 32 of 1998)
- Population Registration Act, 1950 (Act 30 of 1950)
- Prevention and Combating of Corruption Activity Act, 2004 (Act 12 of 2004)
- Prevention of Organised Crime Act, 1998 (Act 121 of 1998)
- Public Finance Management Act, 1999 (Act 1 of 1999)
- Terrorism Act, 1962 (Act 83 of 1962)

INTRODUCTION

This is a book about accountability. More specifically, it is about quantitative accountability and the National Prosecuting Authority (NPA) in South Africa. I am interested in how prosecutors, who have the power to call others to account for wrongdoing, are themselves held accountable. Central to this study is the role played by recently introduced performance measurement systems in the way prosecutors are held accountable. I explore how these measurement systems shape and influence South African prosecutors' understanding of accountability and their prosecutorial practices. I ask whether there are significant implications for legal work, as the language of 'performance statistics', 'indicators', 'targets', 'rates' and 'rankings' is becoming common parlance within the judicial system.

While numerical representations are gaining increasing importance for the demonstration of accountability in many government and non-government settings in the twenty-first century, the effects and consequences of this for our social, institutional and political life are relatively opaque. We know little about what numbers do in and to organisations, or what professionals do with them at work and whether and how they effect operations, decisions, the allocation of resources and their accountability. Numbers provide people with universalised and standardised language, but we know that this does not translate into the purpose and effect of numbers being the same in different settings.

This ethnography follows a small number of court and managerial prosecutors through their everyday work life in the NPA. By ethnographically exploring the role that numbers play in their prosecutorial (account giving) practice and how these prosecutors reflect on the relationship between accountability, quantification and law, I am able to contribute to a more nuanced and textured social scientific understanding of the effect and impact of the increasing use of quantified knowledge in many professional and organisational settings worldwide.

ACCOUNTABILITY AND QUANTIFICATION

Accountability is a watchword firmly established in contemporary politics, policies and the organisational life of many countries worldwide (Munro and Mouritsen 1996; Power 1997; UN 2007; Espeland and Vannebo 2007; Boström and Garsten 2008; Espeland and Sauder 2016). Today, there are frequent calls for greater and more expansive forms of accountability, rarely for less. In its simplest sense, accountability denotes when people, who have been entrusted with power and money, are required to explain and justify their decision, or, in other words, when their resource allocation and their professional and ethical reasoning are scrutinised. However, accountability is rarely that simple and most scholars highlight the concept's obscurity, vagueness and its 'chameleon'-like character (Sinclair 1995: 219). Many different and sometimes conflicting ideas exist, both in popular and scholarly use: When, where, to whom, for what, on what basis and with what consequences someone is accountable can look very different, depending on the involved actors' understandings of the concept (Koppell 2005).

Accountability scholars often point out that expectations of how accountability should be demonstrated are never static (Dowdle 2006) and heated debates around the 'correct' way to ensure that public officials work in the best interests of the public and remain trustworthy are nothing new (von Dornum 1997). Over the last ten to fifteen years, however, various scholars have noted that the rapid increase of *quantitative* forms of accountability in many governmental settings worldwide are radically shifting these debates (Power 1997; 2000; Shore & Wright 1999; Strathern 2000a; 2000b). When being accountable becomes more and more synonymous with using quantitative measures and creating supposedly 'verifiable' accounts, then, they argue, our understanding of how accountability can be defined and rendered becomes narrower. People who are living in an 'audit society' (Power 1997) surrounded by an emerging global 'audit culture' (Strathern 2000a) will be less accepting and convinced by other forms of accountability. It becomes difficult for institutions to practise accountability differently, that is, without performance indicators, rankings, benchmarking and/or audits and with more deliberative and qualitative forms of account-giving (Rottenburg 2000; Espeland and Vannebo 2007: 40).

Although quantitative forms of accountability are in high demand because they appear to have the capacity to simplify complex social phenomena and make these more accessible to outsiders and lay people, critics point out that the increased transparency achieved through this 'information reductionism' is illusory and counterproductive (Tsoukas 1997: 829). Illusory, because when complex phenomena such as 'justice', 'education' or 'health' are reduced to a few 'key' indicators that are selected to represent the issue under scrutiny, equally important dimensions of these phenomena, which are more difficult to quantify but still relied upon in order for the expert system to function, are lost in the quantification process. Included in the latter are dimensions such as tacit and experiential knowledge (Strathern 2000b: 313–314; Power 2004: 774–778). The risk of illusion is especially high when the indicators become so pervasive and influential that they become synonymous with the measured phenomenon itself. In other words, critics warn that indicators do not only indicate some aspect of reality, but are constitutive of this reality: They influence what people take to be real, what they pay attention to and how they (re-)act.

It is argued that this reactivity can be counterproductive because people whose work is evaluated and monitored using performance measurement systems soon change their behaviour, developing a 'compliance' or 'audit mentality', or 'game the numbers' in order to promote their chances of receiving positive reviews – without necessarily improving the conduct the indicators and rankings are designed to measure (Power 1997: 16; Strathern 2000a: 282–287). Thus, they begin to manage the performance measurement systems instead of managing the underlying problems these systems were set up to deal with. Michael Power therefore refers to many of these audit practices as empty 'rituals of verification' (1997). He argues that '[h]ow we are perceived, as organisations and individuals, rather than what we do, has come to be a major preoccupation in late modern societies', warning of the 'potential pathology of societies which invest more in account-giving than doing' (Power 2008: XVII).

Another more distinctive form of reactivity, which various scholars criticise, is performance measurement systems' capacity to *discipline*. For example, Chris Shore and Susan Wright (1999; see also 2011) argue that the increasing demand for numerical representations and quantified accountability reconfigures actor's understanding of what it means to be a professional. They describe quantitative forms of evaluation, monitoring and accountability as 'neoliberal' 'disciplinary mechanisms' (Shore & Wright 1999: 557). The independent professional self is 'disciplined' into an 'auditable', 'competitive' self, a 'docile auditable body' (Shore & Wright 1999: 563; 569), owing to the fact that performance measurement can not only be used to describe professionals' behaviour, but also to exert control, judge or even punish an actor. Constant 'surveillance' makes professionals fearful and stressed and does not provide strong incentives for professionals to think independently and creatively about how to provide their clients with the most suitable service. The fear of falling in rank and status makes actors quickly internalise the measures so that they become part of their professional self-understanding and discipline becomes self-imposed (Shore & Wright 1999: 568). Consequently, it becomes normal for professionals to refer to their work in terms of quantity rather than quality, to choose 'process over substance' (Power 1997: 16) and to be more concerned about 'doing things in the right way than doing things right' (Lindwert 2008: 156).

These points of concern and criticism are frequently repeated and restated when anthropologists and other social scientists talk and write about the consequences of numerical representations and quantitative forms of accountability.[1] While authors like Wendy Espeland and Michael Sauder (2006; 2007; 2016) or Sally Engle Merry (2011; 2016) illustrate in their exemplary work the harmful and detrimental effects of public law school rankings, or globally circulating human rights indicators on many people's lives, a number of quantification scholars, including the last mentioned authors, point out that one needs to be cautious about simply assuming that 'numbers' have the same obvious effects in every organisational setting (Porter 1995; Lampland 2010; Timmermans and Epstein 2010; Davis et al. 2012; Rottenburg et al. 2015). My ethnographic study of how performance measurement systems shape South African prosecutors' understandings of accountability and their prosecutorial practices is an attempt to produce nuanced anthropological knowledge about how a specific set of quantitative measures operates in a distinct social domain.

Mapping multiple ways of understanding the relationship between accountability and quantification in the NPA allows me to problematise the widespread idea that quantitative forms of accountability always and inevitably subsume other more qualitative forms of account giving. I will be arguing in this book that the independent professional self is, at least in this setting, not so easily turned into an 'auditable, competitive' self, who has to sacrifice 'quality' for 'quantity' and/or 'process' for 'substance'.

[1] See Desrosières (2015), for a very insightful and concise summary of two different 'emerging critique[s] of statistics' and the associated 'crisis of confidence' in numerical representations since the 1990s.

ANTHROPOLOGY OF THE STATE MEETS SOCIAL STUDIES OF NUMBERS

My research has been inspired and built on a number of social anthropological and other neighbouring social scientific bodies of work, which laid the groundwork for me to turn quantitative accountability into an anthropological object of study in itself. Certain anthropological colleagues of mine never failed to remind me while I was writing this book that 'quantitative accountability' is not a conventional research topic to be undertaken within the discipline of anthropology. While this is to some extent true, much of the work I am building on comes from studies with a strong interdisciplinary approach. It is important to mention that the starting point for my research is deeply grounded in the anthropology of the state and more specifically in ethnographies of public services. While these studies have not led directly to the topic of this ethnography, they have indeed prepared the ground for my receptivity to it. In order to give an overview of where I am coming from, where I differ and where I am heading to in this book, I would like to mention the specific anthropological and non-anthropological authors and texts which influenced me, highlighting their respective research questions and the relevance to my work.

My interest in the working world of prosecutors was initially inspired by anthropologists who call for the empirical, anthropological and ethnographic study of African state apparatuses (Migdal and Schlichte 2005; Schlichte 2005; Blundo et al. 2006; Bierschenk 2010). For example, Thomas Bierschenk and Oliver de Sardan (2014: 39) emphasise that the working state and its public services have been extensively studied in the Global North but '[e]mpirical studies about administrations, state professions, service delivery, public policy and implementation, and street level bureaucrats are spectacularly lacking for Africa' and the Global South. Furthermore, they level the criticism that if African states 'were studied empirically, more often than not it was from a perspective of deficiency: the focus was on what African bureaucracies were not, as compared with an idealised notion of Western bureaucracy' (Bierschenk & de Sardan 2014: 42–43). They add that the empirical insights from political and administrative sciences and sociology about the working of public services in the North are often ignored in these studies (Bierschenk & de Sardan 2014: 54). As a result of this misinformed analytical lens, but also due to the lack of empirical knowledge,

African states are often described as 'weak', 'failed', 'underdeveloped', 'neo-patrimonial', 'predatory' and so on.

To adopt a less normative, less stereotypical, less exoticising point of view of these states and to empirically explore what these 'failed' or 'weak' state apparatuses actually do when they are working is, according to Bierschenk and de Sardan, a more productive approach. They suggest that an ethnography of African public services should start with the following basic questions (Bierschenk & de Sardan 2014): what are the everyday professional practices of African public bureaucrats? What does their working day look like? What are the conditions of their work? How do they perceive their work and their working environment? What is the emic perspective of these professionals?

Another strand of anthropological state research which shaped my own interest (although more indirectly) in the running of public institutions, attempts to understand the state from 'the margins of the state' (Das and Poole 2004: 8; see also: Buur 2003; Roitman 2005; Hornberger 2009). This body of work is characterised by ethnographies of disciplinary, regulatory and enforcement practices in various states of the Global South. These studies show how the guarantees and protection of state law are uncertain, unjust and unpredictable in these settings; how particularly marginalised people are exposed to the arbitrary power of state officials and regulatory authorities, who, because they act as representatives of the state, can move easily between legal and extra-legal forms of punishment and enforcement; and how in these margins – which these scholars often refer to as 'emergency zones' and, following Agamben, 'state of exceptions' – people struggle to survive, obtain their notions of justice and hold the state accountable.

My research, although much closer in methodology and theoretical background to the 'states at work' anthropologists, is inspired by these ethnographic accounts of unaccountable, unpredictable and arbitrary state power which show that people fear the state, but at the same time invest hope and desire for honest governance and redistributive justice in the state (Das and Poole 2004: 24). It motivated me to bring the idea of accountability to the forefront and centre of my study and to ask what accountability actually means in practice in post-apartheid South Africa. Until recently, only a very small proportion of the population had the power, the rights and the social capital to hold the state accountable in South Africa. Moreover, under the infrastructure of Apartheid, state officials had previously moved comfortably between the legal and illegal use of violence, continuously abusing their state power without sanction (Shaw 2002; Truth and Reconciliation Commission 2003; Davis and le Roux 2009).

Many prosecutors played a central role in the daily administration of Apartheid's repressive, racist and exploitative social order. Close to fifteen million people were prosecuted for pass laws and other influx control offences alone between 1948 and 1981 (Klug 1988: 201).[2] The White minority government furthermore made extensive use of political trials to crush the country's resistance and dissent movements and to publicly demonise their leaders as terrorists (Abel 1995; Lobban 1996). It was common during this period that prosecutors ignored the general procedural safeguards built into the South African system of criminal procedure on a daily basis. Prosecutors covered up the illegal and atrocious practices of the police, or worse, relied on them to obtain convictions (Davis and le Roux 2009). To be accountable to *all* South Africans only became an important and desirable good for the prosecution services after the democratic transition to democracy in 1994 and especially from 1998 when the country's first centralised, National Prosecuting Authority (NPA) was established and came under pressure to legitimise itself in the eyes of those it had, until very recently, suppressed (Schönteich 2001: 30).

While I share an interest with the above-mentioned authors in regulatory authorities in settings where they have never been self-evident, trustworthy and therefore predictable, I differ from this strand of research in that I am focusing on the everyday accountability practices of less visible public servants, but whose accountability lies at the heart of South Africa's criminal justice system. I ask how prosecutors, who obtain key positions within the running of a modern state, reflect on their and their organisations' accountability? What does it mean to them to be accountable and to be held accountable? How do they account and how are they held accountable?

My interest in quantitative accountability and the South African prosecuting authority is secondly shaped by area specialists, namely a number of anthropologists, criminologists and sociologists who explored the organisational transformation of the South African

[2] 'Pass laws' is a commonly used term in the legal and sociological literature about South Africa. The pass laws system entails that all non-White South Africans had to carry a passport at all times. 'It was one of the key instruments of Apartheid and of the economic exploitation of African workers' as Klug points out (1989: 201).

Police Service (SAPS) after 1994 (Marks 2000; 2004; Shaw 2002; Buur 2003; Hornberger 2009; Jensen 2009). They ask whether and how the police have been able to transform themselves from a previously unaccountable state apparatus into an accountable one. Since the transition to democracy, the police have had to change their modus operandi, from their propensity to use violence whenever non-violent policing techniques failed to achieve the desired result, to working within the law and adhering to the human rights-oriented values enshrined in the country's new constitution. However, these authors have demonstrated that despite new legislation and new training programmes attempting to transform the police, there is ample evidence of continued prevalence of serious police misconduct, including the excessive use of deadly force (see also Bruce 2005; Marks and Shearing 2005). Monique Marks (2004) has shown that the police's organisational culture – that means policemen's and -women's deeply held assumptions, attitudes and values – had not transformed in significant ways since 1994 and that there were clear signs of resistance to the new organisational human rights and community orientated demands.

Lars Buur (2003) and Steffen Jensen (2009) point out that in order to understand police violence and the difficulties the South African police encounter in transforming themselves, one has to study the context in which they are operating. They explain that in marginalised parts of South Africa, namely urban townships, not only is violence so prevalent, it is also acts as an important resource that residents draw on in order to restore some form of social and moral order and to prevent future crime. For this reason, many people do not necessarily support the proposed changes for the South African police service: While residents complain about police brutality and admire and desire a representative, accountable and human rights-oriented policing body, when it comes to their immediate problems with the ongoing disorder in their lives, they often rely on violence to reestablish order and to secure their own survival. To some extent, residents expect the police to do the same.

Along with the above-mentioned area specialists, I share an interest in South African criminal justice institutions and the role 'law', specific organization 'ideals' and 'models' play in their transformation processes. My research adds new and fruitful directions to this field, as I am focusing firstly on the understudied and under-theorised South African National Prosecuting Authority. Secondly, perhaps more importantly, I am looking at how a piece of public administrative law, namely the Public Finance Management Act, a much less researched field of law, affects the accountability practices and understanding of a South African criminal justice institution. So, in other words, I am extending the study of criminal justice employees' account-giving stories and practices to the study of their organisation's accounts (for an exception see Leggett 2003; Faull 2010).[3] I argue that this is important because many of the anthropological studies mentioned above have the tendency to treat performance measurement systems as a threat to other seemingly more valued, tangible and human forms of accountability (e.g. human rights law). Performance measurement is often viewed as something technical and beyond the reach of social order, and therefore irrelevant to social scientists who are interested in the accountability of criminal justice actors.[4]

In this work, I aim to bring the anthropological study of public bureaucracies and the state closer into contact with a wide range of scholars that share a common interest in the social studies of numbers. The latter presents an extensive field of study. For example, in the history of science and in science and technology studies, the study of numerical representations and the increasing significance, power, prestige and ubiquity of quantified knowledge has for some time been a central theme (Porter 1986; 1995; Latour 1987; Hacking 1990; Daston 1995). I do not intend to give a summary of this vast field of scholarly work as this is beyond the scope of this book, but for anthropological readers who are less familiar with this field, I would like to mention the specific texts and authors that have significantly shaped my interest in (and receptivity to) quantitative forms of accountability in the NPA.

Firstly, I would like to highlight the book *Trust in Numbers* (1995) written by the historian Theodore Porter. *Trust in Numbers* was

[3] Jean Comaroff and John Comaroff (2006) have studied South African crime statistics in their wonderful article 'Figuring Crime: Quantifacts and the Production of the Un/Real', however not from an emic perspective of professionals, but more as commentators and public intellectuals.

[4] Thomas Bierschenk's (2008: 113) study on the Beninese court system does not mention quantitative accountability and performance measurement systems. He interestingly mentions the lack of formal performance monitoring and career planning. He says, 'attempts to introduce modern performance-based human resource management have failed' in Benin. This makes it difficult for criminal justice actors to predict promotions or demotions and creates further incentives to rely on informal ordering mechanisms. See Rottenburg (2002; 2009) and Anders (2008) for anthropological studies, which look at the role of numbers in the way international development agencies operate and ask their grant implementers and receivers to account.

important for my thinking (as for many other authors in the social studies of numbers) because it provided an interesting explanation for a complex question, namely: Why have numbers become so powerful, seminal and ubiquitous over the last two centuries in many parts of today's world? Porter describes numbers as transportable modes of communication, as powerful 'technologies of distance' and 'persuasion'. They have, as he says, the capacity to create and overcome distance. On the one hand, numbers provide people with a shared universalising language, which allows them to communicate despite vast physical, social or political distances. So, in that sense, numerical representations bring people closer together, help to ease communication, coordinate activities and solve problems. On the other hand, numbers also create distance, namely between the producer and the user of the numbers. This is because when numbers get produced, the local, the personal and the particular of a specific setting is erased. The person who makes the numbers becomes less important and invisible, because it is assumed that he follows an explicit set of rules. That means it does not matter who counts and calculates, because the result would be always the same.

According to Porter (1995), numerical representations became particularly important for public decision-making in political contexts where controversial decisions had to be made and defended and other consensus-finding mechanisms failed. Porter argues that an increased quest for impersonal quantitative expertise has to be seen in relation to the emergence of a changed meaning of objectivity over the last two centuries. Previously objectivity was grounded in personal knowledge, expert judgement, professional and elite discretion (often practised behind closed doors), or divine will. Today, a new understanding of objectivity rejects these practices as distrustful and suspicious; they are often viewed as practices which need to be constrained. The new understanding of objectivity is grounded in impersonal quantitative expertise and numerical knowledge whose authority is based on compliance with explicit and standardised rules. Porter refers to this form of objectivity as 'mechanical objectivity' and argues that it replaces trust in persons with trust in numbers.

Moreover, Porter (1995) goes on to emphasise that the demand for mechanical objectivity struck elites and professionals in different settings differently. While all professionals contested and resisted the curtailment of their discretion and independence, some were more successful in protecting it and maintaining the status quo than others. Porter argues that 'weak elites' were forced to rely more on quantitative techniques to defend their positions and decisions whereas powerful professionals' discretion remained intact and legitimate. Thus, they managed to be shielded from such public scrutiny.[5]

Porter's book is so important because while it is obviously attentive to the normative dimensions of numbers as a powerful, sometimes subtle, and sometimes not-so-subtle means of organising modern life, he teaches one to appreciate the distinctiveness of the power of numerical representations. Porter's book inspired me to look at the variation in the use and effects of quantitative techniques today, and, not to assume that they have the same 'bad' or 'good' effects across different settings. The book forced me to question why some professionals and organisational fields are transformed more by quantitative accountability than others. Why can some professionals free themselves and disengage from the power of numbers whereas others struggle? What are the underlying factors that might help to explain differing developments?

While Porter looks to the past to make us understand and rethink the present, quantification scholars who focus on the current production and communication of numbers also shaped my work. Several sociological and STS (science and technology studies)-influenced studies contributed to the important question of 'What actually has to happen so that something can be counted?' They show that certain preconditions have to be in place so that social phenomena can be counted. Firstly, measurement relies on complex classification systems. Categories of similarities need to be established before things can be made commensurable (Espeland and Stevens 1998; Bowker and Star 2000).

Bettina Heintz (2010: 162) explains that in order to compare something, there always needs to be a perceived similarity and at the same time an observed difference. She says every comparison relies on the combination of these two operations, namely 'Gleichheitsunterstellung und Differenzbeobachtung', which have to be analytically differentiated. The criterion of the comparison makes difference despite similarity possible. What follows is that where there is no perceived

[5] For example the US Army Corps of Engineers were under far greater pressure to rely on cost-benefit analysis to defend their far-reaching decisions of where to build bridges, canals and railroads than their English counterparts. High ranked members of the British civil service, all educated in Cambridge or Oxford, who were running the treasury department had the freedom to negotiate the budgets without relying on standardised and formalised knowledge whereas their American politically appointed counterparts were unable to make decisions without basing them on these quantitative techniques (Porter 1995: 194).

similarity, phenomena cannot be compared because they are incommensurable.

For example, during Apartheid where people were classified as White, Black and Coloured on nearly all occasions of public life, they were not compared, as their common personhood was not perceived as somehow more significant than their differences. Today all previously White, Black and Coloured people are classified as human beings, South African citizens, equal before the law etc. Another example, which shows the historical contingency of quantification and commensurability, is the South African Truth and Reconciliation Commission (TRC). The TRC granted amnesty to offenders who could prove that they were committing a politically motivated crime. The classification 'political violence and crime' and 'other violence and crime' was very controversial and contested, because by singling out political motives as a privileged reason for granting amnesty, the TRC somehow suggested that political crimes appear to be different to and disconnected from every other crime and the morality of politics different to and detached from the morality of everyday life (Dixon 2004).

Geoffrey Bowker and Susan Leigh Star (2000) have also shown in their widely read book *Sorting Things Out. Classification and its Consequences* that it is not self-evident whether a phenomenon is perceived as commensurable or otherwise, but that this is the result of social, cultural and political ordering efforts, making any system of classification highly controversial. Further, although classification systems ignore 'inessential' differences, reduce complexities and are highly selective, once accepted, such systems appear natural and incontestable. That is why they are often underestimated phenomena in scholarly research, because they are 'just there' as Star (1999: 43) says as 'lists of numbers and technical specification in the background, sunk in below level of visibility'. The social and political work that has gone into the construction of that kind of infrastructure often is quickly forgotten.

An infrastructure is the second precondition which needs to be in place before social things can be counted, rated and ranked. Various scholars show that while counting can be a simple act, it takes large amounts of financial resources, intellectual skills, trained people and discipline in order to count complex social phenomena on a large scale. As Sally Engle Merry states, 'what gets counted depends on which groups and organisations can afford to count' (2011: 6). That is why quantification work is often done in large, well-funded bureaucracies and why poor countries of the Global South often struggle to generate sophisticated quantified data (Desrosières 1998; Espeland and Stevens 2008: 410–412; Merry 2016).

My research into prosecutors' quantitative account-giving practices touches on the history of the NPA's performance measurement system, but my work does not focus on the recovery of the social and political efforts and negotiations out of which it arose. My focus is rather on the 'doing of numbers', another important topic in the social studies of numbers (Espeland and Stevens 2008: 405). I follow the approach of these studies by asking 'What do numbers do in the NPA?'; 'What gets done with them by prosecutors and managers?'; 'What effects and consequences do they have for prosecutorial work?'; and 'What are prosecutors' attitudes towards them and how do they react to being evaluated and monitored with numerical representations?'. I pay particular attention to authors who study the 'doing of numbers' in the field of law.[6]

Wendy Espeland and Michael Sauder (2007; 2009; 2016) showed how the widely publicised law school ranking that the magazine *U.S. News & World Report* (USN) produces transformed the whole organisational field of higher legal education in the United States. While law school leaders deeply resented the rankings and perceived their USN's methodology as so flawed and meaningless that when they first came out in the 1990s, they doubted that they could be of any real informational value to anyone interested in studying law; they were soon forced to realise that external audiences relied on the rankings to make far-reaching decisions (Espeland and Sauder 2007: 24). They were losing top students and financial resources to other law schools when their own school's rank had dropped. Although many law school deans strongly criticise that USN ranking imposed on them 'universalistic and elite-based criteria' of law school quality (Espeland and Sauder 2007: 33) and that it penalises law schools for having diverging views on how to define it, they felt they could not afford to carry on ignoring the ranking and started to manage the effects they had on their school.[7] Espeland and Sauder show that the rankings

[6] For the medical field, see for example: Abraham 2012; Timmermans and Berg 2003. For the education field see: Kipnis 2008; Shore and Wright 1999; Shore 2008; 2010. For social work see: Lipsky 1980; Evans 2011. For international governance see: Arndt 2008; Arndt and Oman 2006; Davis et al. 2010. For public administration see: Hood 2007; Hood et al. 2008; van de Walle 2008.

[7] Law school 'insiders' strongly criticised USN for not taking into consideration many factors which make up a good law school and which are, according to their experience, important to

changed how resources were being allocated, how admission decisions were taken and thus how discretion was being exercised, and how academics in this field trusted each other since some schools started to improve their rank by manipulating their USN scores with gaming strategies (2007: 11).

Lastly, my deliberations for this book were built on the work of social scientific authors who explore how rationalisation actually occurs in practice. They show that quantification processes are often embedded in larger social projects. People use them to communicate, collaborate and to coordinate work; to settle disputes; to accomplish something larger like improving public health (Geissler, Rottenburg and Zenker 2012), setting up urban water supply systems (Rottenburg 2000; 2002; 2009), modernising agricultural production (Lampland 2010), expanding banking business to unknown territories (Kalthoff 2000) or managing a powerful scientific laboratory (Law 1996). These studies point to the reflexive competences of organisational actors to juggle different, and not always coherent, institutional logics and accountabilities simultaneously. While the depicted actors account with numbers for their work, quantitative accountability is not the only account form they adhere to or worry about when making decisions in order to accomplish. After situating this ethnography within the scholarly body of work upon which this study has been built, I will now provide a short overview of my chapters.

OUTLINE: WHAT IS TO COME?

Chapter 1 begins by looking at the power, independence and wide discretions prosecutors enjoy in order to make clear why the accountability of prosecutors is a topic of much debate in many countries worldwide. The chapter then moves on with a discussion of prosecutorial accountability relationships in South Africa during the twentieth century, with a focus on the Apartheid era (1948–1994). Following this, it traces the major changes that have occurred since South Africa's transition to democracy in 1994. I show that the accountability relationships of the prosecuting authority became more diverse and

students. For example, the racial, gender and economic diversity of the student and faculty body is not counted; neither is the location, the cost of studying, the specific mission of the school (e.g. commitments to religious traditions, public service or to providing 'access' for socially and economically disadvantaged students), nor the availability of funding, the social atmosphere on campus or the teaching quality (Sauder and Espeland 2006: 205; Espeland and Sauder 2007: 17).

complex from 1994 onwards, and that these relationships rely on a wide spectrum of accountability definitions, techniques and instruments. I will discuss the most prominent ones of this change, namely accountability as *separation of power*, as *professionalism*, as *representation* and as *performance measurement*. I then briefly explain the genesis of the NPA's performance measurement system and give an overview about the different performance statistics, indicators, rates and rankings the NPA is working with, including their users and purposes. The aim of this chapter is to raise awareness that the accountability of the NPA is multi-levelled. The introduction of a new form of accountability does not merely encompass or end previous forms. They can often coexist. Lastly, the importance of the discussed concepts differs in time and space. Each form has their own distinct logic and effects and reflects different concerns and constituencies. In others words, accountability can mean different things to different people in different organisational units of the NPA.

Apart from introducing my field (NPA), the field sites (courts, regional and national head offices) and the research participants of this ethnography, namely court prosecutors and managerial prosecutors, Chapter 2 provides an overview of how my research was conducted. I discuss the challenges of gaining access to such a highly restricted, expert dominated and multi-sited organizational setting where space for passive observers is usually not provided, and where actors are able to regulate the outsiders' access to the confidential and classified realities of their working life with ease. I then describe the limits and limitations of using traditional ethnographic working methods at the top of the NPA where opportunities of data collection are not easily repeated, where the 'getting-to-know phase' of a field contact has to occur simultaneously with the 'getting-the-information phase'. While I discuss the challenges of 'studying-up' and 'through' the NPA, I also put forward a more general argument, namely that an ethnographic approach, which aims at the participation of the inner logic and self-conception of social situations is well suited to explore relatively gated organisational settings and the (in-)formal rules that shape how actors think and work, and the norms that underpin practices in such settings.

Chapter 3 forms the beginning of the ethnographic part of this book. The chapter starts with a discussion of what role performance statistics, indicators, rates and targets play in lower court prosecutors' working life in South African courts. I present examples which show that the observed and interviewed prosecutors have internalised the language of performance measurement and that numbers play an important part in the way they account for their work and are held accountable. However, I argue that to accept this as evidence of reconfigured and changed prosecutorial practices, or of prosecutors' reduced or narrow understanding of accountability, is to ignore the strength of other forms of accountability and evaluation that guide these professionals' work in the NPA (professionalism, ethics, responsibility, legal accountability/ liability, constitutional ideals). I will show that performance indicators are not exclusively indicative of prosecutorial performance, and that they were not the only legitimate measure of performance. Furthermore, this chapter highlights that they have not become a proxy for justice in that context.

Chapter 4 asks the question: 'How does it come to be that the NPA prosecutors of my study have a more conciliatory attitude towards performance measurement, quantitative forms of accountability and evaluation in comparison to many other professionals in other organisational fields?' The deep resentment, scepticism and fear of performance indicators and rankings described in other social science studies researching professionals were absent amongst the prosecutors in the South African magistrate courts. I move on to highlight the institutional and historical reasons for these different reactions and expand on two reasons why prosecutors held a more positive stance towards the quantification of their work. Firstly, the fact that allocated resources are not tightly coupled to the NPA's performance measurement system means that prosecutors perceive it not as a threat to their professional discretion and values. Secondly, certain legal principles and provisions of the South African Criminal Procedure Act and the Constitution, as well as the lack of sophisticated and well established quantification chains, provide some form of buffer against the encroachment of numerical power on prosecutors' legal work.

Chapter 5 leaves the world of lower court prosecutors and examines whether this wider and more nuanced understanding of performance and accountability was also shared in other parts of the organisation, namely among NPA managers, who have different tasks and responsibilities and where the pressure of numbers might therefore manifest differently. I show that expressing their work in terms of numbers, targets, rates and rankings is also widespread and common amongst NPA managers. They use the performance measurement system for internal management purposes, 'to see what is going on', for economic control and for adhering to external accountability demands. I will be arguing that while they also internalised the language of numbers, it would be wrong to interpret this as a sign of their 'audit mentality' or of an auditable disciplined professional self. I will show that this form of analysis ignores the numerical knowledge, competence and reflexivity these prosecutorial managers rely on when dealing with numbers.

Since the last three chapters map multiple ways to understand the relationship between quantitative accountability and prosecutors' legal practices. Chapter 6 asks: 'What does it all mean for the South African public?' Are they convinced that the performance measurement system is holding the NPA to account? I will be focusing on a specific performance indicator in this chapter, namely the NPA's conviction rate. Various public representative bodies have criticised the NPA's conviction rate counting standard as 'misleading', 'creative' and 'inflated'. The NPA is accused of manipulating their performance measurement and for creating confusion and obscurity instead of accountability and transparency. While it is common among anthropologists to associate the 'doing of numbers' with 'cooking the books' and 'chasing statistics', I will argue that it makes little analytical sense to speak in this context of 'misleading numbers' or 'wrong numbers'. I present examples in which prosecutorial managers reflect on the NPA's conviction rate and its purpose and meaning for their work. I will end the chapter by arguing that these 'misleading' numbers might contribute more to the NPA's public accountability and the public's knowledge about the NPA than critics allow.

THE LACK OF INDEPENDENCE OF THE NPA AND THE CASE OF JACOB ZUMA

Before I move on to the chapters of this book, I want to make one point regarding the scope of this study clear. The NPA is an institution whose proper functioning determines the efficacy of the entire criminal justice system in South Africa. This is due to the fact that the NPA alone decides which criminal cases go to trial. The accountability and independence of the NPA has been a matter of deep public concern since its establishment in 1998.

Despite mounting incriminating evidence collected by both external and internal crime fighting units, the head of the NPA failed to prosecute high level government officials for corruption, fraud and other related charges, especially after 2009. The inaction led to ongoing doubts over the leadership of the NPA – its integrity, competence and independence as the National Director of Public Prosecution (NDPP) is appointed (and suspended) by the president. The widely held perception that the NDPP is not independent enough from the executive to carry out his job without 'fear, favour or prejudice' and to make sure that 'everyone is equal before the law' was strengthened when prosecutorial powers were abused. For instance legal commentators complained loudly about the misuse of prosecutorial powers when widely respected state officials who stood up to the encroaching state capture or NPA top prosecutors pursuing high-profile fraud and corruption cases were being prosecuted on shady grounds.[8] However, it is above all the never-ending case of Jacob Zuma, Deputy President between 1999 and 2005 and President of South Africa between 2009 and 2018, and the simultaneous disbandment and/or weakening of corruption and commercial crime fighting units in the NPA and the police during his presidency, which are nurturing these doubts and fears.

Shabir Shaik, the financial adviser to Jacob Zuma, was convicted in 2005 of bribing Zuma, who was at the time Deputy President of the country. In addition, Shaik had solicited a bribe from an arms company on behalf of Zuma. Only in 2008 was Zuma charged with eighteen counts of corruption, money laundering and racketeering, after an earlier prosecution attempt of 2005 was unsuccessful for procedural reasons. This was also after NDPP Bulelani Ngcuka had decided in 2003 not to prosecute Zuma, even though he announced that there was *prima facie* evidence of corruption. In 2009, the acting head of the NPA NDPP Mokotedi Mpshe withdrew the 2008 charges against Zuma, because he had then complained that the charges against him were part of a political conspiracy to prevent him becoming president. While the country's opposition party asked immediately for a legal review of

[8] For example, South Africa's former Finance Minister Pravin Gordhan was charged with fraud on 10 October 2016. A lobby group 'Hands off Pravin Gordhan' gained quickly momentum on social media plattforms. The charges against Gordhan were withdrawn on 31 October 2016. Or Glynnis Breytenbach, regional head of the NPA Specialised Commercial Crime unit working on the fraud, theft and corruption case against former police crime intelligence head Richard Mdluli, was suspended in 2012 and then later criminally charged with perjury, fraud and obstructing and defeating the ends of justice. She was cleared on numerous disciplinary charges, but left the NPA in 2014. A court decided in 2018 that she did not obstruct and defeat the ends of justice, and the prosecution withdrew also the perjury and fraud charges against her during that trial. (de Vos 2013; Underhill 2015; Madibogo 2016)

the NPA head's decision and for the publication of the records on which that decision was based on, that review only took place years later, because Jacob Zuma and Mokotedi Mpshe went to the courts themselves to fight the legality of these demands. In 2017 the North Gauteng High Court however declared the NDPP's decision of 2009 irrational and this was then later that year also confirmed by the Supreme Court of Appeal (Zuma v DA (771/2016); ANDPP v DA (1170/2016) [2017] ZASCA 146 (13 October 2017)).

How far the announcement of the current NDPP Adv. Shaun Abrahams at the beginning of 2018 to reinstate the charges against Zuma, and to prosecute the Guptas, a family who is being accused of being at the centre of South African state capture and to have benefited due to their close ties with the Zuma family from 'preferential treatment in state contracts, access to state provided business finance and in the award of trading licenses' (Public Protector 2016: 30) will help to ease such concerns about impunity and lack of accountability can only be told with time. Media articles celebrated Zuma's and Gupta's day in court and the punishment that would potentially follow, but reporters also raised concerns about the capability of the NPA to take on such complex cases of corruption after years of inaction and avoidance. During the spring of 2018, the NPA lost several confiscation orders to have the Gupta's assets frozen. The judges in this matter were highly critical of the quality of the NPA's evidence and seriously questioned its ability to secure convictions against the Guptas in the future (see e.g. Davis 2018; Du Toi 2018).

For the prosecutorial accountability discussion of this book, however, it is important to note that the NPA receives hundreds of thousands of cases from the South African police service per year and handles close to a million. The bulk of the cases involve ordinary people committing offences like burglary, assault, robbery, theft or murder against other ordinary people. Very few involve prominent members of the executive or well-known businessmen. Very few demand the involvement or intervention of the NDPP. The amount is insignificant in comparison to the amount of other cases. Career prosecutors work on the bulk of cases under immense time and resource pressure, and they are heard at the country's magistrate and regional courts under the guidance of senior and chief prosecutors. The prosecution services of each of the country's nine provinces are overseen by a director of public prosecution (DPP), that is a permanent

NPA position which is not politically appointed. It is this part of the NPA where performance statistics, indicators, rates and targets were a common feature in the working world of most prosecutors I observed and interviewed between 2007 and 2012. It is this part of the NPA the book is mostly concerned about.

1

FROM APARTHEID ADMINISTRATORS TO LAWYERS OF THE PEOPLE: A HISTORY OF ACCOUNTABILITY INSIDE THE SOUTH AFRICAN PROSECUTION AUTHORITY (1948–2018)

INTRODUCTION

Prosecutors are powerful actors in the South African criminal justice system as in many other jurisdictions worldwide (UN 1990; Schönteich 2001; 2002; Jehle, Wade and Elsner 2008; Luna and Wade 2012; Tonry 2012a, 2012b). In South Africa the National Prosecuting Authority Act 32 of 1998 and Section 179 of the Constitution of the Republic of South Africa 1996 equip them with extensive powers of discretion to initiate or discontinue criminal proceedings on behalf of the state, backed by the power of the state.

They decide who to charge with a criminal offence, what charges to file and when to dismiss or withdraw a case. The type of criminal charge a prosecutor chooses to bring against the accused can, in some cases, make a difference between life imprisonment and a much lower prison sentence for the offender, once he or she is found guilty of a crime (e.g. murder versus attempted murder; indecent versus sexual versus common assault). Whether a case involves plea bargaining or an alternative form of dispute resolution, and which type of criminal cases should be prioritised (e.g. organised crime, domestic violence or cases of racial discrimination) and consequently, how the state's scarce prosecutorial resources are allocated, lies predominantly within the prosecutorial sphere of discretion.

Bail applications are another part of the criminal court process in which prosecutors make far-reaching decisions affecting the wider workings of the criminal justice system in South Africa (Ehlers 2008). Lapses or negligence in the bail application process can lead to the injury or death of a complainant or state witness. But if release and bail conditions are applied too strictly, this may result in awaiting trial prisoners experiencing overcrowding and other objectionable and potentially life-threatening prison conditions (Fagan 2005). Lastly, prosecutors in South Africa, and many other countries, also guide police investigators on legal issues in criminal cases. They, for example, decide on search and arrest warrants and have the power to safeguard the legality of the police's arrest, interrogation and custody practices.

Looking at the power and wide discretions prosecutors enjoy, it is not surprising that the accountability of prosecutors, and closely related to this, their independence, is a topic of much debate in many countries worldwide (Gordon and Huber 2009). However, how prosecutors' accountability is envisioned, demanded or practised in different countries, what forms of account giving are perceived as desirable, seminal or insufficient, depends to a large extent on the respective political and juridical systems of these countries (Tonry 2012b: 2). While in many jurisdictions they are expected, across different societal spheres, to act independently, impartially and non-politically (and do this more or less also in practice) (Fionda 1995; Johnson 2012). In countries where the top-prosecutors are elected, it is more common that prosecutors make decisions about cases not only 'on the merits of the case' but also by taking into account public attitudes and political considerations (Huber and Gordon 2004; Davis 2007; Gordon and Huber 2007; 2009). Similarly, in countries where there is an institutional dependence of the prosecution's authority on the executive, for example when high-ranked prosecutors are presidential appointments, accountability relationships can again look different. Here it is more common that politicians expect that they can use the power of prosecutors to pursue their own political interests and might call prosecutors to account if they refuse to do so by removing them from office (Tonry 2012b: 2–3; Krajewski 2012).

What prosecutorial accountability and independence means or should mean, to whom it is owed, to what end, according to which standards and mechanisms and with what consequences are questions which were time and again central in the history of the prosecution services in South Africa (Schönteich 2001: 15–22). These questions are indeed as old as the office itself. The history of South African prosecution services goes back to 1652, when shortly after Batavian laws were implemented by the Dutch East India Company in the Cape the first prosecutor-like office or 'fiskaal' was imported from the Netherlands to the Cape (Ross and Schrikker 2012: 29; see also: Schönteich 2002: 82). The first 250 years are permeated with battles over how many formal liberties the position should be granted, with concerns over lack of accountability and attempts to silence the fiskaal and later, the attorney general. Salary disputes and fraud, since the fiskaal was entitled to a fee from the disputing parties, were also frequent reasons for friction. There were periods of great formal independence and in the administration of the Cape the position of the fiskaal was almost as powerful as that of the governor and the secunde (deputy governor). The position was well remunerated and fiskaals were highly respected amongst the colonists (Ross and Schrikker 2012: 32). But there were phases, particularly between 1926 until the early 1990s, during which literally no formal or substantive separation of powers between the attorney general(s) and the executive existed; and where the office was perceived as weak and unattractive because staff were badly paid and received little respect from the public (Schönteich 2002: 87–88).

This chapter will give a historical overview of the accountability set up of the South African prosecution authority. A focus will be on the historical developments between 1948 and 2018. The first part of this chapter describes prosecutors' accountability relationships during Apartheid – that means between 1948 and 1994. During that time, the prosecuting authority became increasingly dependent on, and accounted to, the White minority government that progressively controlled all spheres of state and society. Courts and prosecutors functioned as an integral part of the country's oppressive, exploitative and racist social order because they obsessively enforced it and thereby legitimised it. As a result, courts and prosecutors were deeply distrusted by most South Africans. I will provide specific examples of ways in which lower and High Court prosecutors failed to fulfil their prosecutorial duties and violated the country's criminal procedure act on a constant basis, with little consequence or sanction.

In the second part of this chapter, I describe how the predominance of the executive-orientated accountability of prosecutors came to an end around the time of the transition to democracy in 1994, and how the country's new national prosecuting authority was established in 1998. I explain that attempts to turn prosecutors into 'lawyers of the people' in the new democratic South Africa, in other words into an organisation people can trust and predict, relied on various forms of accountability. I will discuss the most prominent concepts of this change, namely accountability as *separation of powers*, as *representation* and as *professionalism*. *Quantitative* accountability in the form of a performance measurement system was an additional form of accountability introduced only at the turn of the new millennium, as I will show in the third and last part of this chapter.

The exploration of the history of South African prosecutors' accountability during the twentieth and twenty-first century provides important background information for the discussion of the central question of this book. Namely, how recently introduced performance measurement systems shape South African prosecutors' accountability understanding and prosecutorial practices. I show in this chapter that the accountability relationships of the prosecuting authority changed radically and became more diverse and complex since the transition to democracy and that these relationships rely on a wider spectrum of accountability definitions, techniques and instruments. Historicising account-giving practices of the prosecutorial workplace assists me to situate the effects and consequences that these new forms of quantitative forms of accountability have on this organisational setting more adequately.

LACK OF INDEPENDENCE AND ACCOUNTABILITY, ABUSE OF POWER AND INDIFFERENCE: THE PROSECUTION SERVICES DURING APARTHEID

Prosecutors occupy an important function in the court process where the accountability of people who are accused of having committed a crime is discussed, interpreted and established. They can be pivotal in assisting victims of crime to seek 'protection' from further harm and to obtain 'justice'. It is up to them to ensure that 'everyone is equal before the law' by holding also the 'rich, powerful and well-connected' to account for wrongdoings. And it is amongst their responsibilities that every accused receives a fair trial.

During the most part of the twentieth century, many South African prosecutors had a different function, far away from the above-mentioned ideals. The right and duty of prosecution until 1926 was vested in the office of the Attorney General.[1] This independence and freedom from political control and interference was removed in 1926 when, after legislative amendments initiated by the then government, the highest

[1] The office of the 'attorney general' can have different functions and responsibilities in different jurisdictions worldwide (Tonry 2012b). In South Africa, the highest prosecutor of the country was called 'Attorney General' until 1998 and then renamed in 1998, once the first national prosecuting authority was established, the 'National Director of Public Prosecution' (NDPP).

prosecutor of the country was placed under the control of the Minister of Justice, who was from then on authorised by law to reverse prosecutorial decisions and from 1935 onwards, after further legislative amendments, to act even as a prosecutor himself (Redpath 2012: 3; 1–10).

During the heyday of Apartheid in the 1970s, when strident protests took place against the country's racist and oppressive social order and the Apartheid government countered the resistance movement with escalated repression, including added pieces of repressive legislation, the 1935 position was reiterated in the then new Criminal Procedure Act of 1977. Formal separation of powers between the Attorney General and the executive were reconstituted only in 1992 via legislative amendment (Redpath 2012: 10). That means that the power and independence of prosecutors were severely curtailed between 1926 and 1992.

The courts and the prosecuting authority functioned, especially after 1948 when the Nationalist Party took power, as an integral part of the racist, exploitative and segregationist apartheid system. They obsessively applied, enforced and reinforced Apartheid's laws, which basically criminalised the everyday life of the majority of the South African population. As a result, prosecutors and courts were deeply distrusted by the majority of South Africans (West 1982; Klug 1988; Maylam 1990; Tshehla 2001).

While racial segregation and influx control had a long history of existence in South Africa and racially discriminatory laws and regulations existed from the end of the eighteenth century and increased and became more overtly racial during the turn of the nineteenth century, they were only systematically and more ruthlessly enforced after the Nationalist Party came into government (Ross 1999: 122ff.; Worden 2012: 75). Furthermore, the Population Registration Act of 1950, which enforced the classification of people into four racial categories,[2] together with the Group Areas Act of the same year, legislating and legalising separate racial residential urban areas, made the existing enforced separation of Whites and others in the spheres of work, residence and government more comprehensive, uncompromising and therefore compulsive (Maylam 1990: 58; 67).

[2] There were four racial classifications under the Population Registration Act of 1950, namely 'Natives or Bantu/African/Black', 'European/White' and 'Coloured/Mixed' and 'Indian'. The 'Office of Race Classification' was managing the classification and reclassification process. Decisions were made based on appearance, but also social standing. See also Bowker and Star 1999: Chapter 6.

This bundle of old and new racially discriminatory pieces of legislation regulated almost every aspect of indigenous Africans' lives. They were indeed the scaffolding for the oppressive Apartheid system. People who were classified Black were restricted economically on a massive scale because the laws determined where Africans were allowed to own, rent and use land; where they could attend school and university; in which professions and economic sectors they might find a career; which public amenities and facilities they were allowed to use; with whom they could have sexual intercourse and marry; and where they could build a home. Access to the most basic forms and rights of political organisations and representations was also denied to Non-whites (Worden 2012: 73–103; see also: Wolpe 1972; Posel 1997).

These racially discriminatory laws created an illegal population, as the mere presence in a White-designated area of a person classified as Non-white who was not in possession of a valid permit was deemed to be a criminal offence which could be prosecuted. None of these laws applied to Whites or, as Klug (1988: 184) puts it, the 'condition for criminality' was being 'Black' because 'a person cannot be accused of certain crimes, such as residing outside of a Bantustan without permission, unless he or she falls into a particular racial category, in this case, unless he or she is Black'.[3][4] Maylam (1990: 78) states that between 1916 and 1984 almost eighteen million Africans were arrested and prosecuted for pass laws and other influx control offences. Nearly thirteen million of these prosecutions were conducted between 1948 and 1981 (Klug 1988: 201). And nearly six million pass law offences were prosecuted during the height of Apartheid during 1965 and 1975 (West 1982; Savage 1986). The available statistics have to be viewed with some caution as Michael Savage (1986) suggests, because the state artificially lowered the statistics because the number of pass law offenses was already so high.

[3] Except the Immorality Act of 1950 which prohibited mixed marriages and any sexual contact between Whites and other South Africans. However, Whites usually received less heavy penalties (Bowker and Star 1999: 198–199).

[4] A Bantustan, also later referred to as Homeland and finally even National States, refers to the land the Apartheid planners set aside for Black South Africans. Every Black South African was supposed to be assigned to a Bantustan according to her or his 'ethnicity'. During Apartheid, millions of people were forcibly removed to these mostly impoverished and not very fertile rural areas. The Nationalist Party used the Euphemism 'separate development' to justify these forced removals. Each race can develop at its best in a location where it can develop separately according to its own natural pace, needs and skills (Abel 1995: 385–434; Worden 2012: 48–50; 120–122).

These prosecution figures give an indication of the scale of involvement of prosecutors in the daily administering of Apartheid. Klug states that South African courts were 'engaged in the process of legitimising South Africa's social order, applying and giving legalistic credibility to the enforcement of apartheid laws' (Klug 1988: 177–180). And with regards to the Commissioners' Courts, also referred to as 'special courts' or 'pass courts' where most pass law and influx control offenders appeared, he states that they merely had a legal 'veneer' (Klug 1988: 177–180; see also West 1982: 474).[5] West (1982: 472), who observed court proceedings in the late 1970s and early 1980s, states for example that the speed of the process was more important than ensuring a fair hearing and that the Commissioners' Courts 'appear to operate on the premise that cases will be undefended, and the prosecutor is usually unprepared or unable to continue a case where a plea of not guilty has been entered and a basis of defence disclosed'. Free legal representation for the accused offender was in theory available, but neither the police nor the prosecutors and magistrates gave the accused the opportunity to appoint an attorney (West 1982: 469–70). The relatives of those arrested were often not able to arrange a defence since the whereabouts of the detained person was frequently unknown to them or they were themselves illegally in an urban area which restricted them in their ability to act. The speediness of the whole procedure was a further limiting factor to arranging legal representation in time as the accused would be held in police custody overnight and usually appeared in front of the court the next day. The case was heard and sentenced on the same day (West 1982: 469).

During the trial, the accused were often not informed about the charge(s) against them or did not understand them due to language barriers and lack of interpreters, but the onus was on them to convince the court of their innocence. Most pleaded guilty in order to get out of the court as soon as possible and to return to work to avoid further loss of income after they paid their fines or did their time in prison (West 1982: 470). Nearly half of those sentenced could not afford to pay their

[5] The Commissioners' Courts were set up by the Apartheid state in an elaborate manner and developed separately from the ordinary South African court system. The Department of Justice was in charge of the operation of the Commissioners' Courts, which were established on a district basis, and it also appointed the prosecutors. Commissioners and prosecutors in these courts were often less qualified and trained than their colleagues working at ordinary magistrates' courts, and in certain instances they were appointed without any legal qualifications. Despite this, the Commissioners' Courts had the same jurisdiction as magistrates' courts in criminal offences committed by Blacks (Lewin 1944; Klug 1988).

fines.[6] People who appeared in the courts included people who were unlawfully arrested; however, they lacked the resources and the knowledge to sue the state for wrongful arrest. The prosecutors and magistrates who discharged them did not assist or inform them about such a possibility and right (West 1982: 472).

West states that the rapid and at times unlawful administrative processing of cases at three-minute intervals was severely interrupted when the accused were legally represented, which became more common in the 1980s when a growing number of 'human rights' or 'anti-Apartheid' lawyers offered their assistance to illegal township dwellers. It became then more difficult for prosecutors and magistrates working at the Commissioners' Courts to only pretend to follow due process of law and to give the accused a fair trial (West 1982: 470; see also Abel 1995: 23–66).

While the lower court or Commissioners' Courts upheld the unjust and repressive influx control laws, and were thereby involved in the criminalisation of Black everyday life, so the higher South African courts, like the country's High Courts and the Supreme Court of Appeal, were implicated in the criminalisation of the political life of Black South Africans (Abel 1995; Lobban 1996). The aim of these prosecutions and trials were to prevent the political activities of the ANC and other anti-Apartheid organisations and resistance movements from fighting for a non-racial democracy and to publicly demonise their leaders as terrorists, as it was done at the famous Rivonia trials of 1963 and 1964, during which a large number of ANC leaders, including the late Nelson Mandela, were charged under the country's Sabotage Act and sentenced to life imprisonment. The details of these often highly publicised political trials have been analysed in depth (see e.g. Davis and le Roux 2009: 36ff.).

Cases in the Commissioners' Courts described above were speedily dealt with in an administrative way by prosecutors with little legal knowledge. The prosecution practices in political trials heard in the High Court were rather different. Here, there were cases where Black political leaders and resistance fighters refused to plead to the charges –

[6] It is important to notice that the painful and discriminatory consequences of influx control prosecutions did not stop people coming to the cities to look for work and to live together as families. West (1982: 472–473) argues that the level of impoverishment in the homelands was so high and the chances of finding employment in the rural areas so low that it was still economically more advantageous for people to work part-time 'illegally' in the city. He states that this was the case 'even if she or he [was] fined and imprisoned fairly regularly. (…) Arrest [was] therefore an occupational hazard' (see also Wolpe 1972).

often treason and sabotage – thereby rejecting the Apartheid state's right to exercise jurisdiction over them, and protesting against the methods of the security police and security forces, which in the first place had brought them and their cases to court (Klug 1988: 175–176). When attempts were made to force the accused to plead guilty they would plead not guilty and then a lengthy trial would ensue, which could take months or years, even under the repressive Apartheid regime. As Davis and le Roux (2009: 40) note, '(...) even during this bleak legal period, the law of procedure guaranteed a measure of fairness for the accused'. For example

> the State was obligated to let the accused know in clear terms what case they were required to meet in court. The accused were thus entitled to object to the charge sheet on the basis that the charges set out were vague in describing all of the necessary particulars or that it failed to specify elements of the crimes for which they stood charged. Where a court sustains such an attack, the State must be given a chance to remedy the charge sheet by amendment and failing which the charge will be quashed and the accused freed.
>
> (Davis and le Roux 2009: 40)

Political accused were in many cases represented by well-known and experienced attorneys and advocates who argued every legal point they could find to free the political activists, or at least in unwinnable cases to prevent the worst: the death penalty (Abel 1995). The state was also represented by experienced prosecutors in these political trials. For example, in the Rivonia case, the second most senior prosecutor of the Transvaal province, Dr Percy Yutar, was in charge of the trial. For him it was, according to Davis and le Roux (2009: 24), of great importance for his career to win this trial and to 'show his usefulness' to the Apartheid executive in order to achieve his ambition to become the highest ranked prosecutor of the province, the Attorney General of the Transvaal.[7]

Indifference to the immorality of the Apartheid system was one area in which these High Court prosecutors failed to fulfil their prosecutorial duties. However, there were also other instances of more tangible legal negligence in the everyday actions of these prosecutors whose main aim was to obtain a conviction, and which had disastrous consequences for

[7] Transvaal used to be one of the provinces of the Union of South Africa (1910 until 1961) and then of the Republic of South Africa (1961 until 1994). After 1994 the province was dissolved and parts of it belong today to the following provinces: North West, Limpopo, Mpumalanga and Gauteng (Ross 1998).

the accused in these political trials. Most importantly, prosecutors hardly questioned the fallibility of the police (Abel 1995; Davis and le Roux 2009). They used evidence which was often obtained illegally; they did not follow up potential cases of abuse of police power in which the accused complained that they had been assaulted or tortured by the police while under arrest or held in custody.[8] They used as witnesses other political accused who had been detained without a trial for lengthy periods of time, which was legal during Apartheid, but who often only agreed to testify against their former comrades after they had been coerced and tortured, even though this was illegal under Apartheid.[9]

Having said that political trials were often lengthy and involved with accused who pleaded not guilty, there were also many less publicised political court cases where activists confessed at their first court appearance. Again, these confessions were often coerced as a result of torture, but this was not taken into account and followed up by the prosecutors and the judiciary. In other words, prosecutors sanctioned, with their indifference and in their working practices, the use of violence as a legitimate investigative technique. Consequently, they severely violated the rights of the accused in terms of the Criminal Procedure Act (Truth and Reconciliation Commission 2003: 6/5/2).

[8] Detainees had been complaining for a long time that they were tortured while being held in police and/or prison cells. 'Mysterious' deaths in custody had occurred from the 1970s onwards and detainees' relatives protested against the police's suggestion that incarcerated political activists committed suicide or died while trying to escape. Academic research had confirmed the torture allegations against the police. However, denial from the government and the police was widespread, brushing these allegations off as '*unscientific*' and '*ammunition for the communist enemies*' (Davis and le Roux 2009: 86–87).

[9] Davis and le Roux state that between 1960 and 1990 the police detained 80,000 South Africans without a trial, as they show 'a parallel system of incarceration existed' (2009: 81). The General Law Amendment Act of 1963 introduced detention without a trial for 90 days to the South African legal system, but the permission to detain people for 90 days was extended to an indefinite period of time when the Terrorism Act of 1967 was introduced. For example, in 1975, at the age of 28, the well-known founder and leader of the South African Students' Organisation (SASO) and of South Africa's Black Consciousness Movement, Steve Biko, was detained and held for 137 days without charge or trial. In 1976 after the Soweto uprising he was detained in solitary confinement for 101 days. In 1977 he was arrested, detained and released in March and rearrested in July, charged and acquitted, and again arrested in August. He died in custody in September of that year. The official state inquest into Biko's death was heard a few months later. Despite evidence that Biko had been tortured and murdered by members of the Security Branch, the magistrate ruled in favour of the policemen and acquitted them, available at: http://www.sbf.org.za/Main_Site/steve_biko_timeline.php, [4 June 2018]; See also: http://untreaty.un.org/cod/avl/ha/cspca/cspca.html; http://daccessddsny.un.org/doc/RESOLUTION/GEN/NR0/297/01/IMG/NR029701.pdf?OpenElement; http://www.un.org/documents/scres.htm [4 June 2018].

The police's systemic torture practices over the last thirty years were exposed in a widely publicised case before a state court in 1985–1986 (Abel 1995: 211–258; Davis and le Roux 2009: 88–96).[10] An interim order against the police was granted in 1985 by the Port Elizabeth High Court, which restrained police officers temporarily from assaulting detainees. The police did not admit any liability in this case – it ended when the applicants succeeded in gaining a restraining order – but did for the first time pay a large amount of compensation to the assaulted detainees in an out of court settlement.

While the case did not stop police torture practices, it became more difficult for prosecutors to bluntly ignore these horrific allegations. This did not mean however that policemen and generals were called to account. Commentators criticise the lack of adaptations of the prosecution authority in this transition period. Fernandez, for example, states in 1993 that although pass courts have been abolished in 1986, a number of prosecutors still did not follow criminal procedures correctly and still covered up the illegal practices of the police and were reluctant to initiate prosecutions against them (1993: 23; see also Barrell and Soggott 1998).

Ending this impunity and lack of accountability and moving away from the predominance of the executive orientated accountability of prosecutors, and becoming accountable to all South Africans by transforming into 'lawyers of the people' only increasingly became important and a desirable good for the prosecution authority after the transition to democracy, and especially from 1998 onwards when the country's first, centralised, National Prosecuting Authority (NPA) was established and came under pressure to legitimise itself in the eyes of those it had, until very recently, suppressed (Schönteich 2001: 5; 30). Quantitative forms of accountability in the form of performance measurement systems did not feature much in the accountability set up of the new prosecution authority until the beginning of the new millennium. Prior to this, other mechanisms were envisioned and introduced to make the prosecution services accountable in the new democracy, as we will see in the following section.

[10] Wendy Orr, a 25-year-old medical doctor who worked at the District Surgeon's office in Port Elizabeth had first-hand knowledge of the police's brutality since she had to examine prisoners on admission, transfer and release. When prisoners complained, her job was to keep a record of each complaint. These records were used in evidence at the High Court to have an interim order against the police issued in 1985, which restrained police officers from assaulting detainees ('The Case for Police Reform', 1987). For a detailed summary of the trial see Davis and le Roux 2009: 88–96).

AFTER 1994: ACCOUNTABILITY AS SEPARATION OF POWERS, REPRESENTATION AND PROFESSIONALISM

Accountability as Separation of Powers

Accountability was initially, between 1992 and 1998 in the time period around the democratic transition in 1994 and before the establishment of the National Prosecuting Authority (NPA) in 1998, hotly debated in terms of institutional independence and separation of powers. To who should the head of the new prosecuting authority be answerable and who should have the final say in prosecutorial decision-making and policy? These questions were once again on the agenda because the separation of powers between the Attorney General and the executive, reintroduced in 1992 via legislative amendment, was perceived to be under threat, or as a threat in itself, depending on one's point of view.

During the drafting process of the South African Constitution of 1996, which made provision for a single national prosecuting authority for the country, and of the National Prosecuting Act No. 32 of 1998, which laid out the details of the new South African prosecutorial system, this new or regained institutional independence was again restricted. South Africa's 1996 constitution and the NPA Act No. 32 of 1998 provide the NPA with the 'power to institute criminal proceedings on behalf of the state' and further ensured 'that the prosecuting authority exercises its function without fear, favour or prejudice' (NPA 1998: 2). But the constitution also makes provision for South Africa's president to appoint the country's highest prosecutor. In the new democratic set up this office was renamed from attorney general to 'National Director of Public Prosecutions' (NDPP). An additional change was that the 1992 provision, which also provided security of tenure for this central state office until the age of 65, was amended to a ten-year tenure in the new legislative framework (Redpath 2012: 3; 1–10).

The provision in the Constitution which empowers the President to appoint the NDPP was especially controversial at the time it was certified.[11] Opponents of this new constitutional clause questioned how far the country's top prosecutor would be able to defend controversial prosecutorial decisions in which the NPA holds for example 'the powerful, rich and well connected to account' when there is an

[11] See: Certification of the Constitution of the Republic of South Africa, 1996 (CCT 23/96) [1996] ZACC 26; 1996 (4) SA 744 (CC); 1996 (10) BCLR 1253 (CC) (6 September 1996) pp. 83–85.

institutional dependence on the executive (Schönteich 2001: 26–30). They challenged its constitutionality on the basis that it contravenes the doctrine of separation of powers between the legislature, executive and judiciary, which allows for appropriate checks and balances to ensure accountability, responsiveness and openness (Redpath 2012: 1–10). Proponents in contrast welcomed this institutional dependence because, at the time when the new constitution was drafted, most members of the prosecution services, especially at the top, were old-order prosecutors and, as already mentioned, were entrenched by the legislative amendment of 1992 for security of tenure until the age of 65. At the time of the transition there was concern amongst the new democratic elected leaders that public servants who occupied central state functions during Apartheid might not be accountable and responsive to their commands and may try to maintain the status quo, or even turn their power against them as they did in the past (Redpath 2012: 10; see also Shaw 2002).

The Constitutional Court rejected that objection, stating in its 1996 judgment that the prosecuting authority is not part of the judiciary and 'the mere fact' that the head of the NPA is a presidential appointment is not 'in itself' a contravention of the doctrine of separation of powers (Certification of the Constitution of the Republic of South Africa, 1996 (CCT 23/96) [1996] ZACC 26; 1996 (4) SA 744 (CC); 1996 (10) BCLR 1253 (CC) (6 September 1996) p. 83). The court stated furthermore that the national constitutional provision that an act of parliament had to 'ensure that the prosecuting authority exercises its function without fear, favour or prejudice', was a 'constitutional guarantee of [prosecutorial] independence' (Certification of the Constitution of the Republic of South Africa, 1996 (CCT 23/96) [1996] ZACC 26; 1996 (4) SA 744 (CC); 1996 (10) BCLR 1253 (CC) (6 September 1996) p. 85).

Accountability and Representation

A potential lack of responsiveness amongst the old prosecutorial guard was not only discussed as an accountability issue at the top of the new prosecution authority, but also in the context of the whole prosecutorial workforce of the country (Redpath 2012: 78–84). Being mostly White and male, there was also concern that they might not share the new leaders' vision for a democratic South Africa. As mentioned before, the obvious lack of commitment of some old order prosecutors to the new state and its constitutional and human rights orientated legal framework was criticised from time to time between 1992 and 1998 (e.g. Fernandez 1993; Barrell and Soggott 1998). Accountability was therefore also discussed in terms of creating a more representative workforce through affirmative action policies, which the new Employment Equity Act of 1998 made provision for. It was also argued that an NPA more representative of the racial composition of South Africa would also help to overcome the mistrust and suspicion the wider public felt towards prosecutors. It would mold the prosecution services more convincingly into 'lawyers of the people' in the words of the first NDPP, Bulelani Ngcuka, in 1998 (in Schönteich 2001: 5).

The Employment Equity Act of 1998 states that its purpose 'is to achieve equity in the workplace' and that 'affirmative action measures' should be implemented in state organs and by employers who employ more than fifty people in order to eliminate and redress the 'disadvantages in employment experienced by designated groups' in the past. A designated group refers to 'black people, women, or people with disabilities'. The Act meant that positions must be given preferentially to members of these 'designated groups' even when candidates from non-designated groups had the same or equal qualifications. Merit is not the overriding principle on which employment decisions have to be taken. The employer is also required by the Act to specifically train members of the designated group in order to eliminate potential employment barriers and increase the 'diversity and representativeness' of the workforce.

Between 1994 and 1998 many prosecutorial posts were left vacant by the Department of Justice and Constitutional Development, despite available qualified White prosecutors and law graduates, because the Department complied with affirmative action policies. As a result, it was reported that many of the White male prosecutors were 'disillusioned' (Schönteich 2001: 89ff.). They were concerned that there would be no future for them in the organisation and they left their positions. In 1997, in the Western Cape office of the Attorney General and in the greater Johannesburg area, almost a quarter of the professional staff resigned (Mvoko 1996; Sogott 1997). According to Schönteich (2001: 90), White prosecutors' 'promotional concerns' about their future in the NPA increased when sixteen White male prosecutors with experience ranging from four to twenty-one years were apparently excluded from consideration for appointment to thirty senior posts advertised by the Department of Justice and Constitutional Development. In particular, the appointment of a

Black woman with only one year's experience in the state attorney's office and limited experience of the law elsewhere as a deputy state attorney caused anger and frustration amongst the excluded applicants. These men took their case to the Pretoria High Court, which decided in 1996 that the appointment process they were complaining about and felt victimised by was discriminatory and ordered the appointment process to be frozen (Sogott 1997).

When the NPA was established in 1998 its first NDPP made clear that he was attempting to redress the current imbalance of lack of Black senior staff members, speaking to a group of senior prosecutors in 1999 he said (in Schönteich 2001: 91):

> If I look around this room it is obvious to me that we still have a long way to go before we more closely reflect the demographics in this country! Not only will we require vigorous affirmative action policy to achieve this but we will also need each and every person in this room to be committed to such a policy. What it means is that when vacancies open up, the people in this room will do their best to find black people with potential to fill those vacancies.

Despite the need to change the NPA's faces and make space for 'designated groups' in the NPA who were previously excluded from management and other senior positions, Bulelani Ngcuka in 1998 appointed experienced White old order prosecutors and new White anti-Apartheid lawyers to central NPA positions. Ngcuka was quoted as saying that he 'would have liked some of the appointments to key positions in the prosecution service to have been black. But we do not have the people. There has to be a balance between skills and representativeness' (quoted in Schönteich 2001: 91).

Accountability and Professionalism

Professional (skills) development was therefore another important key dimension to how accountability was discussed around 1998. While fresh and more representative faces were an important factor to create a more accountable prosecution authority, in order to reach its organisational vision of 'becoming lawyers of the people' the NDPP emphasised that 'a new breed of prosecutors' was needed (Schönteich 2001: 5), namely, ones which receive extensive legal, professional and ethical training. The new constitutional setup of South Africa in which the rights of the accused were drastically strengthened – the onus to prove the accused's guilt beyond reasonable doubt was for example moved onto the state – required a prosecutor with more advanced legal skills and knowledge. So a law degree became increasingly the uniform entry-qualification to become a prosecutor, which was a major change for the profession from previous training practices.[12]

During most of the twentieth century, many prosecutors had no legal tertiary education and were usually drawn from the ranks of the clerks, or in smaller towns local police officers were frequently used to conduct prosecutions on behalf of the state (Fernandez 1993: 120). Clerks and police officers would be authorised by magistrates to act as prosecutors and would be trained informally on the job. Prosecutors were ranked as legal assistants in the department's occupational classification system (Fernandez 1993: 119). In the late 1970s the status of prosecutors started to change. Then, in order to act as a prosecutor, a university level legal qualification was required. The professional group of public prosecutors was formally recognised by the Department of Justice in 1979. However, police officers were in the early 1990s still used in rural areas to process postponements of cases or cases that involved petty offences (Fernandez 1993: 119). Only after the transition to democracy did these informal training practices came to an end and were officially replaced in 1997 with coherent professional training for aspirant prosecutors (NPA Aspirant Prosecutor Programme; Fernandez 1993: 120). These twelve-month courses were envisioned to prepare future prosecutors more adequately with the functions and responsibilities of prosecutors in court and acculturate them into professional legal values like e.g. impartiality, objectivity and independence. Thus, they were designed to act as an additional safeguard against prosecutorial misconduct and abuse (Schönteich 2001: 57).

The remunerated in-service training programme includes classroom tuition, practical or in-court training during which trainee prosecutors have to demonstrate their competency in real cases in court and a final

[12] In the seventeenth and eighteenth centuries, during the time when the Dutch East India Company ran the Cape, the 'fiskaal', the prosecutor-like office which was imported from the Netherlands to the Cape, needed to have a law degree from a Dutch University (Ross and Schrikker 2012: 30). I was not able to find information on when this requirement ended. Many of the younger prosecutors and older ones I had contact with had LLB degrees, however it is still not an educational requirement for prosecutors. The Acting Chief Executive Officer of the NPA stated in 2012 in front of the Parliamentary Justice and Correctional Services Committee that the DOJCD is encouraging prosecutors who were without such a degree to obtain one, see: http://pmg.org.za/committee-meeting/15032/ [22 June 2018]. The high prevalence of law degrees in the province I was mostly working in might be related to its popularity amongst the prosecutorial workforce. That made it potentially a more competitive work environment, which made additional qualifications necessary/beneficial to secure a position.

written assessment. A course which focused on the introduction to human rights issues and the effects of the latest Constitutional Court decisions on prosecutors' work was also included in the programme's curriculum. A senior prosecutor conducts the training and successful candidates are offered entry-level positions within the NPA. Thus, for the first time (and ever since), a coherent standardised training system was established where people who are interested in pursuing a career as prosecutors are trained and guided in practice by senior prosecutors and not by magistrates, and before they start prosecuting on their own and not, as was previously the norm, after they had already started (Fernandez 1993: 124).

From 1998 onwards the NPA not only concentrated more efforts on consistently developing prosecutorial legal skills, but also on keeping its skilled prosecutorial staff members and countering the existing high staff fluctuation. There was a focus on introducing more incentives for people to become career prosecutors, such as more attractive career pathing and remuneration systems (Fernandez 1993: 112).[13] In the past, prosecutors were often withdrawn from the prosecutorial position to become magistrates after a relatively short period of time or used the job as a springboard for private sector work. Thus, being a prosecutor was for many people only a transitional position (Fernandez 1993: 119). It was a very unattractive position due to the low salaries, the lack of advancement opportunities and due to the administrative dependency on the magistracy, which caused friction between prosecutors and magistrates. Magistrates not only trained prosecutors informally, but until 1995 also had administrative control over them, which led to the widespread perception that prosecutors were not independent of the judiciary (Schönteich 2001: 90ff.).

[13] It is important to keep in mind that the problem of lack of experienced staff is not a new phenomenon that was only connected to the democratic regime change, but one which was observed seventeen years earlier in 1981 by the Hoexter commission of inquiry into the structure and functioning of the South African courts. The commission stressed the need for the Department of Justice to keep its skilled prosecutorial staff members and warned that the high staff fluctuation and connected to that, the lack of experience among prosecutors, was cause for concern. Inexperienced prosecutors might lose their cases, especially when an accused was represented by a more knowledgeable and skilled attorney or advocate. Prosecutors needed practical experience in order to know how to apply the law to a specific case, feel at ease in court and sum up quickly what had been said. Cross-examination techniques and the presentation of evidence needed be learned in practice over time. The Hoexter commission also mentioned that one of the biggest problems for the state prosecuting services was the low salaries they were paying their prosecutors, compared to the better-remunerated jobs in the private sector. In the report the low salaries were called a 'national disgrace' and the main reason for the high fluctuation and high number of resignations of more experienced staff members during the 1970s and early 1980s. (Hoexter in Fernandez 1993: 117)

Despite working under a senior prosecutor, for example, prosecutors had to ask the senior or chief magistrate of the court where they were stationed for permission to take leave, get a transfer to another court or to attend training courses. The magistracy also determined promotions and administered the court's budget. Prosecutors also had to consult with the senior magistrate if they needed to send faxes and make long distance telephone calls, or when they needed new stationary – all simple non-legal everyday activities. Limited office space, furniture and parking lots and the available hours of typists were also often distributed in a way that was to the advantage of magistrates. 'The preferential treatment given to magistrates over prosecutors served to place the latter in a psychologically subservient position to the former' as Schönteich (2001: 92) put it and contributed to the unattractive image prosecutors had within the hierarchy of the civil service. He stated that when the administrative dependency on the magistracy ended in 1995 and separation of powers established in 1998, this was viewed as an important step in the independence and professionalisation process of the South African prosecuting authority.

The last point I would like to mention which was used to improve the status and occupational identity of the profession and increase levels of professional skills and therefore of accountability was the introduction of specialised prosecuting units. The National Prosecuting Authority Act of 1998 created the office of the NDPP, but also made provision for a series of special investigating units which would operate within the structures of the NPA and would focus on specific categories of crime, like sexual offences, corruption and fraud, organised crime, terrorism and crimes against the state. All of these units assisted the NPA to prolong employees' commitment to the prosecution authority because they diversified prosecutors' career opportunities and offered them more areas of specialisation in which they can develop and deepen their specific skills (Schönteich 2001: 112).

The NPA Special Investigative Units 'the Asset Forfeiture Unit' and 'the Directorate of Special Operations' (DSO), subsequently called the 'Scorpions', both deal with high-profile economic crime and corruption cases and were particularly successful in attracting highly skilled and experienced personnel. This was the case because they were in the position to pay much higher salaries and benefits and provide employees with a more modern, much better resourced and equipped working environment than other NPA members had to cope with (Broughton 1999; Le May 2000; Shaw 2002; Basson 2012). Another reason was that new pieces of legislation, like the Prevention of Organised Crime Act (POCA) which was adopted in 1998, provided these NPA investigating units with powerful legal tools; POCA provides, for example, for civil forfeiture. Thus they made the work of these units a lot 'easier' and more 'successful'.

Civil forfeiture allows the AFU to confiscate the proceeds of crime, whether it is property acquired or property used to commit the crime, independently of the outcome of a criminal trial. A civil action means that they are 'only' required to prove their case on a balance of probabilities and are allowed to use circumstantial evidence to seize assets. Therefore, they are able to confiscate assets before the accused is found guilty beyond a reasonable doubt. This makes civil forfeiture, despite the complex civil litigation it nevertheless involves, a very powerful tool for the AFU in their efforts to investigate economic and organised crimes and corruption, including their aim 'to take the profit out of crime' as the long-standing head of the unit Willie Hofmeyr was often quoted in the media or when appearing in front of parliament.[14]

The Scorpions' and the AFU's work was widely published and celebrated in the media and positively positioned the NPA as an organisation which was seriously committed to control crime and violence in the country (Shaw 2002: 133).[15] This positive feedback from the media was apparently another reason that made positions

[14] Hofmeyr 2007; see also: Hoyfmeyr, Head of the AFU, during the NPA briefing of the Parliamentary Committee on Justice on its Annual Report 2012/2013, available here: https://pmg.org.za/committee-meeting/15032/ [1 June 2018].

[15] For example in the NPA's 2014/2015 Annual Report it is mentioned that the AFU had its best overall performance since its establishment in 1999 recorded during this period. They had a success rate of 93.1% and completed 436 forfeiture cases with a value of R1.9 billion and 342 freezing orders to the value of R2.7 billion; Freezing Orders to the value of R 2.2 billion and recoveries of R1.5 Million relating to cases where the amount benefited from corrupt activity was more than R5 Million; R 1.6 billion were paid to the victims of crime and R11.1 million were recovered in cases where government officials were convicted of corruption and other related offences. While these figures do not clearly indicate how much money is potentially 'made' through organised crime and 'lost' through corruption during 2014/2015, nor do they tell the public exactly how efficiently and effectively the AFU is working, they are without doubt high and substantial enough to count as an AFU, and therefore a NPA success stories. That the money the AFU confiscates also comes from high-profile 'serious criminals', 'fraudsters' and 'racketeers' and is used to 'fight crime' and for payments to victims of crime, it means that 'criminals themselves are paying the price of law enforcement' is possibly another compelling and attractive reason why the AFU's work is widely published and celebrated in the media (Challenor 1999; Gifford and Krost 1999; Flick 2001; 'Forfeiture Unit goes after the big fish' 2001; Broughton 2002; 'Assets worth R24m seized from ANC MP' 2012; 'NPA returns stolen money to Kouga' 2012; 'Asset Forfeiture Unit eyes R50 Billion in state capture loot' 2018; 'NPA's AFU sets eyes on Gupta linked companies' 2018).

within these specialised units more attractive and sought-after for qualified lawyers (Broughton 1999; Gifford and Krost 1999; Le May 2000; Basson 2012).

This was the case at least within the first decade after the establishment of the NPA. The Scorpions were dissolved by parliament in 2008 after the ANC took a decision at its annual conference in Polokwane in December 2007 that the Directorate of Special Operations should be disbanded. A new special investigative unit, the Directorate for Priority Crime Investigation (DPCI), otherwise known as the 'Hawks', was established in 2009 within the organisational structures of the SAPS and under the control of the National Police Commissioner. When I started my fieldwork during 2008 I already met in Pretoria two former 'Scorpions' who had left the NPA and were employed now in the private sector and academia because they were unsure what place they would have in that new special investigative unit or whether they would find it attractive to work for the South African police service. While in other countries the move to bundle all investigative state organisations within the national police service might not be contentious, especially in countries where the police enjoy public acceptance and trust, this was not the case in South Africa. Levels of distrust in the police continue to be high: so the disbandment of the Scorpions was highly controversial – and remains so today.[16] The AFU

[16] Commentators argued that the Scorpions' critics had accused the NPA of being politically biased and not strong enough to prosecute every corruption suspect with the same vigour. They agreed with the Scorpions' critics that the NPA might not have been totally independent from political interference. They emphasised, however, that the new unit, the Hawks, would in all likelihood be even less independent and even more vulnerable to political interference (de Vos 2012; Kinnes and Newham 2012). The Constitutional Court ruled in 2011 that the new priority crime unit was not a sufficiently independent anti-corruption entity and therefore not in line with the Constitution, the Bill of Rights and international agreements on fighting corruption which had been accepted by Parliament, and which require countries to have such an independent body (Glenister v President of the Republic of South Africa and Others (CCT 48/10) [2011] ZACC 6; 2011 (3) SA 347 (CC); 2011 (7) BCLR 651 (CC) (17 March 2011)). The Constitutional Court judges found that because the Hawks' activities are co-ordinated by Cabinet and that a ministerial committee determines policy guidelines and influences which national priority crimes should be investigated, that this makes the new unit vulnerable to political interference. In addition, the court found that the head and other senior members of the Hawks enjoy inadequate levels of employment security and the National Police Commissioner controls the unit's budget, which means that they are not independent and protected enough to do their jobs with commitment and vigour. The Constitutional Court gave parliament eighteen months to rectify these shortcomings in the new national priority crime unit. Various civil organisations made submissions to the respective parliamentary portfolio committee to establish a structurally and operationally independent anti-corruption fighting unit outside of the SAPS (see e.g. Law Society of South Africa; Helen Suzman Foundation; Institute for Accountability; Kinnes and Newham 2012). While parliament made some changes, the Constitutional Court intervened in 2014 again and declared sections

still exists today. However, there were also attempts to weaken it. Firstly, NDPP Adv. Menzi Simelane, who was in his previous role at the DOJCD overseeing the disbandment of the Scorpions, announced when he presented the NPA's Strategic Plans in 2010 to parliament that he intends to disband the AFU by decentralizing it. This plan however caused a public outcry and was in the end never put into action ('Radebe puts on hold plans on AFU' 2010). Secondly, Adv. Willie Hofmeyr, who is one of the four Deputy National Directors of Public Prosecution and headed the AFU since its inception in 1999, was forced out of this position. The new NDPP Adv. Shaun Abrahams removed Hofmeyr in August 2015 from the AFU for unknown reasons despite his widely acknowledged success, experience and integrity and demoted him to the Head of the Legal Affairs Division (Underhill 2015). The widely held concerns that the top of the NPA lacks independence from the executive will be addressed in more detail in the concluding remarks of this chapter.

Performance Measurement System

That prosecutors' accountability was also talked about and secured in the form of performance measurement systems and became an organisational fact only after the enactment of the Public Finance Management Act of 1999 (PFMA). This additional accountability demand came at a time when there was a general shift in attention in South Africa from policy development to 'efficient' and 'effective' and 'friendly' service delivery and the means of improving it (Chipkin 2011). A perceived growth in crime and its wide discussion in the media put the departments responsible for safety, security and justice under immense public pressure to improve their performance (Shaw 2002; Leggett 2003; Ehlers 2008: 123).

of the South African Police Services Act as invalid, because the Act failed to establish an independent corruption fighting unit as required by the Constitution (Helen Suzman Foundation v President of the Republic of South Africa and Others; Glenister v President of the Republic of South Africa and Others (CCT 07/14, CCT 09/14) [2014] ZACC 32; 2015 (1) BCLR 1 (CC); 2015 (2) SA 1 (CC) (27 November 2014)). The judgment stated that it is the National Head of the Hawks and *not* the Minister of Police who has the authority and discretion to decide which national priority offences and which suspects for corruption to investigate. That the National Head of the Hawks is still appointed by the Minister of Police curtails however the independence of that office. De Vos (2016) writes for example that the Minister of Police removed shortly after the Constitutional Court announced its 2014 judgement, the current National Head of the Hawks and replaced him in 2015 with a General, who was described in a High Court judgement in another matter from the same year as lacking 'integrity and honour'.

The PFMA requires that state departments cascade their five-year strategic plans into annual performance plans. In these plans they are required to report about anticipated service delivery targets and corresponding financial projections over the Medium Term Expenditure Framework (MTEF) period. The budget tabled in Parliament has to include measurable key performance indicators for both non-financial and financial performance information. By aligning plans and budget closer to each other the PFMA is envisioned to assist parliament to assess how well state officials implemented their department's annual performance plans based on the budget they received from treasury. That the NPA was able to conform relatively quickly to the requirement of the new Act was due to the 'court management unit'. It was established in 1998 and for the first time in the history of the country's prosecution authority started to collect 'court management statistics' in mid-1999.

In 2002 the NPA submitted its first annual report for the 2001/2002 financial year including performance indicators to Parliament and Minister of Justice and Constitutional Development. The following national statistics for individual courts were collected: (1) the number of court hours in session; (2) the number of outstanding cases on the courts' rolls; and (3) the number of finalised cases and how they had been finalised (e.g. withdrawn, removed from the court roll, conviction or acquittal of the accused). So when the performance indicators had to be chosen and presented, the NPA were able to rely on this already existing administrative data. Over the last fifteen years additional data was collected and more performance indicators have been created, but the ones relying on the above-mentioned statistics remain, together with the number of received dockets, number of decision dockets, number of cases finalised by way of alternative dispute resolution mechanisms, the most important performance indicators for the National Prosecuting Services (NPS) (see: NPA Annual Plan 2007–2008; 2008–2009; 2009–2010; 2010–2011; 2011–2012; 2012–2013; 2013–2014; 2014–2015; 2015–2016; 2016–2017; NPA Performance Plan 2012–2013; NPA Quarterly Performance Overview 2011/ 2012).

The NPS is the largest business unit of the NPA, in which the bulk of the country's criminal cases are dealt with. Each court prosecutor in the country captures every day the data on the so-called 'prosecutor's daily court return' form. At the end of the month the form is handed over to the court's control or senior prosecutor. All the data is then captured at the regional head office and is monitored and controlled by a chief prosecutor. The data from each court is calculated to arrive at an overall cluster efficiency rate, meaning the data from all the courts in one cluster is added to arrive at one aggregate rate, and then the different clusters in one province are ranked according to their achieved rates. It is important to notice that the annual reports only contain national aggregated rates, so the counts of court hours or conviction rates of a specific prosecutor, court, cluster or province, for example, are not made public.

Within the NPA the used set of indicators which I just mentioned one can distinguish, following here Sally Engle Merry's distinction, between *counts*, *ratios* and *composites* (Merry 2016: 14–15). Number of finalized, diverted cases, court hours etc. are all counts. They refer to a specific number of actions the prosecutor did and/or concluded and are more or less descriptive. How the NPA decided on what to count and how to define and what constitutes prosecutorial performance will be discussed in Chapter 5 where I show that these decisions where predominantly shaped by the costs of counting and that the NPA used already existing administrative data as proxies for what they would like to measure. Ratios, in contrast to counts, compare two numbers with each other. Conviction rates, for example, do not only count the number of convictions a prosecutor achieves, but it counts them in relation to another number, e.g. the number of cases which the prosecutor receives from the police or decides to send on trial. Chapter 6 will show in great detail the heated discussions amongst different stakeholders about the correct way to calculate the NPA's conviction rate, which illustrates well that ratios do not only describe performance, but they also evaluate it. Lastly there are composites. The cluster efficiency rate is composite since it is made up of separate systems of counts and ratios and then these numbers are converted into a score, which allows the NPA to rank the different clusters according to their score performance. How the NPA decided to merge and weight the constituents part of the efficiency rate is not known to me since this number played in the part of the NPA I researched and in the public debates about the NPA's performance a non-existing role and was therefore not further explored.

With regards to the origin of the Public Finance Management Act it can be interpreted in the context of globally circulating public service idea(l)s like 'new public management' or 'evidence based governance'. They can be summarised as idea(l)s that promote business management techniques, which rely heavily on quantitative knowledge as the basis for decision-making, for the public sector. The promise is that state bureaucracies run more efficiently and effectively when they are managed 'like businesses' with goals, strategic plans, benchmarking, bottom-lines, more stress on outputs than process, more flexible hierarchies and pay structures and more contract based competitive provisions, etc. (Power 1997). These idea(l)s had their origin in Anglo-Saxon countries and are in many fields, most advanced in the US and the UK. It is important to notice that while there is the allegation that these new and/or old repackaged ideas led to a global paradigm shift, there is also evidence that there is a lot of variability and degree in the implementation of these ideas in different countries (Hood 2007).

For the South African context, it is further important that these global ideas were not foreign to the country or forced on it through donors or development agencies. The managerial prosecutors, who were responsible at the NPA Head Offices in Pretoria for the introduction of the performance measurement system in the NPA, were furthermore trained in South Africa (prosecutorial training and MBA training) and were familiar with global management concepts and practices. Their social and cultural distance from the global was not an issue. In contrast these actors were themselves sometimes global players in this specialised field of performance measurement of the public justice sector.

Furthermore, the South African government was among the first in the world to be interested in performance auditing. The South African Exchequer and Audit Act of 1975 already included provisions that mentioned the concept of performance audits and added it in that piece of legislation to the Auditor-General's work tools. While this Act could already be seen as a sign that the future of government audits would include practices where the AG controls whether the state receives 'value for money' and would test the merits of expenditure, it took some time until these forms of audits could become practicable (AGSA 2014). For example, the South Africa's Crime Information Analysis Centre (CIAC) started to collect information about South African courts' conviction rate only from 1996 onwards. Other court related performance statistics were not collected before that time. I further traced the first parliamentary critic of the lack of commitment within the Department of Justice to collect statistical data on the work done by prosecutors to the late 1980s (Fernandez 1993). As I mentioned above the first NPA annual report, which included performance indicators that can be used to assess the organisation's compliance with their annual stated delivery targets, was submitted to Parliament and the DOJ only in 2002.

The ethnographic chapters of this book will deal in great detail with what role the performance statistics, indicators, rates, targets and rankings play in the way observed and interviewed prosecutors are held accountable. How have the quantitative measures shaped and influenced prosecutors' everyday work practices and their understanding of accountability? They will show that these various numerical representations differ in terms of their everyday presence and relevance for court and managerial prosecutors' internal and external accounting work. Before I move to these chapters and this question I want to make three points in summary.

CONCLUSION

This chapter illustrates firstly that the expectations and demands of how prosecutors should be held accountable, and to whom, and with what mechanism and consequences has changed and diversified tremendously over the twentieth century. During much of the twentieth century the power of prosecutors was abused on a massive scale by the country's White minority government – to which the head of the prosecuting authority was accountable. The political leaders used it for their own and the White population's political and economic interests. After South Africa's democratic transition in 1994, power and accountability relations between the different arms of government were newly distributed and constitutionally entrenched. The newly introduced separation of powers strengthened independence but also extended the accountability demands on the prosecution authority. Additional checks and balances were introduced to ensure that the abuse of power and the constant violations of the country's criminal procedure act, so prevalent during Apartheid, would come to an end. Accountability was discussed, as I showed, by making the prosecution authority more representative of the overall population, by professionalising the work force and by making its working more effective and efficient through performance measurement systems.

Secondly, although I presented the various forms of accountability separately in this historical overview, they are not to be understood as an absolute succession in time. One form did not merely encompass or end previous forms. That means that different forms of accountability co-exist, have their own distinct logic and reflect different concerns, but that at times, new forms of accountability can also transform the existing form without necessarily superseding them. New forms lead more often to a 'web of accountabilities' as Boström and Garsten (2008: 6) suggest 'which, in turn, creates greater and greater fuzziness'.

Thirdly, and this is the most important point, the different forms of accountability I presented here were not equally important at all times for all parts of the prosecuting authority. Accountability demands can emerge from different constituencies and therefore have dissimilar effects on disparate parts of the organisation. Although I referred very generally to 'the NPA' and 'prosecutors' and 'cases', in the following chapters I will paint a much more detailed picture of specific parts of the NPA and its 3,000 employees working in hundreds of courts and additional buildings in nine different provinces and dealing with over a million cases per year. In other words, it makes a difference, when thinking about the NPA's accountability relationships, to keep in mind which part of the organisation we are referring to.

Accountability through representation was, for example, not a talking point when White prosecutors were working in the NPA's Special Investigative Unit dealing with economic and organised crime and investigated and prosecuted some of the country's 'top criminals' or 'serious gangsters'. When the same group of prosecutors initiated criminal proceedings against popular and highly ranked politicians and government employees, all distinguished struggle heroes, the prosecutors' race became a topic of public conversation in relation to their accountability or more specifically as a sign of their lack of accountability (Matisonn 2001).[17]

Accountability through institutional and political independence does not play an important role when the accountability of lower

[17] The Scorpions investigated corruption allegations against popular high-ranked ANC officials – amongst them Toni Yengeni, chief whip of the ANC from 1998 until 2001; Jacob Zuma, the country's Deputy President from 1999 until 2005 and President of South Africa after 2008; and Jackie Selebi, South Africa's National Police Commissioner between 2002 and 2009 and President of Interpol between 2004 and 2008. Tony Yengeni, convicted in 2003 of fraud after he failed to disclose to Parliament that he had received a 47% discount on a SUV Mercedes Benz vehicle from Daimler-Benz Aerospace, a company who was bidding at the time for South Africa's arms procurement deal ('Judgement day for Tony Yengeni' 2005), complained, for example, about the 'number of white people there [in the Scorpions]. The same guys who persecuted us are in control [...]. So it's not surprising that the attention of the unit has changed from cracking serious syndicates and criminals. [...] I told them they were being insensitive to the history of the country, that it was against the spirit of the constitution, because it reminds me of whites judging blacks. We know there is racism; whites thinking blacks driving a car are thieves or drug smugglers' (in Matisonn 2001).

court prosecutors, who are mostly involved in the prosecution of 'petty criminals' (thieves, robbers, burglars), drunken rowdies or wife beaters, is discussed. It more usually receives attention when prosecutors are involved in more controversial prosecutions and when the NDPP is personally involved in the decision-making process. The prosecution of Jacob Zuma, the country's deputy president from 1999 until 2005 and President of South Africa between 2009 and 2018 (when he was forced to step down) is such a case where the independence and accountability of the NPA was and still is furiously debated, as I already indicated in the introduction. Critics question how independent the NDPP could be, when he was appointed by a president who may again have to face serious corruption charges once his presidential term ends. The NPA's specialised investigation unit has been investigating Jacob Zuma since 2001. His personal financial adviser, Shabir Shaik, was in 2005 found guilty and sentenced to fifteen years in prison for paying bribes to Zuma in return for his support for an arms contractor in one of the largest arms-deals in the history of the country (S v Shaik and Others (Criminal Appeal) (62/06) [2006] ZASCA 105; [2007] 2 All SA 9 (SCA); 2007 (1) SA 240 (SCA) (6 November 2006)).[18]

Zuma was charged with corruption in 2005. The case was stuck from the court's roll by the presiding judge in 2006, but the NPA recharged him after further, more in-depth preparation and investigation of the case in 2008. In April 2009, however, two weeks before the national presidential election, the acting NDPP, Mokotedi Mpshe, announced that he was dropping the charges against Zuma because of accusations that the timing of the recharging of Zuma was manipulated by Mr McCarthy, then the head of the Scorpions, for political reasons. The NDPP decided that is was not fair and just to carry on with the case. Two weeks later Zuma was elected as the country's new President. Since then he enjoyed immunity from prosecution.

The case raises critical accountability questions, namely whether the NPA complies with its mandate to be politically unbiased and whether the executive respects the NPA's independence. Critics accused Zuma of instating lawyers to this strategically important position – the head of the NPA – who are well disposed towards him in the event that his

[18] In 1999 South Africa bought, for R43 billion, various types of arms from several European manufacturers. In 2000 Patricia de Lille, opposition party leader, told Parliament that she was in possession of information which implicated ANC politicians of receiving considerable bribes. In 2000, a parliamentary committee also reported irregularities in the way this arms deal had been processed. For further information see: Marais 2011.

corruption charges resurface, but which are not fit and proper persons to do the job. For example, the appointment process of Menzi Simelane, a former Director General of the Department of Justice and Constitutional Development (DOJCD), to the position of the NDPP in 2009 was found to be irrational and invalid by the Constitutional Court of South Africa in 2012 (Democratic Alliance v The President of the RSA & Others (263/11) [2011] ZASCA 241 (1 December 2011)). The court stated that Zuma had failed to pay attention to evidence, including the findings of the Ginwala inquiry into the conduct of then-NDPP Vusi Pikoli, where it was specifically mentioned that Simelane gave contradictory evidence to the inquiry and where doubts about his honesty and integrity and credibility were raised. Critics also accuse the 'Zuma camp' of playing an active role in the disbandment of the Scorpions in 2008.

The DA, South Africa's official opposition party, tried shortly after Zuma's case was withdrawn in 2009 to hold the NPA to account for their decision-making processes – the NPA was being forced to make the material and records, which lead to the withdrawal of the charges against Zuma, public in 2017 – another form of account giving which does not come into play in most cases the NPA deals with. The party also applied for a judicial review of the Mpshe's decision to withdraw the charges. It took nearly seven years until this review was finalised in April 2016. The main reason for the delay in this review application was that Adv. Mpshe and Zuma challenged the DA's *locus standi* in this matter and questioned the reviewability of the decision as well as whether NDPP Mpshe was compelled to disclose the material and records of his 2009 decision to the DA. Both cases were only finally decided at the Supreme Court of Appeal and in favour of the DA (Zuma v DA (771/2016); ANDPP v DA (1170/2016) [2017] ZASCA 146 (13 October 2017)). The judgement states that the decision of the NDPP at the time was 'irrational'. In March 2018 the head of the NPA Adv. Shaun Abrahams reinstated the charges against Zuma and on April 6 was Zuma's first court appearance in this matter. The court date for the start of the trial is 12 November, 2018. However, a side battle over Zuma's legal costs might further delay and complicate the case. South Africa's opposition parties, the DA and the EFF ('Economic Freedom Fighters'), accuse Zuma of abusing state funds to obstruct and delay the administration of justice and avoid public accountability. They are asking the courts to review the right of the state to fund Zuma's legal battle since 2006 with the aim to make him personally liable to pay his costly and ever-increasing legal bills.[19]

President Jacob Zuma's case has been one of the most publicised cases of the NPA. It has, to some extent, become a litmus test for the NPA and for the South African constitutional democracy. Three NDPPs stepped down, were fired or were suspended over the controversies this case attracted. The amount of time and resources, which went into this case, is unprecedented. In the next three chapters I will move to the less publicised side of the NPA: to the everyday work realities of prosecutors stationed at the lower courts, the district magistrate courts. Prosecutors working for the NPA's specialised units who prosecute high-profile cases like that of Zuma usually concentrate on a few cases for extended periods of time. Prosecutors in the lower courts deal with up to thirty cases a day, hundreds of cases per week, close to a thousand cases per month. Their offices are more modestly furnished and equipped, and they have fewer resources to spend on each case. Their cases are barely commented on in the media, although this is the criminal justice system that the majority of South Africans comes face to face with, if at all.

[19] Zuma had an agreement with the Presidency (then under Thabo Mbeki) that the state would fund his defence and if he was found guilty he would pay back the state the money. While it is common that a state covers its employee's legal fees if that person was charged with a crime allegedly committed while exercising his or her official duties, this arrangement can be repealed when it turns out that the employee was actually not exercising his public duties, but only promoting his private interest when committing the crime. Then the person has to refund the state for the legal costs the state covered for him or her. One application has already been granted by the High Court in Pretoria in December 2017, although this one is not related to the corruption trial. The Court ordered that Zuma needs to pay personally the legal bill (around R10 million) for trying to prevent the publication of public protector Thuli Madonsela's 'State of Capture' report (which examines the ties between the Gupta family and specific state officials/institutions), herby trying to interfere with the constitutional obligation of the former public prosecutor.

The other two applications are asking for the legal review of the agreement between Zuma and the Presidency with the aim to declare it invalid, set it aside and make Zuma personally pay for his legal costs. The North Gauteng High Court is still processing them. The current president Cyril Ramaphosa has already announced in May 2018 that he is not opposing the DA applications and that he will leave the matter in the court's hands. It is expected that he will do the same in the EFF application, which deals with the repayment of costs Zuma has already incurred (Maughan 2018). Ramaphosa's spokesperson announced end of June 2018 that he will adhere to the agreement that taxpayers' money is used to fund Zuma's legal costs until a court orders the Presidency otherwise. Commentators estimate that the legal review of the agreement will take up to two years and there is concern that Zuma will use that time and Ramaphosa's insurance that his costs are covered by the state to continue to delay the trial with further litigation (Hunter 2018). However, there are also voices which think that due to a recent landmark judgement of a Durban High Court Judge (Westwood Insurance Brokers (Pty) Ltd v Ethekwini Local Municipality and Others (8221/16) [2017] ZAKZDHC 15 (5 April 2017)), personal cost orders for public officials might become more frequent in the near future and that this potential threat or change of legal climate might prevent reckless public officials from using 'frivolous litigation' to avoid being held accountable (Herselman 2017).

2

ETHNOGRAPHIC RESEARCH IN A MULTI-LOCAL ORGANISATION: ACCESS, CHALLENGES AND METHODS

INTRODUCTION

The ethnographic study of multi-local organisations provides the researcher with a challenge, 'given ethnography's focus on local places, on small scale, more or less observable social units and the cultural meanings and practices that constitute them' as Merry states (2006: 980; see also Czarniawska 2008: 5). The ethnographer's units of observation – her field sites – are harder, for example, to locate within a national state organisation like the NPA whose over three thousand employees work simultaneously in nine different provinces in national and regional head offices and in hundreds of district, regional and high courts, scattered around South Africa. One approach to make the running of larger organisations more amenable to ethnographic research is to focus on a single aspect of their working reality, which is both observable in specific locations and central to linking different organisational actors and settings, and the way they communicate and work together (Merry 2006: 981; Czarniawska 2008: 13; Breidenstein et al. 2013: 48). I focused on the single aspect of quantitative accountability.

The aim of this chapter is to provide methodological clarification and specification of how this research was conducted. Where did I study quantitative accountability? Where did it happen and materialise? Who or what exactly did I follow? What kinds of methods were used? What factors influenced the research? To begin with, I provide background information as to how my research interest in quantitative accountability and the South African National Prosecuting Authority came to be. Fieldwork, as it often does, shifted my interest slowly to these numerical representations. My focus emerged in the field, where I had been for months, and not while I was planning and conceptualising my research sitting at my desk. The chapter then moves to the introduction of the three central types of locations for my fieldwork: several magistrate courts, an NPA regional head office and the NPA's national head office. The prosecutors I worked with in these settings can be divided into two groups: firstly, prosecutors who are involved in immediate prosecution, and secondly, prosecutors who are involved in the senior and upper management of the NPA. My empirical analysis thus covers different organisational levels. In the last section of this chapter I discuss the specific challenges and problems I encountered when doing research in these different settings, and how they and the people who worked in them shaped the data collection and findings for this study.

IDENTIFYING THE OBJECT OF THIS STUDY

My interest in the workings of the South African criminal justice system was formed during my Honours and Magister research, where I studied private crime prevention and security strategies in various locations in the Western Cape over ten months between 2003 and 2005 (Mugler 2005; 2006). There was never a day in the field when my research participants, coming from a wide variety of social, economic and racial backgrounds, did not complain about the country's criminal justice system. When they shared their personal experiences with crime and violence with me, or when they showed me their physical security devices in their homes or explained their strategies on how to move around safely through the city, there was almost always a moment where the state's criminal justice system was criticised for failing to provide South Africans with a safe and secure living environment. Comments like 'Crime pays in this country'; 'Our criminal justice system is useless'; 'It is a complete joke. It keeps on postponing cases forever. It lets criminals off the hook too easily'; and 'It is not working' were commonly made by observed and interviewed South Africans, and shocking personal accounts of experiences frequently followed. Out of this extreme frustration of my research participants with the country's criminal justice system grew my interest in exploring South Africa's criminal courts: What do courts actually do when they are at work? That was my initial, and then still broad, research question.

When I began conducting fieldwork in various South African magistrates' courts in 2007, it struck me how often my prosecutor informants mentioned their 'stats'. This conversation was nothing I had initiated, and nothing I initially paid much attention to, since I was at the time interested in more classical legal and political anthropological topics circling around the exploration of how 'the' state works in practice in the new South Africa (see Bierschenk and de Sardan 2014). Thomas Bierschenk's (2008) exciting research amongst prosecutors in Benin had, for example, shown how important various informal and privatising practices were for the everyday functioning of Benin's under-resourced state courts. He described corruption as one of several informalisation and privatisation strategies 'which simultaneously resolve and reinforce the functional problems of the Beninese legal system in a kind of negative feedback loop' (2008: 3).

I was also hoping to contribute to questions Jean and John Comaroff (2004: 189) were raising in their writing like 'where are the [South African] state's "limits of legal tolerance?"' and 'how does the country's criminal justice system "accommodate difference" and make space for "African jurisprudence" while at the same time promoting "one law for one nation?"' I was interested in finding out what 'African jurisprudence' means in these urban courts, since the Comaroffs were suggesting that South African state courts were being transformed in rural areas by Black African magistrates who were socialised in different milieus than their White counterparts who were unfamiliar with the power of witchcraft accusations or the complexities of bridewealth payments. None of these authors had mentioned the relevance of performance measurement systems, targets and indicators for their research participants.

While I listened attentively and feverishly took notes of prosecutors' and magistrates' 'stats talk', I often secretly hoped that our conversation would move on to these legal and political anthropological, and for me more interesting and more relevant, topics. It took me some time to realise: firstly, how central those numerical representations, which prosecutors talked about and waved about my face, were for my general question of 'How South African state courts work?' and more specifically 'What does accountability mean in this setting?'; and secondly, how much more most complainants in these urban townships were interested in state courts' speedy response to their cases rather than taking the time or energy to worry about 'African jurisprudence'. The courts were less perceived by local Black African residents, according to my observations, as an alienating and inappropriate forum for dispute resolution than scholars previously had pointed out a decade ago (Burman and Schaerf 1990; Wilson 2000; Tshehla 2001). Only after this recognition did I begin initiating conversations with prosecutors around their attitudes towards quantitative forms of accountability and consciously digging for any available information on the topic.

The fact that I decided to shift my initial research interest in the 'Africanisation of state law/courts', which was not an ongoing concern in the settings where I was conducting my study, to something which was part of the everyday working life of the people I observed made it easier to identify suitable units of observations for exploring quantitative accountability. In other words, I was already immersed in various field sites when I noticed the significance of quantitative accountability for the working world of my research participants. That is characteristic for the ethnographic method, which starts from the premise that the researcher discovers and derives her more specific research question from her involvement with empirical work (Breidenstein 2013: 45–49) and takes the stance that it is more difficult to find the right questions than to answer them (Merton 1959: 27ff.). In the following section I want to now present the three main field sites where the material for this study was collected, as well as the actors with whom I worked in these different settings.

FIELD SITES AND RESEARCH PARTICIPANTS

I conducted ethnographic fieldwork within the NPA over eighteen months between 2008 and 2012. Research participants were promised anonymity: information such as their names, places of work and other identifiable information would not be disclosed openly in the study. In order to protect the identity of research participants their real names and the name of the geographical location of their workplaces are therefore not revealed in this study. It is important to keep in mind that without this confidentiality agreement, the majority of the prosecutors I worked with would have not have given me the permission to observe them at work and to answer the hundreds of questions I posed to them. For this reason, I will only sketch out my research settings.

My main field sites were: (1) five different magistrate courts, all located in the metropolitan area of a major South African city with two located in two different townships 25 kilometres outside the city centre, two located in the city's CBD and one located in a large suburb; (2) one regional head office, located in the CBD of the same city; and (3) the NPA's national head office, located in a suburb of Pretoria.[1]

[1] In addition, I paid several visits to the national and regional head office of the Department of Justice and Constitutional Development (DOJCD), to five police stations in the province where I was conducting the research and one visit to the South African Police Service's head office in Pretoria. My aim was to collect data on how other key South African criminal justice

My research participants can be roughly divided into two groups of prosecutors. Firstly, I worked with prosecutors who are involved in immediate prosecution. In the NPA's organisational hierarchy they are referred to as 'prosecutors' and 'control prosecutors'. The second group I worked with were prosecutors who are involved in the senior and upper management of the NPA, namely 'senior public prosecutors', 'chief prosecutors' and 'deputy directors of public prosecution', 'deputy directors of national prosecution' and 'directors of public prosecution'. These two organisational levels were researched with different methods. Periods of stationary, non-moving research alternated with periods of mobile research (where I would follow a specific prosecutor or case around).

Seven prosecutors and one control prosecutor, who are stationed at five different magistrate courts, were shadowed at work, sometimes on a daily basis, over eighteen months between 2008 and 2012. I shadowed an additional five prosecutors stationed at two other courts over shorter periods of time. In total I got to know fourteen different courts and observed and spoke to twenty-six court prosecutors in three different provinces. By 'shadowing' I mean that I followed a prosecutor through his or her entire working day; I observed their work but did not participate actively in the true sense of the word in their work activities (Czarniawska 2007; 2008). Furthermore, the prosecutors' private lives, although much was revealed to me during the course of my fieldwork, were not a focus of the research.

I got to know prosecutors' working environment by spending hundreds of hours 'hanging out' in different courtrooms observing prosecutors in action when they were busy prosecuting cases between nine o'clock in the morning and four o'clock in the afternoon. I was either squeezed between the visitors, accused and witnesses on the courts' benches in the public section of the court, or, when the spatial arrangement of the court allowed and I became more familiar with the respective prosecutors, on a free chair directly next to them. Once I spent more time in the non-public sections of the courts, I listened to prosecutors' interaction with witnesses and complainants, and to their conversations with colleagues and with other members of the court during their tea and lunch breaks and during court adjournments. Other members included interpreters, (legal aid) attorneys, clerks,

organisations collect performance data, how sophisticated the data is and in what ways it shapes their everyday work and accountability understanding in order to see more clearly the NPA's specifics.

policemen and to a lesser degree magistrates and security guards. I would also spend hours chatting with prosecutors informally in their offices while they were preparing their cases or doing other forms of paperwork, either before they would start their court work or after they had finished it.

In addition, I shadowed a control prosecutor on a daily and later on a weekly basis over the entire time of my research. I sat many days in his office and observed him at work screening dockets and interacting with witnesses and police investigators. His office was also a central focal point for other prosecutors from the same court, but also from other courts who came to visit and would talk about work, which made his office a particularly interesting and important field site for me. When the control prosecutor left the court building during working hours, I followed him whenever he granted me permission to join him. I was able, with him, to attend management meetings at other courts, meetings at police stations in the jurisdiction of the court, training sessions at the regional head office, workshops organised by NGOs which had the aim of improving the safety and security of the townships surrounding the court, outreach events organised by the NPA or by the Department of Justice and Constitutional Development, for example, in local schools or city halls and social work gatherings.[2] Lastly, I also shadowed a senior public prosecutor from time to time over the period of this research. I sat in her office at a busy urban magistrate court and followed her to a wide variety of meetings and NPA outreach events as she also acted as a community prosecutor[3] for about thirty per cent of her working time. It was also through her that I was able to attend meetings at the regional head office, where I came into contact with members of the NPA's upper and executive management.

The material I collected within the more senior and upper management spheres of the NPA was gathered during management meetings I attended at an NPA regional head office where seven NPA managers were observed in action and, to a lesser extent, during NPA's public outreach events and training sessions, and through formal interviews which I conducted with five managerial prosecutors. Senior and upper management prosecutors working at the national head office in Pretoria were introduced to me via a South African law professor. During three

[2] State advocates who prosecute at the High Court and have their offices at the regional head office did not form an important part of this study. I only spoke to them informally during trials I attended at High Court in the province where I conducted my fieldwork.

[3] See Chapter 3 for explanation of a community prosecutor.

days in 2008 and three days in 2010 I paid several visits to the head office. During my first visit, my key contact, a senior prosecutor working at head office, arranged interviews for me on an ad hoc basis. That means that she knocked on peoples' doors and shuffled me into their offices and I was able to conduct an unexpected interview marathon. I interviewed seven senior and upper management prosecutors. She also arranged further meetings with prosecutors at her home and with her husband who was an ex-Scorpions prosecutor. When I visited the head office for the second time, I arranged two interviews in advance and was hoping that my key contact would again assist me in opening further doors since I was also staying with her. Unfortunately, this time this contact became silent when I arrived in Pretoria. All interviews with managerial prosecutors were recorded. Interviews with court and control prosecutors took more the form of informal conversations in passing. Most of the time I had to take notes while I was in a private place like the court's bathroom or in my car, or in a public place like the visitor's benches in the courtroom where I would record what people had told me while court was in session and listening to the court proceedings.

In addition, two former senior public prosecutors, who now act as magistrates, were regularly asked for comments on my research findings during my research. I would sit in their offices and chat to them, either before their court work starts (between eight o'clock and nine o'clock) or during their lunch break. These two magistrates acted as 'mentors' for my research, since they were no longer directly involved with the NPA, but still had had important insights and contacts which they willingly and less restrictedly shared with me.

Three judges, four magistrates, three private attorneys, three legal aid attorneys, one police station commander, various policemen, four members of SAPS' senior national management, three social workers, two high ranked members of the Department of Justice and Constitutional Development and five South African criminal justice researchers were also interviewed in order to collect material which would assist me to triangulate my data and sources.[4] That allowed me to corroborate, elaborate and disconfirm evidence and gain a more

[4] These criminal justice actors were especially interviewed at the beginning of my research during the exploratory phase where I tried to create as many accesses to the field as possible and where I tried to understand who actually is involved in the working of a specific lower court and how knowledge and responsibilities are distributed. Members of the SAPS' management were interviewed with regards to their organisation's performance measurement system.

nuanced understanding of motivations and contexts (Flick 2011: 51). The change of perspective I obtained through the contact with these non-NPA actors also assisted me to intensify and specify my observations in the NPA, since it became much clearer to me how the NPA 'ticks' when talking to these other criminal justice experts.

The dominant research language of this study was English. Although I studied Xhosa, one of South Africa's nine official languages and the one African language that is, next to Zulu, the most frequently spoken, I usually used it only when contacting people via email and text message or when introducing myself. The courts' working language is English or Afrikaans, so in order to become a prosecutor people have to at least be fluent in English. During conversations Xhosa-speaking people would quickly turn to English since their English was so much better than my Xhosa. While my research would have benefited from greater language skills, the constant switch between different languages, lack of understanding and need for translation is a frustrating South African court and civil servant experience I shared with many of my research participants. For example, many Black prosecutors, magistrates or accused were not fluent in Afrikaans. That I was able to converse rudimentarily in Xhosa as a White German woman made an enormous difference in terms of ease of access to the field. While I encountered much less racism in prosecutorial working environments, compared to the South African private living worlds I studied in my previous research on private crime prevention strategies (Mugler 2005; 2006), being a White person in South Africa is still associated and experienced by many coloured and Black South Africans with enormous privileges and also brings up negative associations and reactions. Most White urban South Africans are unable to speak any African languages, so it was perceived by many of my Black research participants as something positive that I was at least trying. 'Ndiyazama noko' (Xhosa for 'I am trying at least!').

To be able to speak some Xhosa was also very useful for doing research in the courts, which were located in townships where predominantly Xhosa-speaking South Africans were living. It is well known that according to reported crime statistics over the last two decades, South Africa has repeatedly been listed as one of the most violent, crime-ridden countries in the world. However, it is often overlooked that the burden of crime and violence is distributed very unevenly in the country. The least economically powerful sector of the South African population carries the largest burden of it. A large amount of that crime and violence occurs in urban townships. The country's highest murder rate is for example frequently recorded at one of the police stations in close proximity to and within the jurisdiction of the two courts where I began my research.[5] That the police find bodies discarded in open fields or that residents claim they are used to the sounds of gunfire are unfortunately not exceptions in these residential areas. Every month high numbers of assault, attempted murder, robbery, theft, rape and domestic violence cases are reported at the three police stations surrounding the courts.

Despite the repeal of the Group Areas, Land and Population Registration Acts in 1991, White South Africans are an absolute scarcity in these previously Black-designated areas surrounding the court. I was constantly sticking out. The economic disparities between these suburbs and the more affluent, mostly White or 'mixed' areas are huge and amongst the main reasons for the lack of desegregation and integration of these poor neighbourhoods into the wider metropolitan life of South Africa's urban centres. The high violent crime rate in these townships, their geographical and socio-economic distance from urban centres and persisting racist factors are all reasons why most White South Africans perceive large urban townships as 'no-go areas'. Being able to speak and understand some Xhosa made it easier for me to feel more comfortable, more normal and less at risk of being attacked on my way to and from the courts and during lunch breaks, or when I had an after-work drink with prosecutors in the area or gave them a lift home (some of them lived in close proximity to the court). Having some knowledge of the local language also helped me to develop my own personal security strategies. I quickly learned from prosecutors who were living or used to live in the areas surrounding the courts to differentiate between 'quiet' and 'not so quiet' township areas.

Having now introduced the settings and the research participants of this study, I want to move on and discuss the challenges I encountered while studying quantitative accountability in the NPA. I want to acquaint the reader through that reflective discussion with the specificities of my field sites. The following section of this chapter focuses first on the obstacles I had to deal with when studying court prosecutors, and

[5] For reasons of anonymity and protection of the identity of research participants, the court's actual geographical location is not revealed in this study. Crime statistics indicating the crime rates of these areas are with the author of this study. See:
https://www.saps.gov.za/services/crimestats.php for crime statistics per station and per province. Access 5 July 2018.

in a second step reflects on the difficulties which emerged when researching managerial prosecutors.

METHODOLOGICAL CHALLENGES WHEN DOING RESEARCH ON STATE ORGANISATIONS

Access and Mobility

Organisational settings, like a state prosecution service, as I mentioned in the introduction of this chapter, can be difficult to research using traditional ethnographic working methods. Unlike in many other field sites, I was not able to 'just hang out in prosecutors' offices' and go somewhere else or ask someone else if things do not work out as planned, simply because there is only a limited number of organisational actors in each setting to talk to (see Whyte [1943] 1993; Czarniawska 2007; 2008). For example, there are only a couple of courts in each South African city, no more than three prosecutors work at small district courts, there is usually only one chief prosecutor responsible for a cluster of courts and only one DPP manages the prosecution services of a whole province. If these actors dislike the researcher, or are afraid of her findings, or are too busy and therefore too tired to talk to the ethnographer, research becomes difficult.

For example, in the beginning of my research and after I had spent days and weeks building up a very good working relationship with a prosecutor at a small court where he was the only prosecutor, he was suddenly transferred to another nearby court. His successor in contrast was not very talkative and did not grant me permission to sit in her office and observe her at work. She literally always had her door closed whereas the other prosecutor would leave his door open most of the time and invite me inside. I was torn between keeping my established observer position at 'my' first field site, where I was already familiar with the working and rhythm of this specific court and its staff members, and following my key contact and start anew at another court.

Moving between different field sites is conceptually a much-desired method – multi-sited and de-territorialised ethnographic research is currently often called for (Marcus 1995; von Benda-Beckmann and Griffiths 2005; Büschner and Urry 2009; Merry 2006). In practice, however, it is a time-consuming undertaking, especially when it is not intended and planned for at the beginning of the research, because building up trusting working relationships with research participants requires the researcher to spend a considerable amount of time in one location. It was only when I realised that it is common for prosecutors to move between courts in their specific cluster (few worked permanently at the same court during the entire research period) that I felt more at ease in extending my field sites and moving around various courts in a specific geographical area and following the prosecutors with whom I had developed the most trusting relationships.

Having said that prosecutors' and control prosecutors' mobility was something I had not sufficiently anticipated in the beginning of my research, this group of prosecutors is far less mobile than more senior prosecutors. Once lower court prosecutors are stationed, the times they will be present at court is far more predictable in contrast to more senior NPA members, who were often 'already elsewhere' (Strannegård and Fridberg 2001): for example, travelling, in parliament, at functions, at head office or participating in national or regional criminal justice management gatherings, or attending last-minute meetings or 'crisis situations'. I will mention more about the difficulties of gaining access to senior and executive NPA members and the conundrums of having to rely for analysis on relatively short formal interviews and limited situational observation below.

In contrast, court and control prosecutors attend meetings less frequently, and if they do, these activities usually take place in the same locale, so they spend the majority of their working hours in one specific geographical area – their cluster. When these lower court prosecutors had meetings with other criminal justice role players in their locale, their professional image and the authority which is attributed to the office allowed me to accompany them to these non-NPA meetings without many questions being asked by, for example, the police, social workers or non-governmental organisation (NGO) employees. Within the structured and hierarchical world of the civil service, they occupied a higher position to the former.

Despite courts being open to the public, they can be intimidating public institutions. At the entrance every court visitor has 'to go through security', which means I had to walk through a metal detector, undergo a body search and my bag was screened and in some instances searched. I had to make sure that I was not in possession of food, weapons or cameras, otherwise they would be confiscated; if one is lucky they will be secured in a safe, but often there is no safe, so I was asked to hide them in the entrance area. This is not a feasible option because these items will be gone when one returns to reclaim them.

When I got friendly with the security guards at certain smaller courts and they recognised me as a regular visitor to the courts' prosecutors, they spared me the security check most of the time and waved me through.

Once one is inside the court building, every court has a different atmosphere depending on the purpose, size and history of the court. In some courts the intimidating rattling of the keys of the iron cell gates can be heard the moment one steps into the building. Some courts are located in grand nineteenth century buildings that carry an aura of colonial suppression or, depending upon one's view, the charm of a past era. Others have a more sterile, soundproof, modern design. The cells are below the courtrooms and one hears much less of what goes on inside them. The atmosphere in court also depends on the type of cases which are being heard. When people are charged in regional and high courts with offences that may result in long prison sentences, the intensity and nervousness amongst court visitors and staff members is much higher than in cases where the accused is more likely to end up with a fine or suspended sentence. Accused who have been awaiting trial for a long time or face a possible life sentence are also more inclined to try secretly exchange information or goods with family members or friends or even to try to escape. The police court orderlies in these cases are more alert.

Courts were initially intimidating for me too because, as an outsider, it was not clear to me which areas were open to the public and how I was to behave in a courtroom where special procedures are followed. In some courts, due to space constraints, the accused, witnesses and court visitors have to sit next to each other. Being in close proximity to people who are accused of having inflicted horrendous pain or stress on others was at times threatening and nerve-racking. However, after having visited fourteen courts during the course of my research and after becoming friendly and close to numerous prosecutors, magistrates, policemen and -women, interpreters and clerks, these unpleasant memories are almost forgotten.

While I have focused so far on the more difficult aspects of gaining access to prosecutorial working environments, I would also like to mention the convenient aspects of doing research in state courts. They are public institutions and therefore open to any visitor. Access to the public spaces of court buildings including courtrooms was therefore, with some exceptions, easily obtained and allowed during the entire time of this study. Only a small percentage of cases are heard *in camera*, meaning that the complainant can decide whether she or he will accept court visitors. Being present in the public areas of the court assisted me in gaining access to the non-public areas of the court. When I began to sit next to prosecutors in court, thus entering a non-public space, it was usually necessary to inform the magistrate about my research, but no one ever opposed my presence.

It is further important to keep in mind that to some extent prosecutors are obliged, due to their public role and mandate, to listen to members of the public (although whether a curious German PhD student belongs to that group is obviously debatable). Thus, their public role and the public character of state courts makes it difficult for people who find the presence of a researcher disconcerting or even perceive it as a surveillance threat to 'hide', knowing that I must be somewhere in the court building. People who work for non-state institutions or private individuals or even the more senior NPA members who work at the NPA regional and national head offices can hide more easily. Their places of work are not open to the public so my opportunities to gain their trust were restricted because they could refuse the researcher access to their premises. Limited face-to-face contact made it easier to decline or ignore my email or telephonic requests for access.

Confidentiality and Classified Information

While I was able to 'hang out' in the public areas of the court and gain prosecutors' trust relatively quickly, which enabled me to sit in the non-public court spaces and in their offices, the challenge with lower court prosecutors was more in the detail. Prosecutors, like most organisational actors, are able to regulate outsiders' access to the realities of their working life (see Lau und Wolff 1983; Peters 2000; 2001; Mosse 2006; Boyer 2008; Breidenstein et al. 2013: 51–53). They could easily restrict access by saying they were not permitted to talk about certain 'confidential' issues or could not give access to 'classified' documents. They could also restrict access to specific segments of their working life: For example, if they did not want to bluntly refuse access to certain meetings and documents or if they wanted to disguise the restriction, they would state that 'it would not be interesting for your research to attend the meeting', even though I had explained in detail how beneficial the attendance would be for this study.

The general challenge in these situations was for me as an outsider to firstly identify the documents, meetings and topics that are open to the public and which are closed, and identify who is authorised (or willing, in the case of confidential information) to grant me access to the desired data and setting and who cannot authorise, or is unwilling to take the risk of, sharing organisational insights. Secondly, I needed to be constantly aware that some situations are more complicated and that it would be a mistake to interpret the phrase 'not interesting for you' always to be about power relationships, hierarchies and therefore restriction of access and redirection of my ethnographic attention.

For example, it would probably be right to say that the ontological centre of a prosecutor's work life revolves around legal knowledge and court action because most of them see themselves primarily as litigators and lawyers and not as administrators or managers. Many presumed that trials – particularly the regional and high court trials of 'serious criminals' or the newly-introduced alternative dispute resolution mechanisms – would be most interesting for me as a researcher. So there were different ideas embedded in different professional and intellectual communities about what the real object of my study was, or should be. It may be that prosecutors thought that my interest in performance statistics and indicators was mundane, not part of their core work and therefore inconsequential. To get across that I am interested in the mundane, the non-legal part in their work was a constant challenge because of their expertise being strongly embedded in the legal field. It took also some time until I learned the performance measurement vocabulary and the lines of authority within the NPA in order to show convincingly that I am really interested in the accounting part of their work.

Another constant problem for organisational researchers, who shadow people in their working environment rather than in other settings outside of work, is that they have to ensure that their presence does not cause trouble at the workplace. In my opinion this point is often overlooked. For example, Czarniawska (2008: 11) states that 'the possible effects of shadowing for and on the person shadowed can vary from one study to another', but also says that 'shadowing has boosted the morale of the person' she shadowed and that 'shadowing usually enhances the status of the person who is shadowed in the eyes of co-workers'. While this might be true, police court orderlies frequently teased me, for instance, about why I did not visit their courtroom or court more often instead of 'always visiting court X' and 'Mr. Mafunda', a control prosecutor and one of my key contacts.

However, it is equally true that some senior prosecutors indicated, although never spelling it out directly, that they would prefer it if I did not distract their staff from their prosecutorial duties with my presence and endless questions. And lower-ranked prosecutors were also often concerned about how it might affect them if higher-ranked prosecutors found out what confidential information they were sharing with me or to which work meetings they were taking me. Once I began to attend NPA management meetings more frequently and to interview more senior NPA members who were in some instances the lower court prosecutors' superiors, the concern that comments prosecutors made could 'come back and bite them' if I passed them on to their managers became more prevalent. On the other hand, it also assured some lower-ranked prosecutors that if higher-up prosecutors trusted me, they could trust me too.

Trust and Distributed Knowledge

Most prosecutors, while initially very friendly and accommodating, often seemed nervous about answering more specific questions about the NPA and sharing personal ideas about their work with me. They were afraid that more senior members might reprimand them for doing so and they were unsure about whether NPA official directives permitted them to do so. Once prosecutors understood that I was not an investigative journalist – South Africa has quite a number of them and they are known for their ruthlessness – who might be interested in exposing the NPA's 'internal matters', they were less guarded about what they said to me.

In many cases lower ranked prosecutors also gave me the impression that they were afraid to answer my questions in case they said something which might be wrong. For example, they were unsure about the reasons behind the latest organisational changes and were concerned that an incorrect answer might reflect badly on their professional knowledge, but also on the consistent image every organisation attempts to portray of itself. Also, that people were unable to answer my questions often had something to do with the dispersed and distributed knowledge in an organisation; in other words not everyone is supposed to know, or is authorised to know, everything and it takes time for an outsider to figure out 'who knows what' and to handle that insight with sensitivity.

Some NPA employees were worried that their emails were being read or telephone conversations tapped, especially after 2009 when the police's Director of National Intelligence, Richard Mdluli, was alleged to have committed several offences which pointed to abuse of his power, and when rumours were circulating in the media in 2012 that the acting NDPP was suspending the well-known regional head of the NPA's specialised commercial crime unit who was investigating, at the time, charges of fraud and abuse of state funds against the controversial head of crime intelligence. Consequently, they only felt free to share their views in a private environment or in one where it was difficult to take notes, for example while I was driving or having something to eat. Many prosecutors also disliked being taped on a dictaphone. It was difficult to determine in which situation it was beneficial to be more 'pushy' with my questions and requests for more semi-structured conversations and when it was inappropriate and would scare people. Sometimes reliable field contacts whose trust I had gained quickly turned unreliable and silent the moment I suggested sitting down and talking instead of talking 'on the move', which is extremely tiring. Thus, in my research contexts it was not necessarily the access to people I shadowed which had to be continuously renegotiated, but rather every new topic of conversation. It required continuous diplomatic skills and a huge amount of patience to find the right moment to interpose another of my numerous curious questions into the conversation.

For example, one of my key contacts, a control prosecutor, never grew tired of my visits or of explaining the criminal justice procedures to me, but when I asked him more sensitive questions, for example about rumour or gossip I had heard from other 'justice' employees or in the media, he would quietly change the topic. He explained to me several times that it was 'unethical' and 'unprofessional' for a prosecutor to talk negatively about one's colleagues and he emphasised that prosecutors were trained to arrive at an opinion not on mere snippets of what they had heard or on what someone had told them. Once he trusted that I took his professional work ethic seriously and did not just treat it as an avoidance strategy on his part, he became more open and to some extent less defensive when we touched on more sensitive points during the conversations.

Experts Studying Experts: What Is the Object of My Study?

A last challenging point which is important to mention is that attempting to understand experts or professionals requires a different kind of research mindset than when one interviews individuals who are not experts (Boyer 2008; see also: Ho 2009; Bourgoin 2012). First of all, in order to be taken seriously by other experts, one needs to acquire a considerable amount of expert knowledge and that takes time.

In my setting I was often mistaken for a lawyer, not because of my knowledge of criminal law and the country's criminal procedure act, but more because research subjects thought no other professional would voluntarily spend so much time at court. Once prosecutors and other court employees were aware that I was an anthropologist, I had already obtained some basic understanding of their work and was accepted as an untrained but eager-to-learn outsider.

What was more difficult to deal with was the misleading illusion or presumption that there is a common interest between ethnographers and lawyers. To absorb another expert's regime into one's own was more challenging than anticipated. While there is a similarity between ethnographers and lawyers – both being interested in cases in a wider sense – the difference in this setting is that prosecutors in district courts are often dealing with thirty cases a day. Dockets move quickly over prosecutors' office desks, on to the court and back to the police station and only return to court when the case is heard again (in a few weeks' or even months' time). Being an anthropologist, trained to explore and work with detailed case studies, it was difficult at the beginning of the research to decide whether I should follow the prosecutors or the docket. But being interested in understanding prosecutors' working environment, responsibilities and accountability relationships, it was clear that the focus had to be on them and their work.

I had to 'let go' of my first inclination to learn more about the individual case and its disputants, their expectations and experiences of state criminal justice and punishment. With thirty cases a day in front of you, these are not necessarily the questions a prosecutor has time and energy to ponder. The individual case is important to prosecutors, but the constant 'flow of cases' in and out of court is as vital in the lower courts. At the beginning of the research when I was still thinking about one case that the observed prosecutor had just dealt with (trying to understand its details, who was accused of doing what and to whom, surprised about the weapons people use – hot water or human faeces for example – and shocked by the brutality and poverty that people suffered and that these cases revealed), the prosecutor had already moved on and was already busy with the next case. Only with time did I get used to the specific pace and rhythm of prosecutorial work. On the one hand prosecutors do focus on specific details of cases at great length. It is not always immediately obvious why they would quibble over details laypeople might find irrelevant or unimportant. And at the same time prosecutors can quickly screen over a dozen cases so that an outsider fears that the prosecutor may have overlooked or missed something in the case. After having now discussed the most important factors, which shaped the material I was able to collect amongst prosecutors working in magistrate courts, I want to in the last section of this chapter discuss the obstacles I encountered when exploring quantitative accountability amongst members of the NPA's upper management.

'STUDYING-UP' AND 'THROUGH' THE TOP OF THE NPA

Access

The regional head offices are usually located in the city centre of each province's capital or primary city and are in close proximity to the High Court of each province. The national head office is located in Pretoria, South Africa's administrative capital, in a suburb twelve kilometres outside the city centre. Entering a regional or the national head office of the NPA is a much more complicated undertaking than visiting a district, regional or High Court. Since the NPA offices are not open to the public, I required an appointment scheduled with one of the employees working inside the NPA premises. Without this, one struggles to gain entrance to the building. Firstly, the security guards are more alert: They scan one's body and belongings thoroughly and have new and sophisticated-looking machines to do their job. Secondly, and more importantly, the receptionist takes down one's personal details, including ID numbers, and double-checks telephonically that the person one has the appointment with is willing or ready to see the visitor. Once the person or his/her secretary gives permission, the receptionist calls another security guard, who guides one through the building to the respective office or in most cases to the respective secretary or secretaries, and then disappears. That means I never had a chance to wander around the building by myself. When I entered buildings without an appointment but with head-office employees or regular visitors to the building, the receptionist tried to intervene and questioned my presence, but my NPA contacts were always able to use their authority or diplomatic skills to shuffle me into the building without telling the receptionists my exact position.

The air-conditioned NPA buildings, cooled on hot summer days or warmed on cold winter days, are in stark contrast to the sticky heat or freezing cold of the courtrooms I sat in, which often did not have the luxury of air-conditioning. What is also in stark contrast to the courts

I have described so far is the newness of these buildings. While many of the courts are old, and sometimes run down, or housed in some kind of off-the-wall or low-cost structure, the NPA head offices I visited are brand new. The materials which have been used to construct the buildings come across as solid and long lasting. The white walls, glass doors and dark steel and chrome finishes differ a great deal from the colonial buildings or the administrative-office style buildings of apartheid days, mainly built in the 1960s and 1970s, where many courts, offices of the Department of Justice and Constitutional Development and the police's regional and national head offices were housed. These new offices manifest to some extent the new start of South Africa's prosecution services in 1998 in the built environment.[6]

The offices of highly ranked NPA staff members also stand out in terms of their size, their comfortable furniture, sound absorption and in some instances their view. Actors' knowledge about or influence in the organisation was however not automatically linked to their office size and interior. Head office staff members all had functioning technological facilities like a computer, telephone and an internet connection in their offices, something which was not the norm for district court prosecutors.

The appointments made with members of the head office were often difficult to set up. But once they were, I was seldom asked to reschedule an appointment. That an emergency or someone more important bumped me off the schedule only happened frequently with managers at the Department of Justice and Constitutional Development and SAPS. It is worth mentioning that unlike personnel of lower segments of the NPA, executive managers and other higher ranked prosecutors in the organisation tend to be relatively easy to identify and even to locate. I usually found their names, ranks and contact details with a quick look on the NPA's organogram published on the organisation's website, or in other available hard copy or online NPA publications, for example in the 'list of attendees' of the NPA conference brochures. However, as organisational sociologist Robert Thomas (1993: 81) points out '[u]nfortunately, visibility is not the same as accessibility'.

As I mentioned earlier on in this chapter, to establish relationships with head office personnel was more difficult than in the public court setting, as I could only contact research subjects via mail, email or telephone, and I was not able to 'hang around' the premises. So it was

[6] Before 1998 no national prosecution body existed in South Africa. Each province had an attorney general that was responsible for the prosecution in one province. He and his prosecutorial team were stationed at the respective High Courts in each province.

easier for them to ignore me and deny my attempts to talk to them. I was introduced to most managers through other NPA members I met in district, regional and High Courts and/or through a South African law faculty member whom I met through the Southern African networks of the distinguished legal director of my research school. My status as a member of a research school in which social anthropologists collaborate together with lawyers of the legal research institutes of the Max Planck Society has many times helped to ease the point of entry. Amongst various South African criminal lawyers, the Max Planck Institute for Foreign and International Criminal Law in Freiburg was a recognisable affiliation.

Time Constraints, Eloquence and Smartness

When I was able to arrange a meeting time for a conversation, time was always a serious constraint. Since I had no knowledge of managers' personal schedules I could not estimate how much time they could spare. The awareness that I had been waiting for an interview for months and that this might be my only chance to interview this person, in other words that the opportunities for data collection are limited and not easily repeated, also increased the difficulty of creating a relaxed communicative atmosphere. The 'getting-to-know phase' of a field contact had to happen simultaneously with the 'getting-the-information phase'. In my other field sites there was usually more time for these phases to occur naturally over a longer period. Although I also quickly realised that Ulf Hannerz (2003: 209) is right when he points out that 'to some extent personalising encounters in the modern, multi-site field, comes not so much from deepening particular interactions as from the identification of common acquaintances – from placing the ethnographer in the translocal network of relationships'.

Similar to Hannerz's foreign news correspondents, who appreciated it, as he said, when he told them he had spoken to one of their colleagues somewhere else in the news-making world, the NPA managers seemed to be pleased when I dropped snippets of conversations I had with colleagues known and familiar to them, but who are based at another NPA regional head office, the NPA national head office or in the Department of Justice and Constitutional Development. This fact helped in my multi-local research to avoid not starting anew again at each new location. On average the interviews, conducted between 2008 and 2012, lasted between one and three hours. All interviews were taped and transcribed.

In addition to the time constraints, the intellect, eloquence and in some cases the charisma, as well as the expert knowledge of my interlocutors also made those interviews particularly challenging. Unlike lower court prosecutors, the chief prosecutors and in particular the deputy directors of public prosecution and directors of public prosecution (DPPs), are expected to speak on behalf of the NPA. So they are trained and experienced in representing the organisation to the outside world and to talk about official views in an articulated manner. If one does not redirect or interrupt them, they can easily talk for ten to fifteen minutes nonstop about something one could have read in the NPA's annual reports or numerous press releases. Some respondents probably did that to circumvent answering my questions, but with others it seemed they were slipping, out of habit, into that particular style of talking. Only time in the field in the form of shadowing and observation and meticulous interview preparation enabled me, after a while, to ask very specific questions and to surprise these high ranked prosecutors with my in-depth experience and to some extent knowledge of the inner logic of one of the central parts of the NPA they were overseeing: the lower magistrates' courts.

Having an idea about the (in-)formal rules of how prosecutorial actors think and work and the norms that underpin practices in lower courts helped me to tame, in a way, the unruly and vast mind of difficult to access expert interview partners and to signal to them the level of expertise I would like to talk on or are able to talk about. This technique assisted me to keep those moments where one worries about wasting precious interview time, because one could have collected the data through means other than spending scarce research resources on getting to the manager's office in the first place, to a minimum. I would even say that it was only once I had reached the stage where I moved beyond just listening and could talk to managerial prosecutors and exchange ideas and observations and did not feel I was wasting their time that these interviews became very fruitful. Due to their eloquence, quick- and smartness, we were often able to cover a lot of ground in a very short time.

CONCLUSION

I said at the beginning of the chapter that studying the working of large organisations is a challenge when using an ethnographic approach and that I hesitated to get involved in multi-sited fieldwork, because I feared that I would be unable to retain, as Merry (2006: 981) writes, 'the genius of ethnography: its ability to look closely at a small social space, to listen to the language, to pay attention to social linkages and information exchanges, to notice power relationships, and to pay attention to the cultural constructions of social life at play in everyday interactions'. However, combining periods of stationary fieldwork where I would spend extended periods of time at one place with periods of mobile research, where I would move around and would follow people or documents, and would often have as a result only short encounters with people, e. g. at a regional head office or at the national head office, also offered me new and important perspectives. I was able to explore the organisational linkages, such as how lines of authority and responsibility are distributed, and how actors are able to communicate and work with each other and make sense of what is going on while being located at different places all over the country.

The working worlds of lower court prosecutors and head office members were very different, but there were also clear links. For example, one of my first encounters with one of my key contacts was at a regional head office during a restorative justice training session. He was also the control prosecutor of a district court, which was set up as part of a pilot project and which promoted and tested 'community', 'restorative' and 'alternative justice' approaches. The DPP of this province was responsible for this countrywide project. A senior prosecutor would see the control prosecutor on a regular basis about the progress of the court and would tell him about the steering committee meetings at the regional head office, which she (and I) attended on a regular basis and where she would report on the courts. Furthermore, at these meetings she would make use of the monthly court statistics the control prosecutor and his team were compiling every month. By venturing back and forth between these organisational levels, I was able to overcome the moments which were prevalent at the beginning of the research where what was going on or not going on at court or at a management meeting was often totally obscure and cryptic to me and where I was overwhelmed by the complexity and speed, but also by the slowness, of what I was observing and experiencing.

While I suggest that my methodological approach makes it possible to gain insights into the working of large state institutions and contributes to social anthropology's interest in 'how states work', it is important to keep in mind the methodological constraints discussed above when reading the rest of this book. It was very much up to the

NPA employees to grant or restrict access to segments of their working reality. The material presented here has thus been subject to this external influence. Secondly, what will be presented in the following chapters thus tackles only a very small part of a large fragmented organisation. I could have focused on the tensions around the NPA's high-profile prosecutions and connected to that the dismantling of the NPA's elite prosecution unit, the Scorpions. The local ongoing concerns in these units – for example, that they are not entirely free to prosecute cases in which the accused has close ties to specific parts of the political elite of the country or that they are forced to prosecute political enemies of the same elite or will be removed from office if they resist these actors in their endeavours – might be very different to the ones I am describing in the following chapters. However, as I mentioned before, it is at the lower courts where the majority of South Africans come face to face with the country's criminal justice system. The next chapter now moves to the everyday working world of court prosecutors and to a discussion of the role of performance statistics, indicators, rates, targets and rankings in their work and their practices and understanding of accountability. Here NPA employees worried constantly about the thousands of cases their courts and clusters had to deal with and not about political interference in their work. At the time of my research the independence struggles at the top of the organisation had not affected the morale of the whole organisation, as commentators in the media often stated. For me this simultaneity of different organisational spheres and events is also an important insight into our understanding of the running and working of the state.

3

'STATS TALK' AND ALTERNATIVE EXPRESSIONS OF ACCOUNTABILITY: NPA LOWER COURT PROSECUTORS AT WORK

INTRODUCTION

Performance statistics, indicators, rates and targets were a common feature in the working world of most prosecutors who I observed and interviewed. During the hundreds of hours of ethnographic fieldwork conducted within the NPA between 2008 and 2012, they often discussed their work and their daily concerns in terms of NPA statistics or with regard to specific NPA performance rates and indicators, both with each other and with me. For example, lower court prosecutors would refer to cases which could be finalised quickly – namely cases where the offender pleaded guilty at first or second appearance or where the case would be mediated or diverted away from the criminal justice system – as 'good for the stats' or as 'assisting them in achieving their target' during these informal tea or lunch break conversations.[1]

When their court work was interrupted – for example when attorneys, investigators or magistrates were not ready to proceed or were unavailable; or because there was a power failure preventing the court's recording machines from functioning; or when heavy rain played havoc with the courtroom's acoustics and resulted in fewer witnesses showing

[1] 'Guilty pleas' are good for statistics because when an accused pleads guilty and the court accepts the guilty plea, the case moves straight to the sentencing phase of the trial. That means the time-consuming part of the prosecution and the defence presenting evidence and opposing legal arguments is avoided, as there is no need to prove the accused's innocence or guilt beyond reasonable doubt. When a case gets diverted, the prosecutor withdraws the case before the official commencement of a trial and the accused will not be asked to plead. The case gets withdrawn on the basis of certain conditions: for example, that the accused undergoes drug or alcohol treatments, participates in specific skills or anger management programmes or fulfils a given amount of community service hours. The amount of time a prosecutor spends on a diverted case is also much lower than when the case goes to trial, as the bulk of work in these cases is done by social workers. When a case gets mediated the situation is different. A mediated case is also withdrawn by the prosecutor in court before the accused pleads. But the mediation process in which the disputing parties come together is guided by a prosecutor, usually one who is assigned to exclusively do mediation, and takes between thirty minutes and a couple of hours. The time advantage is that the mediation prosecutor can usually finalise a few cases within a day.

up – prosecutors would comment 'there go my good stats out of the window'.[2] Court postponements and adjournments would most often mean that they would be able to finalise[3] fewer cases that day and would sit fewer hours in court, which in turn would then impact badly on their monthly 'finalisation rate' and/or their 'court hours'.

Likewise, lower court and regional court prosecutors would, during interviews, or when I observed them screening their case dockets in which the police investigators in their opinion failed to link a suspect to the offence, complain that 'oh, no, they are chasing stats again'; 'they are pushing up our withdrawal rate' (prosecutors are instructed not to continue with a prosecution in cases which are not well-founded upon admissible and reliable evidence). Similar phrases were used when prosecutors encountered dockets in which the police arrested people without proper documentation or for crimes like 'riotous behaviour' or 'loitering in public', which is now no longer unlawful conduct as declared by a South African court a while ago.

Furthermore, prosecutors' descriptions about 'working hard' or 'doing well' would often entail a reference to a reduction or an increase of a specific performance indicator, for example, to the 'number of outstanding cases', also called 'backlog rate' or to the 'number of mediated and diverted cases'. In many of these conversations, interlocutors would also physically wave the statistical sheet(s) in my face. This happened in particular on the so-called 'stats day' where each prosecutor had to calculate his or her monthly 'stats' and hand them over to the court's control or senior prosecutor. 'Stats' was an abbreviation frequently used to refer to the information collected on the 'prosecutor's daily court return' forms.[4]

[2] South Africa is a multilingual society. The first language of many of my research participants is not English. Grammatical errors are not corrected in the quotes.

[3] The number of finalised cases refers to the cases which a prosecutor has finalised in that month – or year, depending on the reporting period – by verdict or through the use of alternative dispute resolution mechanisms (ADRM) such as diversion or informal mediation, irrespective of the date of enrolment of the case. When a prosecutor finalises a case by ADRM or verdict, it means that either a verdict of not guilty is given, or that the prosecutor stops the prosecution in terms of Section 6(b) of Act 51 of 1977 (CPA), or a sentence is imposed in the case of a guilty verdict. Every day he or she captures this information on the so-called 'prosecutor's daily court return' form (NPA Quarterly Performance Overview Report of Public Prosecutions. Quarter 2. 2011/2012).

[4] The following national statistics for individual courts were collected on the monthly statistical sheet: (1) the number of court hours in session; (2) the number of outstanding cases on the courts' rolls; (3) the number of finalised cases and how they had been finalised (e.g. conviction or acquittal of the accused); (4) number of cases finalised with alternative dispute resolution mechanisms and (5) number of withdrawn cases (see NPA Annual Report 2008/2009; 2009/2010; 2010/2011; 2011/2012; 2012/2013; 2014/2015; 2015/2016).

Monthly and quarterly performance statistics also played a central role in meetings in which prosecutors would give accounts of their work to more senior prosecutors. For example, the monthly and bi-monthly management meetings I attended on a regular basis at local courts and at an NPA regional head office would almost without exception start with a prosecutor reading out loud the monthly performance statistics of the courts under discussion. These 'stats' would always serve as a basis and starting point for the subsequent conversation in meetings on how the respective prosecutor, courts, cluster of courts or the whole province were 'doing'.

When the respective monthly targets were not reached, the lower ranked prosecutor would then explain to the higher ranked prosecutor the reasons for the 'bad' numbers. For example, court hours or finalisation rates were low because the court's presiding officer is at that moment responsible for two different courts concurrently, and as a result, court would only begin around lunch time once the magistrate had completed his cases at the other court; or because the police repeatedly brought the prisoners late to court which caused delays in the morning; or because there was a taxi driver strike so the court's interpreter was late for work and an Xhosa interpreter was needed because the accused's mother tongue was Xhosa.

Amongst prosecutors with managerial functions and with access to more aggregated performance rates and rankings, it was also common to use the NPA statistics in the description of their work and their daily concerns. Comments like the following were made frequently during the informal conversations and interviews I conducted with them:

'We are constantly working towards bringing down the numbers [of outstanding court cases].'

'We intervened with a special project to see whether we can deal with these cases differently, whether we can take them out of the system.'

'The [court roll] rates were out of control, they were skyrocketing, a thousand outstanding cases, we took two prosecutors to screen the court roll and identify pleas and it worked – we did seventy-five cases in that court that month.'

'When the numbers [the conviction rate and the withdrawal rate] don't add up, we know something is wrong, you can see it over the years, it's easy.'

'If the conviction rate is 30%, then there is something wrong, it may be an indicator that there is something wrong [. . .] the conviction rate is really to tell us how we are doing.'

Lastly, managerial prosecutors who held positions in the Strategy Office of the NPA, whose work includes the compilation of the NPA's annual performance plan and the creation of new, or the adjustment of existing, performance indicators, also referred to indicators frequently when talking about their duties. The following statement of the head of the Strategy Office during an interview with me was exemplary:

> [i]t's not business as usual. They [prosecutors] just actually want to have the leisure of just doing their job, but that's not good enough for government. There must be service delivery, and how do you get service delivery? It's by having good indicators. They drive performance.

The above-mentioned observations and statements give an illustrative overview of the ways quantitative performance information forms a central part of the everyday language and account giving practices of many prosecutors. They make it clear how familiar and versed these prosecutors are with the terminology of performance measurement. They also show that prosecutors, depending on their rank and daily responsibilities in the organisation (whether they hold a court based or a managerial and/or executive position), talk and use them differently. The former use them to account for their monthly work, whereas the latter rely on them not only for attending to external accountability demands to parliament and the minister of justice as prescribed by the PFMA, but also for internal management accounting purposes.

However, what does it mean in practice when prosecutors' everyday work and thinking is shaped by performance statistics, rates and targets? What does it mean when they ask themselves questions which focus on the quantity of their work like: 'Am I finalising enough cases?'; 'How high is the outstanding number of court cases?'; 'How long has this case been on the roll?'; 'How many cases have I withdrawn/mediated/diverted?' What does it mean for their understanding and practice of accountability? This chapter and the following answer these questions in relation to court-based prosecutors; Chapter 5 and 6 will continue with the discussion in relation to NPA's senior and upper management.

In the next section of this chapter I show that although I have just stated that certain performance indicators were always somewhere in the back of prosecutors' minds and played a central role in the way they account for their work and form the basis on which prosecutors' performance is assessed, this form of accounting was not the only way prosecutors in this organisational setting practiced and made sense of their accountability. The examples I discuss below show that quantitative forms of accountability do not override or replace other previously existing demands of accountability which prosecutors are trained and obliged to attend to. The power of 'numbers' is, as I will argue, counteracted by court prosecutors' alternative expressions of accountability like professionalism, ethics, responsibility and liability.

ALTERNATIVE ACCOUNTABILITIES: PROFESSIONALISM, RESPONSIBILITY AND LEGAL LIABILITY

The meaning of prosecutors' 'stats talk' and the effect of quantitative accountability on their prosecutorial practices can be best understood when it is placed in prosecutors' wider work environment and accountability relationships. In this section I show that when observing prosecutors at work it became clear that their understanding and practice of accountability was wider than reaching their quantitative performance targets.

The NPA 'conviction rate' performance indicator is, for example, the indicator which receives the most media attention and is often central to debates in parliament and portfolio committees in which the NPA's performance is evaluated, as I will discuss in detail in Chapter 6 (Broughton 2002; 'High conviction rate for 2012'; de Lange 2013; 'NPA secures 88% conviction rate' 2013; 'The NPA's annual report figures show a troubled criminal justice system' 2016). Furthermore, the country's executive have in the past celebrated the NPA's conviction rates and used them to demonstrate their commitment to the country's 'fight against crime' (OSF 2006). The opposition frequently adduces them to criticise the government and thereby also voicing their own commitment to a safer South Africa (Schafer 2012a; 2012b; 2013). The conviction rate, although such a publicly known indicator, was however something which played a more ambiguous role in prosecutors' everyday life at work in lower courts.

Numerous prosecutors emphasised time and again in our conversations, in reference to their work or the outcome of a specific case, that their primary aim is not to 'win cases' and obtain convictions or maximise sentence severity, but rather to assist the court in arriving at a just verdict and that it is unethical to suppress evidence or mislead the court in order to rescue one's case. When I sat in on discussions between prosecutorial colleagues about their cases in their offices or over lunch and during tea breaks, it was apparent that they nevertheless liked or preferred 'winning' and that they took pride in achieving a conviction and a certain amount of punishment for the offender.

The focus in these conversations was however predominantly on how they obtained the convictions, in what kinds of cases and despite what obstacles. Their clever cross-examination tactics, the sophistication of their case strategies or the styles of legal argumentation and case laws they used to 'take apart' the smart private defence lawyer, and the intricacies of the specific case, were in these conversations what counted the most. Targets, figures, 'stats' and the amount of time a trial took did not play a role when prosecutors got excited about or dwelt on specific sections of the Criminal Procedure Act, landmark judgements and the connected 'legal battles' they had 'fought' in court. It was not the conviction in itself or the prospect of a higher conviction rate which made them visibly excited or turned them into a well-performing prosecutor in their own and in their colleagues' eyes. Pride was notably attached to one's legal knowledge and prosecutorial technique and the ease with which one moves through the country's criminal law and regulations.

Prancing around the court's corridors and bragging about their conviction rates and the severe punishments they achieved were actions I never witnessed. The working atmosphere that senior prosecutors promoted in management meetings or when prosecutors came to them for advice in specific cases, time and again, was that an acquittal is as good as a conviction if the court found that this is the right result. Thus, there was no institutional shame attached to losing a case. Various prosecutors laughed at me when I mentioned to them that I had met an attorney who had told me, 'I have never lost a case', and commented on his remark with the words, 'That's easy when you can cherry-pick your cases.'

It is also important to notice that none of the court prosecutors I worked with would describe 'trials' in which they have to prove the accused's guilt beyond a reasonable doubt and which is the most time consuming and laborious way to finalise a case, as 'bad for the stats', meaning their number of finalised cases. Being involved in trials is what almost all the observed and interviewed prosecutors enjoyed the most. They considered 'proper trials' – showing and using their legal litigation (and not their administration) skills as prosecutors as their core function – as their mandate. Many were frustrated that they spend large amounts of their court hours 'doing postponements' instead of 'doing trials'.

Cases often had to be postponed during the pre-trial stage because the police needed more time to investigate the case. Or prosecutors needed to postpone cases because they were struggling with their daily workload as each court can only hear a limited number of cases each day. Once the workload reaches a certain point, the more cases are placed on the court's roll, and the more the prosecutor will struggle to finalise all of them on their allocated court days. As a result, the prosecutor spends more time postponing incomplete cases instead of prosecuting and finalising trials and the number of outstanding cases starts to grow.

The fact that a trial can only run when all role players are present is another reason why prosecutors deal with large amounts of postponements every day. It only takes an accused who absconded, or a witness who was not subpoenaed in time or an investigator who has no time to come to court to give his testimony for a case not to commence or to proceed. While postponing cases is an important part of prosecutors' everyday work, many prosecutors felt it was a rather boring, repetitive and annoying part of it. Something many wanted 'to get over and done with' so that they can begin with their real work, namely their 'trials'.

That prosecutors viewed their job performance and accountability duties to a large extent in terms of strict adherence to the 'law' and their legal profession and its code of conduct was common. Many prosecutors often looked at me in disbelief when my questions showed my ignorance or lack of knowledge about the South African Criminal Procedure Act, and when my questions indicated that I doubted that laws and rules were being strictly applied. Various criminologists and anthropologists had after all described in their ethnographies how members of the South African Police Service had not transformed their *modus operandi* in significant ways since 1994 and relied on old unlawful apartheid tactics to police the streets of the country (Marks 2000; 2004; Hornberger 2009; Jensen 2009). I presumed that this more flexible stance towards 'the law', where state officials move between legal and illegal use of force and where the rights of the accused were not always taken seriously, might be something which permeates through other spheres of the country's criminal justice system. Most prosecutors would not comment on the misconduct or abuse of power of certain SAPS policemen unless they knew the case details more specifically. It was, however, interesting to observe that various prosecutors said they wished 'someone with a law degree' would work at the police station and 'would explain policemen the law' as if they perceived the law degree as a safeguard against misconduct and abuse by the police.

Legal accountability or liability was another dimension of professional accountability many prosecutors mentioned when they explained and justified their work and why they adhere to the laws and regulations and follow prosecutorial ethics and its code of conduct. When prosecutors, for example, rejected requests from the police to *nolle prosecqui*[5] a case, or to sign a warrant of arrest in cases in which they had the feeling the investigators had not done their work 'properly', they explained that they could not accept 'short cuts', their concern being that they could be sued. Charles Mafunda, a control prosecutor in his forties whom I shadowed on a regular basis at work and who has worked for the NPA for the last fifteen years, said to me, for example, after I observed him refusing to sign a warrant of arrest and after the investigator had left his office, with a serious voice,

> you can be sued if someone gets unlawfully arrested and then something happens in the cells, he gets raped or beaten up, you can be sued for signing that document. You need to be diligent. The investigator needs to determine properly whether the suspect no longer resides at the given address or whether he was just not at home when the investigator came around.

Many prosecutors also widely commented on cases in which public servants were involved in internal disciplinary hearings or public cases in which the NPA and the Minister of Justice were sued for damages due to prosecutors' negligence or malpractice. They would also refer to South African case law when explaining that they can be held legally accountable. For example, many prosecutors frequently quoted the so-called 'Carmichele case' (*Carmichele* v *Minister of Safety and Security* (CCT 48/00) [2001] ZACC 22; 2001 (4) SA 938 (CC); 2001 (10) BCLR 995 (CC) (16 August 2001)). It was one of the first cases where a South African court found after a ten-year court battle that the state can be held liable for damages arising out of the unlawful conduct of its civil servants (Davis and le Roux 2009: 167ff.).

The complainant, Alix Carmichele, took the SAPS and the NPA – more correctly the respective responsible state ministers – all the way to the Constitutional Court, which held them liable for acting negligently

[5] *Nolle prosequi*: the dismissal or termination of legal proceedings by the prosecutor.

in releasing without bail the man who brutally attacked her and consequently granted Carmichele damages. The offender was awaiting trial for attempted rape of another woman when he broke into Carmichele's house and attempted to rape and kill her. Despite the man's history of sexual violence, the police investigator and prosecutor in the case had recommended his release without bail. The complainant and her friends were aware of the offender's previous attempts to sexually assault women and complained to the court's senior prosecutor, who acted negligently in failing to follow up these serious complaints. Vusi Mnguni, a regional court prosecutor in his forties, said to me while we were sitting in Charles Mafunda's office and going through the specifics of the case together, which Mafunda had printed out for me:

> the case was an eye opener for us. It made us very cautious. Even our lecturer at the time did not know that our duty is to protect the public from harm and crime. We thought our duty is confined [he made a gesture with his two hands to map a space of 30 centimetres], that the duty of the NPA is confined to prosecute. [. . .] One needs to be diligent otherwise they can sue you.

Vusi Mnguni also knew that, because he was working in the same province as the prosecutor in the Carmichele case, his colleague's career came to an end through her negligence in that case. He did not show much pity for her; he said that her professional conduct was 'completely unacceptable [. . .] She was lazy. She should have done her job properly and followed up the complaints'. Our conversation ended with Mnguni and Mafunda explaining to me what their colleague should have done in the case and how they acted when they were in similar situations where the investigation officer did not oppose bail, but they 'had a feeling' the accused should stay in custody and bail should not be granted. The Criminal Procedure Act was taken out and they began to show me and cite to me the sections and subsections of the Act they used in their own cases and recalled the course of events of these specific bail applications that they were describing.

While for most prosecutors professionalism meant conducting their actions in an unemotional, non-political and non-partisan way and complying with all applicable laws, rules and regulations, for a number of prosecutors being professionally accountable included more than professional ethics, liability and accountability to the law. It involved a personal commitment to specific justice ideals and to improving the service delivery of the NPA. The following two depictions of senior prosecutor Shelly Meyer's and control prosecutor Charles Mafunda's accountability practices are exemplary in this respect.

SHELLY MEYER

Shelly Meyer, a senior public prosecutor (SPP) in her forties who has been working for the NPA for over twenty years and whom I frequently shadowed at work between 2008 and 2009, saw her accountability as related to her strong commitment to fighting violence against women in very poor and violence-ridden communities. While Shelly worked as an ordinary SPP at a busy urban magistrate court for most of her working hours, she also was involved in a nationwide 'NPA innovation project', which placed the prosecutor in direct contact with the community to play an active role in crime prevention. She told me that the idea behind the 'community prosecutions project' is that 'the prosecutor does not sit like a waiting duck in court until cases are brought to him, but is present in the community to prevent crime before it happens'.

Her 'community' was a low-income informal settlement of about 1,300 dwellings located thirty kilometres away from the CBD of a major South African city. The area fell within one of South Africa's most violent policing precincts. Every month serious crimes, including murders, rapes and assaults were reported at the local police stations. Increasing 'women's access to justice' was particularly important to Shelly in this project. I learnt what that exactly meant to her while driving or walking together through the township. She explained and showed me the work she had being doing in this neighbourhood since 2006. I also observed her in action at formal and informal meetings we attended together, for example, at the local police station or with local NGOs dealing with domestic violence.

Access to justice for her meant firstly improving local women's awareness of their rights and understanding of the law. She organised, together with other 'justice stakeholders', regular public education campaigns and workshops in her assigned community. During these well-attended events at local schools or city halls, she spoke out against domestic violence and abuse; encouraged women to fight back and stand up for their rights; introduced the NPA as 'lawyers of the people' and explained the organisation's place within the overall South African justice system; answered women's questions about the difficulties they were encountering in ongoing domestic violence cases and/or maintenance disputes; or provided them with the necessary information in how to proceed to open a case. For her a successful NPA outreach program also meant that everyone had a good time during these events, so she ensured that they always also had some more uplifting items on the agenda like motivational speakers, music performances, small gifts and a warm meal for everyone.

When numbers of domestic violence protection orders rose at the respective magistrate court in the area, for her, that was a sign that her work had made an impact and that more women were becoming aware of their rights and were more willing to speak out. By using her interpersonal and legal skills, as well as her weight as a senior prosecutor, it was observable how she also actively coordinated the different state and non-state stakeholders in these communities to react more quickly and concertedly when protection orders were violated. She frequently quoted one of the NPA's service ideals, which states that it is important to ensure that 'justice is not only done, but seen to be done' for these women. She got visibly excited when cases ended up with magistrates who were 'good at handling' domestic violence and maintenance cases and 'knew how to talk to people', and voiced her frustration when the same magistrates moved to another court and were replaced with less capable or motivated ones. Because she emphasised that 'it makes a difference in these kinds of cases who is dealing with them'.

For Shelly, access to justice secondly meant creating networks of safety and linking people. She made herself available as an important resource person by putting her own cell phone number on an 'emergency list' she put together and circulated in 'her' community. While shadowing her, her phone would constantly ring and amongst the callers were often members of the community asking her for assistance or telling her what was going on in the 'community'. She often used her legal knowledge but also her wide personal and work networks to facilitate responses to the concerned individuals. Shelly also used her networking skills to set up 'crime prevention initiatives'. She organised, together with local women and businesses, food kitchens for schools, established a childcare facility for toddlers and built up a sewing studio and a food garden in her assigned working area. All initiatives were intended to both create safe spaces for children and to set up support networks and employment opportunities for women, thereby strengthening their position in these violent and extremely poor communities.

Another crime prevention initiative Shelly got involved in was the regulation of illegal drinking spots. The police in the area could link many serious offences like murder, assault and rape to alcohol abuse and illegal outlets for the sale of alcohol. Due to her direct involvement with members of the community, she knew that these illegal drinking places are an important source of income for the owners and places of recreation for the clients. To simply close them down, she said, is contentious and not feasible. She therefore provided tavern owners with legislative information and encouraged self-regulation in terms of opening hours and a code of conduct, which included for example security searches at the door for weapons and drugs. While she took note that stricter opening hours and security searches helped to reduce the amount of violence occurring in and around the 'shebeens', it was particularly important to her that the police had thanked her for reducing the hardened fronts between them and the tavern owners and got the communication between the two parties going.

Lastly, ensuring women's access to justice for her entails women having physical access to courts. She created awareness during stakeholder meetings that organisational decisions which determine which court a specific police station is required to forward its cases to has a significant impact on whether a complainant decides to pursue her case or not. Due to her direct involvement in the community she became more aware, as she said, of how important it is that women can walk to court. Public transport was expensive for people with hardly any income and the additional costs of traveling to court located further away makes it harder, according to Shelly, for women to come to court.

Shelly was one of the prosecutors who would at times physically wave the statistical sheet(s) of her 'project' in my face and would talk about crime statistics and the number of protection orders. In other words, she accounted quantitatively for her work when I enquired about her project. At the same time, she also often explained that her work could not easily be measured. She said that her work could have an impact which appeared initially as 'bad stats'. For example, when the number of domestic violence or rape cases rose, this could be interpreted not only as successful NPA outreach programs but also as a rise in occurrences of these crimes. When she talked about the project or wrote about it in the progress reports, she included other forms of accounts, namely direct feedback she received from members of the community and the police and other crime fighting forums in the area, her own experiences, observations and judgement, before and after photographs she took of specific hot spots of crimes to document her work and survey data she received from an evaluator of the project.

It was apparent in the way she was describing her work efforts regarding that project that all these forms of account giving counted, in her eyes, as much to her as her 'stats'.

The second example of a prosecutor for whom being professionally accountable included a more personal commitment to improving the service delivery of the NPA is Charles Mafunda, who I have already mentioned above. He has been working for the NPA for the last fifteen years. I met him at a local court management meeting which I attended with Shelly Meyer in November 2008. It is another case in point that makes it clear that court prosecutors' understanding of their accountability is more complicated than simply having 'good stats'.

CHARLES MAFUNDA

Charles Mafunda was also a prosecutor for whom professionalism was closely related to complying with all applicable laws, rules and regulations. He was proud of his reputation as a 'technical prosecutor', one who is at ease in front of the court, who knows his '[case] law'. His level of excitement seemed to rise in anticipation of potentially more challenging legal arguments, for example, when a private attorney or advocate appeared in his court where the accused usually defended themselves or were represented gratis but often by inexperienced legal-aid attorneys. He was proud of his personal copy of the South African Criminal Procedure Act and kept it in his private locker overnight. Mafunda was usually very even-tempered and reserved. He refrained at all times from any form of 'NPA gossip' and racist and/or moralistic and stereotypical conversations about colleagues and clients. He would rather try to change the topic of conversation or leave the room than participate in what was to him completely unethical and unprofessional behaviour. But he would also start to use the kind of passionate and sharpened warrior language that probably only another litigator could relate to when he talked about his trials or when he appeared in court.

However, for Mafunda, professional accountability also meant that he needed to ensure high levels of courtesy for his 'customers', as he frequently called the complainants. No matter what time it was or how ill-informed and annoying the client's requests or complaints were, he tried to assist them. Although he was often not the person in charge of the cases people were inquiring about, he nevertheless tried to find out who was in charge, where they could find that person and where possible what was going on in their case. He would often say to me 'people like to complain, but it is their right to complain and to follow up their cases. What I am trying to say is called "Batho Pele", "put people first". You need to follow up, fight for them in court, so they don't come and complain'.

Furthermore, when he prepared witnesses for giving their testimony in court, he was aware of their nervousness or fear and tried to make them feel as comfortable as possible by explaining to them the court's procedure in simple language, reassuring them that he would guide them when testifying and making jokes to lighten up the tense atmosphere. That it was important to him to ensure high levels of courtesy for his 'customers' also meant that he wanted to be open and responsive to the needs of his clients. He was a strong believer or promoter of alternative dispute resolution (ADRM) mechanisms, like diversions and mediation. He would often say 'mediation works, they are good for the stats'. For the NPA, mediation is a process which 'does not require formal justice' but where the NPA nevertheless tries to 'deliver justice' by 'resolving the conflict or addressing the harm caused' (NPA 2012). Although cases are withdrawn in court after they have been successfully mediated, they count as finalised: the most important performance indicator for district court prosecutors.[6]

One could interpret Mafunda's statement and his interest and support for mediation as a sign of his audit mentality, developed due to the pressure to account quantitatively for his work. I would like to illustrate why this reading of the situation would be too simple and ignores Mafunda's more extensive understanding of professional accountability, namely, that he wanted to ensure high levels of courtesy for his 'customers', that he wanted 'to make them happy' as he sometimes said. Mediation was for Mafunda particularly relevant for offering a service to complainants who firstly do not like trials and adversarial legal court battles as much as prosecutors do, and secondly do not have the financial resources to do so.[7]

In his everyday work I often observed how he encountered complainants who are not interested in seeing offenders being sentenced

[6] See also Footnote 1.

[7] It is certainly true that some South African complainants or sections of wider society want to see offenders 'rot in jail' or wish the death penalty would be reintroduced to the country (Steinberg 2001; Ehlers 2008). These kinds of harsh retributive demands, which complainants and their supporters sometimes shout or sing out aloud outside the court where the respective cases are being heard, are mostly made at regional or High Courts where people stand trial for murder or rape, and especially when children are amongst the victims. I never witnessed such demonstrations of public anger and frustration at Mr Charles Mafunda's court.

through the courts. Once their allocated trial date comes up, they are no longer interested in pursuing their cases in court: They want to withdraw them.[8] The reasons for that vary. One common denominator amongst the complainants who wanted to withdraw their cases at Mafunda's court and drop the charges – mostly assault, assault GBH, malicious damage to property and to a lesser extent house break-in charges – were that they live, or used to live, in a close, intimate or familial relationship with the accused.

When talking to Mafunda, the person at court who makes the decision over whether a case can be withdrawn or not, complainants stated that they had reconciled with the offender: He or she had apologised, and/or the wider family had got involved and settled the matter. Some also said that they did not want to see the offender get sent to prison because they felt compassion. Some were discouraged from continuing with a case for fear of retaliation they had already faced or might have to face from the offender or his/her family if the offender was sentenced. Sometimes complainants also indicated that they were financially dependent on the perpetrator and therefore could not afford to have him or her go to prison, pay a fine or, more generally, to have a breadwinner with a criminal record because they would lose an important source of income.

Another important reason for withdrawal was that complainants stated that they felt that the opening of a case against the offender at the police station, the inconvenience of having to appear in court, threatening him or her with conviction and the possibility of imprisonment were 'enough punishment' and would serve as 'a warning' for the offender 'not to do it again'. But complainants who were seeking to arrest but not necessarily prosecute a perpetrator and who were more interested in the temporary protection from the offender which the arrest gives them brought Mafunda into a difficult situation. There are

[8] One would imagine that prosecutors would be relieved when people wanted to withdraw their case because every withdrawn case relieves the court's roll. However, that is not the case, as prosecutors are required to apply their mind to every case that comes before them. The number of withdrawn cases is also considered when measuring a prosecutor's performance and counts as a negative performance indicator. The withdrawal rate needs to be kept low, because if it is too high the senior prosecutors in charge will start asking questions, and court prosecutors are expected to account for the withdrawn cases. A high withdrawal rate could, for example, indicate that the prosecutor has not worked diligently enough or that he or she lacks the training to identify a prosecutable case, or that the prosecutor shies away from difficult cases. A high withdrawal rate could also be a sign that too many complainants have decided to withdraw their cases because they are so disillusioned or frustrated by the inefficiency of the courts or because they feel alienated by the way courts currently operate.

no longer any mandatory prosecution policies in place with regard to domestic assault cases, but he still needed to decide in each and every case whether he would allow a complainant to withdraw a case. NPA policies instruct prosecutors to be 'tough' on violence against women. When talking about deciding whether to grant a withdrawal or not, Mafunda stated that they were also accountable to the demands of other potential victims and to the wider public, and that they had a mandate and responsibility 'to send out a message to the public that crime does not pay'.

Mafunda often struggled with these decisions because he did not want to force complainants to continue with their cases; 'that would be too harsh' he often said, but he felt that a trial and a suspended sentence hanging over the accused's head would have greater potential to stop the perpetrator from re-offending than an informal warning, especially in domestic violence cases. Although an informal warning was exactly what a number of complainants wanted or could afford, in other words he was providing the 'customer' with the desired service, Mafunda did not feel, after withdrawing a case, that he 'had done a good job'. It was for him an unsatisfactory prosecutorial outcome for a case. While he wanted to be responsive to the wishes expressed by the complainants, his professional training and identity was closely linked to conducting 'proper trials', 'finding out the truth' and 'ensuring justice and safety' for the complainant. He certainly did not see courts as one forum amongst many which disputants 'shop' for, to manage their conflicts or that courts potentially assisted the complainant with the informal warning to settle the dispute.[9] I suggest that mediation provided Mafunda with an attractive option in these difficult situations. They give him the opportunity to accommodate complainants who demand the informal involvement of an official criminal justice employee. Complainants' desire to have a prosecutor or magistrate – someone with legal authority – 'talk' to the offender or warn him or her could be accommodated during mediation.

During mediation, ordinary reasoning procedures and conversational practice are permitted; the strict special procedures embodied in the legal court system are not relied on to reach an agreement between both sides. The punishment or the guilt of the accused is not in the forefront

[9] Anthropologists have shown in several contexts that 'forum-shopping' is the norm when it comes to how people resolve or manage their disputes, whether they reside in Indonesia (von Benda-Beckmann 1981), the United States (Merry 1979) or South Africa (Tshehla 2001; Lenart 2013).

of the mediation process. Instead, the focus is on restitution. The complainants can tell the offenders how the offence had an emotional, physical and financial impact on them. The mediator assists the two disputing parties to develop a restitution plan. The restitution agreement signed by both parties and the mediator can include apologies, offers to repair the damage or to take part in rehabilitative programs, community work and financial compensation.

Conflict resolution by means of restitution and particularly compensation instead of by punishment is, according to Mafunda, exactly what some complainants prefer. While a court can grant compensation orders, this can only be done by means of a separate court order[10] once the guilt of the accused has been established or the accused has pleaded guilty, which means he or she will be sentenced by the court and will then have a criminal record. But to punish the accused with the far-reaching consequences of a permanent criminal record is, as I have shown above, what some complainants want to avoid. In contrast, when a case is mediated the offender does not get a criminal record because the charges against him or her get withdrawn. Nevertheless, the complainant can be awarded a compensation payment via the restitution agreement.

The other important advantage of mediation at lower courts is that they can usually be done within one day, which spares complainant and accused the long and dreadful hours of waiting and potential postponements which can be counter-productive for people who wish to forget the case and move on with their lives, and who lose income every time they come to court. That is also why mediation 'works' and is 'good for the stats' as Mafunda pointed out. They take less time and are less labour-intensive than other forms of prosecutorial work. I argue however that to accept Mafunda's 'stats talk' and enthusiasm that mediation 'works' as evidence for his audit mentality ignores what is going on in his wider work environment where his wish to 'make the customers happy' by providing them with an informal and less adversarial way of

[10] I never witnessed cost orders in district magistrate courts. Once I observed a magistrate postpone a case of malicious damage to property. The case was ready for trial, but the magistrate postponed it to give the accused time to repay the complainant, his ex-girlfriend, for destroying her TV during a fight. The complainant told me during a court adjournment 'I am very happy so far about how the court has assisted me because I know the accused. I don't want him to go to prison, but I want my TV back'. The magistrate's actions were unusual and many of his colleagues criticised him for acting in that manner, as it is not procedurally correct, because the accused's guilt needed to be established before ordering him to pay damages.

settling their case and to 'serve justice' is as important as his concerns about his performance and the court's statistics.

CONCLUSION

The empirical material in this chapter has shown that the performance indicators which the NPA use to comply with the Public Finance Management Act of 1998 commonly features in the way prosecutors talk and account for their work. Ten years after the act was passed by parliament, performance statistics, indicators, rates and targets form a central part of prosecutors' understanding and practices of accountability.

Does that mean that prosecutors struggle to account for their work with other, especially more deliberative, forms of accountability, as some quantification scholars suggest? Is their definition and practice of accountability becoming narrower? Does quantitative accountability colonise other ideas and ideals of service and justice as it often assumed? Did prosecutors become more concerned and excited about the quantity rather than the quality of justice, and about getting the numbers up than about the substance of the individual cases? Did they start to opt for speedier ways to finalise a case in order to be seen to perform better – to look good? In other words, do they make decisions based on numerical considerations instead of legal ones? Do they adhere to the authority of numbers instead of the authority of law?

The ethnographic material presented in this chapter showed that in this setting the link between quantitative accountability and audit mentality, between quantification and its so-called unintended effects, is more complicated than often assumed. While prominent in lower courts' prosecutors' working life, performance indicators are not exclusively indicative of prosecutorial performance, and were not the only legitimate measure of it. Meeting their target of finalising a certain number of cases per month or reaching a conviction rate of a certain percentage or working in a top-ranked cluster did not necessarily mean that these prosecutors felt that they were performing well and 'doing justice'.

Concepts like professionalism, including adherence to an ethical code of conduct, public responsibility, responsiveness and legal liability, were shaping prosecutors' work practices and the ways in which they explained and justified their decisions. More personal ideals of justice and public service were additional strong alternative expressions of their accountability. I argue, in other words, that to accept prosecutors' 'stats talk' as evidence of their reconfigured professional selves is to ignore that lower court prosecutors had some control and flexibility over how their reputations were defined and what good prosecutorial performance should entail. The independent professional self is, at least in this setting, not so easily turned to an 'auditable, competitive' self (Shore and Wright 1999: 569), who has to sacrifice 'quality' for 'quantity' and/or 'process' for 'substance' (Power 1997: 16).

The question remains: How does it come to be that quantitative forms of accountability were prominent in lower court prosecutors' work life, but that they were not exclusively indicative of prosecutorial performance, and were not the only legitimate measure of it? I will be arguing in Chapters 5 and 6 that this is strongly connected to how their fellow professionals higher up in the organisational hierarchy defined performance and what role numerical representations and knowledge played in their everyday work. The following Chapter 4 will address the political economy of performance measurement. I argue that because financial and human resources are not tightly coupled to quantitative performance information, lower court prosecutors are less stressed and intimidated by performance measurement systems. The fear and hostility other professionals voice against quantitative forms of accountability, and the serious and harmful effects they experience in their organisational fields, seems to be tempered by the multiplicity of accountability relationships and demands prosecutors are trained and obliged to attend to and which govern their everyday work.

4

NO FEAR OF NUMBERS: REACTIVITY AND THE POLITICAL ECONOMY OF NPA PERFORMANCE MEASUREMENT

INTRODUCTION

Social scientific studies, which focus on the effects of performance indicators and rankings on specific organisational fields, often include accounts of individual professionals whose reaction and attitude towards performance measurement can be summarised as critical, cynical and sometimes even fearful. Sally Engle Merry (2011: S87), who investigates the rapid increase internationally of the use of indicators to monitor like for human rights compliance, describes human rights activists who '(u)ntil the 1990s […] resisted the use of indicators because of concern about lack of data, oversimplifications, and bias. […] Indicators measure aggregates, while human rights are held by individuals'. The criticism from activists was that the specificity of the human right, its individual violation and the country's specific context might be overlooked or misrepresented when international organisations begin to use indicators to calculate something like a human rights compliance rate.

Another illustrative example of a professional group critical of performance indicators is anthropologists themselves. Various authors have expressed their concern and frustration regarding the damaging effects of quantitative forms of accountability on the creativity, freedom and collaborative nature of academic work (Shore and Wright 1999; 2011: 20–21; Strathern 2000a; 2000b; see also: Power 1997 for its effect on accounting studies; Münch 2011 for its effect on sociology).

Marylin Strathern's (2000a) critique of the British government's Research Assessment Exercise (RAE) – which has used performance indicators since the mid-1990s to firstly evaluate and monitor researchers' quality, productivity and activity, and secondly to allocate, on the basis of these indicators, scarce national funds to individual university departments – describes the cynicism many academics feel towards performance measurement. She states that

> (w)hat is being tested would seem to be the performance and productivity of academics, but 'everyone knows' that what is being tested is how amenable to auditing their activities are or how performance matches up to performance indicators (309–310). […] Meanwhile, the 'real' workings of the institution, its social structure, cultural values, modes of organisation […] are ignored. (314)

Furthermore, Wendy Espeland and Michael Sauder (2007; 2009; 2016), in their study on the effects of USN law school rankings on higher legal education in the United States, provide a detailed sociological account of a professional group's reaction to being evaluated and monitored quantitatively.[1] They reveal that most law school deans and admission administrators 'deeply resent' the rankings (Espeland and Sauder 2009: 587). The academics 'hate' the fact that USN reduces their law school's quality and ethos in an 'arbitrary' manner to a simplistic ranking score (Sauder and Espeland (2007: 24).[2] They perceive USN's methodology as so flawed and meaningless that they questioned how anyone interested in (studying) law could take the rankings seriously. Although the Yale Law School is consistently among the top three ranked schools, its dean is quoted as calling the rankings 'an idiot poll'; similarly, the dean of the Harvard Law School (another top ranked legal education institution), has described them as 'Mickey Mouse', 'just plain wacky' and 'totally bonkers' (Sauder and Espeland 2007: 8).

Nonetheless, despite the critical stance of these professionals towards the law school rankings and their attempts to simply ignore them, Espeland and Sauder show that the 'common sentiment' among law school administrators and deans is that rankings are 'unignorable and

[1] Since 1990 USN has annually ranked each US American law school based on a calculated score which measures the 'quality' and 'performance' of each school with four weighted indicators: reputation (40%), selectivity (25%), placement (20%), and faculty resources (15%) (Espeland and Sauder 2007: 10). Each indicator is composed of several other weighted measures which, calculated together, create a law school's overall rank. Espeland and Sauder (2009: 593) state 'for example, selectivity, worth 25% of the overall rank, is based on three components: student LSAT scores count for 50% of the selectivity ranking (12.5% of the overall score), GPA represents 40% (10% overall) and a school's acceptance rate accounts for 10% of the selectivity score (2.5% overall)'.

[2] Law school 'insiders' strongly criticised USN for not taking into consideration many factors which make up a good law school and which are, according to their experience, important to students. For example, the racial, gender and economic diversity of the student and faculty body is not counted; neither is the location, the cost of studying, the specific mission of the school (e.g. commitments to religious traditions, public service or to providing 'access' for socially and economically disadvantaged students), nor the availability of funding, the social atmosphere on campus or the teaching quality (Sauder and Espeland 2006: 205; Espeland and Sauder 2007: 17).

are always in the back of everybody's head' (2007: 11). They need to take cognisance of the fact that external audiences such as students, alumni, trustees, journalists or future employers of their students increasingly rely on the easily accessible ranking scores to make far-reaching decisions (Espeland and Sauder 2007: 11), such as whether to apply to law school x or y, the size of donation to the alma mater or which law school graduate to invite to a job interview.

As a result of the increasing power of the USN rankings to define US law school quality, deans and administrators began to manage the most tangible effects which the rankings had on their school, namely, losing top students and financial resources to other law schools when one's rank had dropped. According to Espeland and Sauder (2007), these professionals altered the way they conducted their work: resource allocation, management of the admission process and exercising their discretion while handling these tasks.[3]

These three anthropological and sociological accounts of professionals' attitudes and reactions to performance measurement systems are discussed at the beginning of this chapter as they are exemplary of the complaints and concerns social scientific scholars raise regarding the use of performance measurement in specific hard-to-measure settings. Additionally, they are highlighted as these professionals' attitudes and reactions differ substantially (as we will see in a moment)

[3] For example, one strategy to attract students with high LSAT (Law School Admission Test) scores, which boosts a school's overall selectivity score and therefore its rank, is to offer those students attractive scholarships. As a result, the number of needs-based scholarships for students with lower marks declined at many universities. Admission counsellors are disturbed that they have less professional discretion than in the past to admit students with low LSAT scores, but who show great potential and might make a class more interesting and diverse, since it would affect their school's rank negatively (Sauder and Espeland 2007: 17). Another example of how the university's scarce resources are being reallocated is that schools spent a considerable amount of money on marketing materials to produce 'glossy brochures' which are sent to other universities whose law school professors are asked by USN to rate the reputation of all US American law schools. This is money deans can no longer spend on employing additional faculty members, buying extra books or awarding more scholarships (Espeland and Sauder 2007: 26). Another strategy is that since the increased importance of rankings, university career services personnel now spend more time tracking the employment status of graduate students, which is important for the school's placement statistics, instead of advising individual students on their legal career. They often feel torn between recommending that students wait for the best offer, or advising them to accept the first offer that comes along, which would be better for the university's placement statistics and their own performance, as their work is increasingly geared towards achieving a specific placement target and the rankings have altered the way they are held accountable (Sauder and Espeland 2006: 211). It became widespread amongst schools to manipulate their ranking score by counting non-legal jobs in their placement statistics; by reporting inflated data to USN; or by admitting students with lower LSAT scores to part-time study programs (those students would become full-time students after their first year) (Espeland and Sauder 2007: 29).

from that of the observed and interviewed prosecutors of my field sites. The deep resentment and scepticism of professionals described in these studies towards performance indicators and rankings were absent amongst the prosecutors in the South African magistrate courts. Unlike many US law school employees, these prosecutors do not have the same fear of being judged according to rank in their daily work and have no equivalent to the pressure the USN ranking had triggered to improve the score of their law school. Why is this so?

The aim of this chapter is to answer this question: It begins with a discussion of examples of prosecutors' attitudes towards the NPA's performance indicators, rates, targets and rankings. I show that most prosecutors have conciliatory attitudes towards them. This analysis is followed by an exploration of the possible institutional, legal and historical reasons for the more positive stance of South African prosecutors towards their organisation's quantitative performance management.

ATTITUDES OF LOWER COURT PROSECUTORS TOWARDS THE NPA'S PERFORMANCE MEASUREMENT SYSTEM

Performance indicators and connected targets set by the NPA itself and only published in aggregated form were, as I mentioned in the previous chapter, always somewhere in the back of many prosecutors' minds. The number of finalised and withdrawn cases, the court hour rate and the backlog rate were particularly important for the lower court prosecutors I observed at work at various district magistrate courts. The deep resentment and even hatred towards quantitative forms of accountability, which professionals – according to various anthropologists and sociologists – voice in other organisational settings was absent amongst South African prosecutors. During the hundreds of hours spent with prosecutors in their offices, at court and at meetings and during the interviews I conducted, I encountered only one prosecutor who brought the usefulness and the meaning of the NPA performance indicators into question.

Michael van Niekerk, in his fifties, has worked for over thirty years in different capacities in the South African judicial system: as a magistrate, as a prosecutor, a regional court control prosecutor and as an attorney. When I met him at the NPA head office in Pretoria at the end of 2008, he was working for the 'NPA Transformation Program' called

'Serurubele' (Sesotho for 'butterfly'). We spoke for over three hours in his office. While he spoke at length about how important and beneficial it is that 'lean management principles' and 'standard operation procedures' (both management concepts and activities that rely heavily on quantified information) are implemented in the running of South Africans courts, he also raised concerns about what he described as the 'quantification of justice'. I quote a passage from this interview at length, because the attitudes of prosecutors towards their performance measurement, which I will discuss below, differ substantially to his perspective. The stance of Michael van Niekerk towards the NPA's performance measurement serves as a counter-example and an exception, which, I would suggest, attests to the complexities of the issue at hand. He stated:

> The problem is we generate a lot of paper, and we generate a lot of things on paper that we don't use in practice. We can take all these things and put them in a basket and ask the [...] chief prosecutor or the senior, who sit in the office, if they know what happens in their court, ask them how many times they visit the court, how many times they have sat and listened to what the prosecutor [...] does in court. Has he ever asked any of the witnesses if they were satisfied with the service, did they think that justice was done? [...] On paper we measure a lot of things but we do not measure the service that we deliver as a personal experience.
>
> We want to justify justice as how many cases have we finalised and how many court hours we have sat, we justify or try to justify why we want to pressurise everybody in the system to deliver at the end of the month. And we don't analyse the case, the outcome of the case and the charges brought against the accused to say 'yes everything done in this whole chain of events has justified justice'. The tribal court doesn't worry about the length of time it sits in the rural area. And how many witnesses it has, and how long it takes to make a decision, but if they make a decision it stands and everybody accepts it in that community. [...] What we now do is that we want to say to the magistrates that they have to do 3–4 cases a day for this reason because the workload is such a lot and there are so many cases in the system, that if a magistrate tries to do his job and explain the rights of the accused, everything that he needs to do and that is required by the Constitution it takes him about 15 minutes just to do that, we want him to do it in 2 minutes.
>
> The measurements should be 'Has justice been done? Seen to be done to the accused and to the victim and everyone?' [...] I feel that we want to quantify justice in hours and minutes and conviction rates. [...] We

> go to Parliament and tell them this is the amount of cases we have finalised and this is the conviction rate, [...], but at the end of the day, is it not a question that we try and put a measurement on justice?

The quote extracted from the interview with Michael van Niekerk shows clearly that he is critical of the NPA's performance measurement system. For him the NPA indicators are, for various reasons, an inadequate monitoring and quality control tool for court work. Firstly, they do not capture what is going on at court as they do not communicate to him or other seniors what has actually happened in a specific case, and secondly (and most importantly), whether 'justice has been served'. He is critical of the conviction rate as it does not consider if the conviction has been overturned on appeal or whether the accused has been convicted for the crimes he was charged with, or for less severe crimes which are not as complicated to prove (e.g. attempted murder or assault GBH on murder charges; or possession of drugs on dealing in drugs charges).

Secondly, as the NPA performance indicators do not capture whether the affected parties – namely the accused, the witnesses and the complainant – are satisfied with the process, the result and the work of the NPA. For van Niekerk, this is an important dimension of justice which is ignored when one measures magistrates' and prosecutors' performance with limited selected performance indicators. Thirdly, he complains that by allocating a limited amount of time to each case, one pressurises prosecutors and magistrates to work faster which, according to him, means that other important quality control measures become neglected (e.g. due process of law). Van Niekerk also seems to suggest that the target settings and the related time pressure undermine the legitimacy and authority of state courts as he feels that people adhere more closely to the ruling of traditional courts, which in his view are free from any time constraints.

I interviewed Michael van Niekerk at the beginning of my fieldwork. It is interesting to note that during the course of my research his points of critique were matters of concern which prosecutors observed working at lower courts and managerial prosecutors never repeated and often did not share. While at times lower ranked prosecutors certainly complained that their seniors, the 'people up there', 'don't understand what is going on here on the ground' (often while raising their hand and looking towards the sky), this statement was not an expression of their general feeling or something which regularly troubled them, and most importantly, not something they would specifically say in relation to the simplifications or misrepresentations that accompany quantitative performance indicators.

For example, at one court, various prosecutors made this statement in relation to the general irritation they felt towards their new superior who they considered as 'arrogant' and not a 'hard worker'. While at another court Vusi Rhadebe (an experienced regional court prosecutor in his early forties) frequently made such comments when he was referring to the incompetence of his senior, who he perceived as an 'affirmative action appointment' and not knowledgeable about 'the law', and when he expressed his frustration that he himself had not received a promotion to a senior NPA post.

Interestingly, with regards to Michael van Niekerk's point that a focus on quantitative forms of account-giving and control leads to the neglect of other quality control measures, a number of prosecutors pointed out that it does not bother them that the quality of their court work or their courtesy and respect towards their direct clients is not measured and evaluated by NPA performance indicators. For example, control prosecutor Charles Mafunda said 'it is taken for granted' and indicated that it is 'common sense' for a prosecutor to treat his clients with respect, work with diligence and know his case law when appearing in court. He thought that these were not prosecutorial work activities which needed to be spelt out to everyone and measured every month: 'That would be too obvious.' According to him, being a legal professional, a trained prosecutor and a public servant inherently entails these qualities which contribute to the delivery of justice. Patricia Nokwindla (an experienced prosecutor in her mid-forties) also emphasised that prosecutors are 'officers of the court': They are 'subjected to the rules of the courts, accountable to the court'. For her it seemed to be clear that this core part of their work did not need to be measured.

Various prosecutors also pointed out that the quality and the quantity of their work was not so clearly defined as Michael van Niekerk suggested. While justice takes time, most prosecutors stated that it is their daily experience that the amount of time complainants and witnesses have to wait for their case to be heard and finalised is directly linked to their level of satisfaction in relation to the court's work. They often emphasised that the amount of time between their acquaintance with a case and the finalisation thereof is linked to the ease with which the case can be closed. The more time people spend waiting for the completion of their case/trial, the greater the likelihood that complications might arise, such as the police having to trace and arrest accused who have absconded or who have intimidated complainant/s. Consequently, witnesses and complainants are more likely to forget important aspects of their testimony or lose interest in the case. As prosecutors pointed out time and again, this results in them needing to spend more time preparing witnesses for court – the longer the disputed event lies in the past, the more time the complainant and other witnesses need to reacquaint themselves with their written police statement. When a prosecutor takes more time to finalise a case, the backlog of postponed or incomplete trials consequently increases and fewer cases can be completed. As a result, the prosecutor spends more time postponing incomplete cases, corresponding with investigating officers and dealing with witnesses' and complainants' anger or frustration over the 'slow and inefficient courts' and the endless delays in their case rather than prosecuting and finalising trials. Many prosecutors were familiar with and complained about this 'vicious cycle'. This led many prosecutors to state that it is not clear how to separate the quality and the quantity of their work.

For example, Thabo Hlope (an ex-senior prosecutor in his early forties), who now works as a magistrate at a busy urban magistrate court and whom I regularly visited in his chambers, noted that the relationship between prosecutorial and judicial speed, quality and quantity is not clearly separable. He stated that it does not necessarily mean that 'justice is being served' and 'quality work' is done when a court spends more time finalising fewer cases. He emphasised that in his experience as a prosecutor and magistrate, and echoed by many other prosecutors, that:

> you will find that one prosecutor will read a murder docket in one minute and know what is still outstanding […] and another prosecutor will take at least ten minutes and he is still not sure what is outstanding. […] One magistrate will come to the real issues within five or ten minutes. He has heard enough from the complainant to make a judgment on the facts in an assault case after three to five questions and takes thirty minutes to finalise the case. The other might take up to two hours for a case involving someone who was slapped with an open hand.
>
> Do you know why it will take two hours? The magistrate takes his eyes off the ball. The witness will come; the witness will talk about history. Five years' history he had with the accused, why do you want to hear

> about that? Is it relevant to an incident that took place on 20 December 2008? That's why this case would take two hours – such a simple case like that? You see, there is a lot you can read into why a case takes too long. It might not necessarily be because that court was doing quality work.

Thabo Hlope's quote illustrates that for him a slow working court is not always a sign of careful legal reasoning, as it can also be an indicator of laziness, lack of legal knowledge, experience and competence. During our shared coffee breaks, Hlope was very clear on the point that 'justice takes time' and when I observed him in action in court he certainly came across as someone who cannot be rushed. During more casual conversation in chambers he made fun of colleagues who take 'justice too seriously', take an unreasonable amount of time for simple cases and forget that courts are not equipped with unlimited resources.

Lastly, Michael van Niekerk's critique that performance indicators place undue pressure on justice personnel was a point of view that no other observed and interviewed prosecutor expressed. When I observed prosecutors talking to their seniors about the monthly 'stats', seniors would certainly start asking questions when numbers were low or bad and this created a certain tension, but there was no outright fear or panic as the performance statistics only formed the beginning of a conversation about 'how the court is doing'. Furthermore, there was no clear link between not reaching targets and being sanctioned or punished.

The following comment by Noma Naidoo (a prosecutor in her early thirties and working for the NPA for the last five years) expresses well how many prosecutors felt about their performance indicators and reinforces what I observed during management meetings:

> no one will lose his job if you have not made the target. I am not afraid of them. If you don't make it there will be questions and you have to give reasons, tell them what happened, you need to give reasons, then it is ok, if you continuously don't make it, they will try to figure out why you didn't make it and if it is you, you might receive training sessions to assist you with your work, but you won't get fired for not reaching the target. And anyway the targets are realistic targets. I am not afraid of them.

The examples provided give an illustrative overview of the predominantly conciliatory and unconcerned attitudes of prosecutors towards their organisation's performance measurement system. The stress, fear and frustration which quantitative forms of evaluation, monitoring and accountability cause professionals in other organisational fields is an experience not prevalent amongst the majority of the prosecutors within my study.

The next two sections of this chapter will explore the institutional, legal and historical reasons which possibly counteract the power of numbers to discipline and punish professionals in this organisational setting and which could explain NPA prosecutors' less than hostile, timid and fearful attitudes towards their performance measurement system. The focus will be on resource allocation and quantitative accountability.

The resource (re-)allocation on the basis of selective performance indicators is one of the main reasons why professionals in other organisational fields fear and loathe their performance measurement, especially when actors feel that the indicators are selected arbitrarily and fail to address the core of their work. For example, as mentioned in the introduction, Espeland and Sauder (2007) show that one of the most important effects the USN rankings had on US law schools was the ranking affected the human and financial resources at the school's disposal. Furthermore, the ranking score affected law school leaders' freedom to spend money and in some instances impacted upon the security of their own salaries and positions. Thus, institutional and personal monetary advantages and disadvantages were tightly coupled to a school's rank on a number of levels. This increased competition among different law schools and the pressure for law school personnel to perform according to USN quality criteria. Strathern (2000a) and Shore and Wright (2009: 3) mention the insecurity, stress and fear which the British government's Research Assessment Exercise (RAE) put academics under, who had to compete on the basis of selected performance indicators for national research funds.[4]

By contrast, in the organisational setting I observed this automated correlation between achieving 'high numbers' and receiving financial benefits or achieving 'low numbers' and being sanctioned did not apply. To understand why, I will first focus on the institutional and legal set up of the prosecutorial work environment which does not – as I will be arguing – provide for the straightforward competition for resources, funds and clients via numerical representations, and secondly, in a separate section on the history of performance-related pay mechanism in the NPA. I will show that within the ongoing professionalisation

[4] For further examples of links between resource allocation and performance measurement systems see: Lampland 2010; Rottenburg 2000; Kipnis 2008; Timmerman and Berg 2003; Star and Bowker 2000.

process of the prosecution authority, a twenty-year-old conflict over more recognition and higher base salaries for prosecutors forced the discussion of competitive performance-based salaries to the background. Creating an attractive work environment was more important in that context rather than identifying and rewarding 'hard workers'.

INSTITUTIONAL AND JURIDICAL SET UP OF SOUTH AFRICAN STATE COURTS AND THE NPA

There are various reasons why performance indicators did not increase the competition between different state courts for scarce public funds in South Africa.

Firstly, state courts fall under the authority of the country's Department of Justice and Constitutional Development. They are bound by national laws and regulations and are not independent entities such as the US private and state law schools with their individual missions and characteristics. Certain American law schools enable equal access to higher education by assisting specific underprivileged or discriminated students over others, or they pride themselves in creating a national elite by only admitting the brightest and smartest students. Therefore, these institutions do not have the mandate or claim to treat every student similarly. However, legal equality and due process – central principles of Section 9 of the South African Constitution – ensure that in the working environment of prosecutors, everyone is treated equally before the law, regardless of their race, gender, sexual orientation, religion, etc. without privilege, discrimination or bias. Although that this does not always occur in practice is not my concern here. As a result of this legal frame, all courts are supposed to operate in the same way and are supposed to be equipped with the same resources. Due to historical reasons, the equipment, facilities, furniture and layout of courts differ tremendously in South Africa.

The DOJCD is currently addressing these disparities. However, the approach is not, for example, to reward well-performing courts with a new roof, a new air conditioning system or better protected police cells, or conversely by making badly performing courts wait for these amenities. The DOJCD therefore allocates resources to the various courts on a need basis rather than on merit. I observed in practice that resource allocation also depended on how well the respective prosecutors were able to justify the need or argue for new equipment and how well she or he was connected to people within the DOJCD in charge of the court infrastructure allocation.

Furthermore, courts have no ability to specifically select the complainants who come to court or try to attract certain groups of complainants or accused and neglect others. The provinces in which I conducted my fieldwork have specialized courts such as drug courts, community courts or sexual offence courts. Within that offence category, those working at a specific court cannot decide that they prefer to deal with educated complainants, or poor ones or those who have the potential to make their 'stats' look better because their cases are straightforward and can be quickly dealt with. The ability of prosecutors to select cases and complainants will be discussed below.

I observed in practice that there could be a decision within a cluster to deal with certain types of cases in different ways. For example, due to the inability of laboratories to cope with the volume of drug samples for substance analysis, unfinalised drug charge cases were withdrawn (with the intention to reinstate them at a later stage). The reasoning behind such decisions is that scarce court hours should not be wasted with the postponement of cases whose investigation could not be finalised due to laboratory backlogs. However, these were decisions affecting all courts in the cluster and came from the provincial and/or national level and not from an individual court level.

Thirdly, the court's jurisdiction, the close connection between the place where a criminal offence occurred and the venue where it will be heard by a state court is another important legal and institutional factor which prevents active competition between courts for cases and clients that make their statistics look better. Reporting a crime or going to court is in most instances not a choice once a complainant has decided to take her or his case to the state. Complainants are required to go to the police station in the jurisdiction where the crime occurred and/or where they live. After the criminal offence has been reported and a case opened and investigated, the police are required to send the case to the court their police station is assigned to. Thus, once complainants decide to get the state involved in their dispute, they cannot choose to take their case to the best-ranked court or to the most efficient court.[5] I observed in practice how complainants, even injured ones, who went to the wrong police station were asked to report to the correct

[5] The constitutional right of access to justice dictates further that a person should be tried in a court nearest to the jurisdiction in which he or she lives. So it is not up to the complainants to bring their cases to courts where they will get the best results.

police station, or how cases which were supposed to be heard by another court were sent back to the respective police station in order to ensure that the case is heard in a court with the necessary regional jurisdiction.

Additionally, it is not only the complainants' choice which is restricted in terms of choosing one's dispute forum. Prosecutors, as I have already mentioned, are not allowed to cherry-pick their cases to improve their rank nor can they choose the magistrate which they feel is best suited to finding in the state's favour unlike, for example, law school administrators who can select specific students to boost their selectivity score. From time to time there are accusations that prosecutors choose 'easy cases' to achieve higher conviction rates (see for example Artz and Smythe 2007a; 2007b). To identify what makes a case easy or difficult is less standardised and ambiguous and is therefore disputed among prosecutors, compared to other organisational fields where the tradition of quantifying complex social phenomena is more established. For example, law school leaders could improve their performance by choosing a student with a high LSAT score over a student with a lower score. In contrast, attempts to quantify cases with the aim of classifying easily winnable cases and challenging cases does not exist in the prosecutorial field. Thus far, no one has quantified the complexity of a case beyond differentiating between lower court, regional court and High Court cases. High Courts usually deal with the most complex cases with a great deal of evidence and numerous witnesses and can impose the most onerous sentences regulated by the Criminal Procedure Act 51 of 1977. Trials usually last weeks or months. In contrast, the cases lower magistrates' courts hear have on average one or two witnesses and hardly any complicated ballistic or forensic evidence to deal with, and are therefore sometimes referred to by criminal justice actors as 'petty' while the lower courts are referred to as 'sausage factories' due to the volume and content of the of cases.

By contrast, the 'prospects', 'talent' or 'quality' of a potential law student has been quantified since 1948[6] by means of the standardised Law School Admission Test (LSAT) and is widely used in the American law school admission process. LSAT can also viewed in the context of the tradition of awarding pupils numerical marks – the ideal and practice of evaluating individuals based on objectified criteria goes back to educational institutions of early modern times (Vormbusch 2008: 92–93): documenting their accomplishments on paper in

[6] http://www.lsac.org/aboutlsac/about-lsac.asp

archives and using school leaving examination marks as a central criterion for university entrance.

These kinds of sophisticated quantification and translation chains are less established in the legal and prosecutorial field in South Africa and other countries (see Espeland 1997: 1122–1131).[7] Therefore even if prosecutors were permitted to cherry-pick, they would not be able to clearly and easily identify the winnability of a case. On the other hand, the not deeply anchored tradition to quantify within that working environment has another effect: While prosecutors were thinking and talking about 'stats', targets and rates, and (as I mentioned) in terms of cases which are good for the 'stats', the concept of a case which is bad for the statistics or the concept of a top-ranked court or cluster did not play a seminal role in court prosecutors' working life, in their working language or for their self-image. Being involved in cases where one has to use their legal and not only administrative skills was something most prosecutors I observed did not dread but perceived as their main task, as their mandate (see Chapter 3).

Another reason why this kind of terminology was not prevalent amongst the prosecutors is the fact that the NPA's court and cluster rankings, calculated on court's overall performance and efficiency rates, are not made public. Only national aggregate figures are published. The capacity of performance statistics to be widely and rapidly circulated and thereby transform people's cognition and produce reactive responses is therefore interrupted, since the public does not know which court is the best-ranked court in the country. In other words, the concept of a 'top-ranked court' plays no prominent role in the public talking and thinking about state courts. Due to the withholding of numerical data, individual prosecutors cannot be held accountable or pressured by members of the public for the rank of their court or cluster as the public does not have access to this information.

The final point I would like to mention as to why the legal and institutional setting of the NPA prevents the organisation's performance indicators from increasing the competition between different state courts for scarce public funds is closely related to the first one. While the DOJCD is responsible for the maintenance of court

[7] An exception would be the highly controversial American Federal Sentencing Guidelines, which I mentioned in the introduction of this book. They restrict the discretion of judges in sentencing people convicted of crimes with a so-called 'Sentencing Table' that allows for less individualised sentences. This example illustrates lawmakers' attempts to bring greater quantitative accountability into a state's criminal justice sector (Espeland and Vannebo 2007: 25–33).

buildings, the NPA administers the allocation of prosecutors and workload. Cases and prosecutorial staff members are distributed among the different courts according to a needs-based system and not a merit-based system. A top-ranked court would not imply that the respective managerial prosecutor would reward the court by allocating more human resources to the court or punish a badly performing court with a higher workload. The performance rankings did not create direct competition for more prosecutor posts between different courts as they did not, for example, redirect prosecutor flows from court A to court B because B was ranked higher than A. For example, when a court where I spent extensive periods of time was functioning well (meaning they did not have a particularly long list of outstanding cases), the court received more cases from another court which was struggling with its caseload. As soon as this court was not able to finalise cases due to the high volume of new cases entering the system, a relief prosecutor from court C was allocated to help with the caseload.

In my view, the following factors explain why, in the working environment of NPA prosecutors, the correlation observed elsewhere between quantified performance information and financial favours or sanctions does not apply: the institutional set up of the justice system and the legal framework in which the prosecutors work (guided by strong egalitarian ideals enshrined in the South African constitution and the Criminal Procedure Act, which demand a needs-based allocation of resources), very limited possibilities to select complainants and cases, the still-young tradition to quantify in this field and the largely non-public nature of the NPA performance information. I argue that these factors are the reason why lower court prosecutors had a more conciliatory attitude towards the NPA's performance measurement system. The effect that statistical devices such as non-public court and cluster rankings or public national court hours or conviction rates had on their work environment was in my opinion less tangible and painful than in other professional's work settings.

In the final section of this chapter I explore why performance indicators create, on an individual and personal level, less fear and pressure for prosecutors. I will show that the NPA's plans to institutionalise competition between prosecutors and reallocate resources based on performance statistics has failed.

HISTORY OF PERFORMANCE-RELATED REMUNERATION IN THE NPA

While competition for cases and clients between different jurisdictions or greater freedom for complainants to choose the best-ranked state court over the second- or third-ranked one were never mentioned as something the new NPA performance measurement process was intended to introduce to the South African criminal justice system, it was indeed envisioned that the performance indicators and targets would lead to a more competitive prosecutorial work environment (Schönteich 2001: 56). There were attempts on the part of the NPA, Department of Justice and the government to reallocate resources and to stop the perpetuation of a system where 'good' and 'bad' performances are awarded equally. It was felt that the existing annual seniority-related pay increments, which were often described as rewarding more or less 'everyone', were not up to the task of motivating employees to 'work hard'. At the time when performance statistics were introduced in the NPA in 1998, there was talk of so-called 'performance-based salaries' or 'performance-based bonuses' (Schönteich 2001: 56) However, salaries, bonuses, job (in-)security, promotions, sanctions and demotion are not currently correlated with prosecutors' performance statistics. In this section I discuss how this came about and provide an overview of the history of performance-related pay in the NPA and will show why this attempt never materialised.

In his prosecution service evaluation and analysis written for the Institute for Security Studies (a non-governmental organisation founded in 1996 in Pretoria), Martin Schönteich (2001: 56) states that prior to 1998 '(t)here was no objective way of rewarding a job well done or dealing with those who failed to perform' within the newly established NPA. During this period prosecutors automatically received salary increases after they had worked for the Department of Justice for a certain time and/or more substantial ones when they moved up the hierarchical ladder within that department. Prosecutorial job promotions were to a large extent also automated, meaning that they were linked to an employee's years of service (Schönteich 2001: 81), and/or based on Apartheid's bureaucratic racism and political favouritism (Davis and le Roux 2009: 17–35). Prior to 1998 there was scant prosecutorial statistical information available which the Department of Justice could use to 'objectively' promote or pay prosecutors' additional bonuses or salary increases.[8] Prior to 1998, as noted by Fernandez (1993) and confirmed by various interviewed older prosecutors, only limited regional statistics data regarding prosecution services was collected.

When the NPA was established, it was the first time a so-called 'court management unit' whose mandate it was to create a 'performance management framework' to govern and monitor the work of prosecutors and to assist the office of the NDPP to improve the 'efficiency and effectiveness' of 'service delivery' of the prosecutors working for the new prosecution service was set up (Schönteich 2001: 56). One of the initiatives the new unit developed to enable them to monitor the performance of the country's court prosecutors was the collection of 'court management statistics' and related to that the creation of a database (Schönteich 2001: 57). From April 1999, seven months after the establishment of the NPA in August 1998, the court management unit began to collect statistics pertaining to the performance of the prosecution service for all the country's magistrates courts, and soon thereafter for the High Court. Additionally, the court management unit set up the first national database which captured information about prosecutors' experience levels, academic qualifications and levels of training. Using this database, so-called 'work load evaluation reports' were, according to Schönteich, compiled for each prosecutor's office (2001: 57). The court management unit used these reports and court statistics to allocate, for example, human resources according to the number of cases a prosecutor had to handle in a specific court and the related outstanding number of cases, or the identification of areas in which additional courts needed to be opened or closed due to an increased or an insufficient work load (Schönteich 2001: 57).

The newly collected national statistics also made visible the shortcomings of the prosecution and justice system in general and, according to several interviewed NPA managers, created greater awareness within the NPA of its 'operational difficulties'. For example, the statistical

[8] When Schönteich speaks of 'objective' performance-rewarding and sanctioning mechanisms, I would suggest he refers to what Theodore Porter, as I mentioned in the introduction of this book, describes aptly as 'mechanical objectivity'. According to Porter (1995: 391) 'mechanical' or 'quantitative objectivity' refers to a standardised way of producing knowledge (often statistical information), which is not necessarily 'true to nature' or 'true to reality', but independent of the person who is producing it. It does not matter who does the measurement and when and where, the ideal is that every trained actor using the same uniform prescribed counting rules and official calculating protocols will, in the end, come up with the same result and data. The possibility that another person can recheck and replicate the official standardised counting and calculating operation supports the idea that this form of knowledge is thought to tame and constrain self-interest, prejudice, personal opinions and preferences.

information made it apparent that when prosecutors took longer to finalise cases the number of outstanding cases grew, or highlighted court hours lost due to numerous unscheduled court adjournments (Schönteich 2001: 75). The court management unit responded by setting individualised performance targets for each court in the country in May 2000 and began to closely monitor under-performing courts (Schönteich 2001: 56). That the NPA was able to compare the performance of different courts was also something new, as prior to that time countrywide statistics were simply not available.

The newly collected statistics were not only used to redistribute human resources and monitor courts. They were also used in 1999 by the NDPP to draw up the first so-called 'performance agreements' with prosecutors in which their salary increases or performance bonuses were dependent on specific performance targets (Schönteich 2001: 56). This performance agreement was intended to reward all prosecutors equally and was not an instrument to reward only 'hard working' employees and incentivise the organisation's 'underperformers'. It was established during a time of continuous, intense and unsatisfactory salary negotiations between the Department of Justice and the prosecutorial body.

In Chapter 1 I mentioned that prosecutors' low salaries started becoming an issue of contention from the 1980s. From the late 1990s, prosecutors in particular became dissatisfied with their remuneration for two reasons: Firstly, in 1996 existing salary discrepancies between magistrates and prosecutors widened when magistrates became independent from the Department of Justice and were able to negotiate considerably higher salary increases; and secondly, when prosecutors' hours of overtime (two to four hours per day, which substituted to some extent for their low basic salary) were no longer paid out by their employer (the Department of Justice) due to lack of funds (Schönteich 2001: 84).

Due to these personal remuneration related changes, in 1996 prosecutors initiated several work-to-rule campaigns and some strike action which slowed down and in some instances brought courts to a complete halt. In March 1999, the government and the unions representing the prosecutors signed a performance agreement in which prosecutors would receive an extra three per cent increase in addition of their annual public service increase when they met specific agreed-upon targets.[9] This agreement was reached after several promises to increase prosecutors' salaries or to reinstitute overtime payments were not kept

9 The following performance targets were included in the performance agreement of 1999:

or were honoured later than promised and broken once again. This led to further protest and strike activities in 1997 and 1998 (Schönteich 2001: 84–87; see also: 'Three unions shelve strike for talks' 1999; Otto 2008).

Most of the agreed-upon targets were, according to Schönteich, met in 1999 but prosecutors were not paid their three per cent salary bonus at the agreed time in September 1999. Some prosecutors were paid in December 1999, but following research, it is still not known if the performance bonuses were paid to the rest. However, it is known that the dishonoured agreement caused increasing tension and led to further go-slow actions (Schönteich 2001: 85). This tense situation was exacerbated when in October 2000 the NDPP promised every prosecutor a once-off R1,000 performance bonus to be paid out in December 2000. The prosecutors' union, after consulting the Department of Justice, found out that NDPP's promised bonus had not been budgeted for and that the NDPP was not in a position to authorise such an additional expenditure (Schönteich 2001: 86).

This brief outline describing NPA's first efforts to allocate its resources more competitively highlights a number of issues. Firstly, these were rather sporadic attempts; secondly, there was no competitive selection process of rewarding specific employees, but rather performance-based salary increases for all; and thirdly, the NPA repeatedly did not keep its agreements and/or promises to pay prosecutors more money, which caused immense frustration and tension amongst the workforce. However, there were subsequent attempts to introduce a remuneration system, which would create performance-related salaries for individual prosecutors.

In 2001 a new 'salary dispensation system' to diversify prosecutors' salary structures was announced. Experienced NPA prosecutors who had years of experience earned almost the same salary as starting prosecutors. This caused dissatisfaction among the more advanced employees and was one of the reasons why experienced prosecutors frequently left to find better-paid employment in the private sector

- reducing the number of awaiting trial prisoners who were granted bail of less than R1,000 by 10%;
- reducing the length of time between the first court appearance and the finalisation of the case to three months for awaiting trial prisoners with bail of less than R1,000;
- increasing the average daily time courts are in session to 4.5 hours;
- reducing the number of outstanding dockets and inquest reports;
- reducing the number of cases on the courts' rolls;
- increasing the number of cases finalised with a verdict. (Schönteich 2001: 85)

('NPA haemorrhages key staff' 2005; 'Prosecutors courting pay row' 2005; Ngalwa 2007). The new system was implemented to enable the NPA to offer more diverse career paths within the organisation so as retain and attract much-needed skilled legal professionals. In the past pay progressions within salary bands were difficult to achieve; the revised system would have more intervals between different salary scales. The NPA would not only remunerate employees according to their 'qualifications' and 'scope of work', but also according to their 'performance', while also acknowledging 'experience' and 'seniority'. The old 'single salary structure' allowed for substantial salary increases only when employees were promoted to management, supervisory or specialist posts. By contrast, the differentiated structure of this new remuneration framework would mean that prosecutors – for example, court or control prosecutors – who remained in their position (and gained experience) or out-performed their peers would receive better pay.[10]

However, the NPA failed to implement the changes and it took another six years before a new salary agreement titled 'Occupation specific dispensation for legally qualified professionals' (abbreviated to OSD), was signed in July 2007.[11] At the beginning of this research in August 2008 the OSD had not yet been implemented. While the Department of Justice and Constitutional Development (DOJCD) had signed the agreement, it had yet to obtain the budget from the treasury for the proposed salary increases of the new salary dispensation structure (Ngqiyaza 2008).

New strike action was threatened, and prosecutors went on a silent strike with banners at certain courts. Representatives of the NPA employees, the Public Servants Association, lodged a case against the Ministry of Justice and Constitutional Development due to the non-implementation of the OSD. In September, a day before the case was due to be heard at the country's labour court (Otto 2008; Masemola and Otto 2008), the office of the NDPP announced that employees would receive OSD from September onwards and the payments would be backdated from 1 July 2007 (Maughan 2008a; 2008b, 2008c). The OSD saga continued until 2013 after further strike and court action from the prosecutors against the Department of Justice and Constitutional Development (Witten 2009).

[10] http://www.info.gov.za/speeches/2007/07061811451001.htm Last accessed: 18 May 2018.

[11] http://www.justice.gov.za/legislation/notices/2010/20101202_gg33826_n1146_npa-osd.pdf Last accessed: 18 May 2018.

In January 2013 a number of prosecutors explained to me that they had received their OSD salary increases backdated to 1 July 2007 and expressed anger that it took court action in order for the DOJCD to pay them the outstanding amounts of their salaries (Momberg 2009).

It is interesting to note that between 2008 and 2012 when the research for this study was mostly conducted, the issue of OSD repeatedly entered conversations of the prosecutors. At the time the majority of the junior and lower senior prosecutors did not have high hopes for performance-related pay increases within their salary level, but relied on the previous promotional system. They sought promotion to a higher ranked position within the NPA or applied for magistrate positions, which were perceived by many prosecutors as attractive posts. My research did not systematically explore the factors determining the selection of personnel for these sought after positions. Prosecutors frequently stated that affirmative action policies, networks, and diverse skills (legal, organisational and communication) were important for promotion within the NPA or the justice system more generally. Besides the other above-mentioned factors, they drew attention to the fact that it was often pure lack rather than a considered decision when being appointed at one of the more popular metropolitan provinces/court clusters.

Some prosecutors remarked upon the comparatively high salaries that lawyers earn in the private sector and how they wished for or actively pursued private sector employment. However, the security of working within the public service was considered to be extremely advantageous, especially in the aftermath of the global financial crisis of 2008. At this time, household indebtedness and inflationary pressures were acute in South Africa. Especially prosecutors, who came from poor backgrounds and were sole breadwinners of their (at times extended) families, raised the point that they lacked the necessary funds and networks to become criminal attorneys or advocates.

The system of performance bonuses or awards still existed within the NPA between 2009 and 2012, but it was no longer linked to an across-the-board performance bonus when a target was met, as in 1999. Individual prosecutors received extra payments for an 'outstanding' performance, the definition of which was unclear to many of the lower court prosecutors interviewed for this study. Most prosecutors felt it was not stringently linked to their individual performance statistics, as explained by Charles Mafunda in 2012 when asked about receiving a performance bonus if he reached certain performance targets:

> no, you don't get it. You have to rescue Haiti in order to get it. One does not get the bonus if one reaches the target or is doing well, you have to do some extraordinary, rescuing Haiti, some charity work, you donate money or other goods, then one has higher chances of getting the bonus of the cluster […] It's unfair because you don't really donate something or do something good when you receive a payment afterwards. And it's unfair, only people who have money can afford to do charity, not everyone has the same opportunities […] anyway there are always golden boys and golden girls, they get the bonus.

Daphne Thusini, a senior prosecutor in her forties working at head office in Pretoria, also suggested and criticised the fact that NPA performance bonuses were paid on the basis of criteria which not everyone had equal opportunity to meet and on the basis of friendship or to reward patronage and not on merit. She went on to say that while bonuses are to some extent allocated according to workload and although there is a certain meritocratic element to the process, she complained that only certain sectors of NPA employees received them. She felt that 'historically disadvantaged' employees and women do not have the same prospect as white employees and men to fill positions in the organisation which enable employees to qualify for the bonuses and found this 'demoralising and unfair'.

Charles Mafunda raised the point that performance bonuses can potentially affect the work morale of prosecutors, but did not express dissatisfaction that he had never received the cluster's bonus. There were, according to him, only a few bonuses available, so his chances of receiving one were very slim, and individuals, rather than the whole prosecutorial teams, received a bonus. He perceived this kind rewarding mechanism as potentially counter-productive for the reality of court work and recalled his work in a factory to earn money while he studied, where they also received performance bonuses. However, these were not awarded individually, but granted to the team when they produced additional products in a shift. In his opinion prosecutors also work as a team, as one court building usually houses courts with several different tasks (drug court, domestic violence court, reception court) and to him it made no sense to single out an individual's efforts. He was concerned that individual rewards were 'not good for the spirit of the team' and suggested that collective promotions would be far more suitable for the prosecutorial mode of working.

CONCLUSION

This chapter has shown that NPA court prosecutors' attitude towards their performance measurement system is less critical, fearful and hostile than the reaction and stance of professionals in other organisational settings to being evaluated and monitored quantitatively. While court prosecutors certainly were aware that performance statistics, indicators, targets and ranks could not comprehensively capture everything they were doing at work (as certain simplifications or misrepresentations accompany numerical representation) most prosecutors did not perceive this as something negative, but rather as inevitable when one is evaluated and monitored using numerical representations. The majority did not perceive that the performance statistics, indicators, rates and targets diminish their professional discretion or undermine the authority of law. They were not pressured to make decisions which were 'good for the stats' but 'not good for justice'; some even felt there was not always a contradiction between the two.

I argued in this chapter that prosecutors' more positive stance towards the quantification of their work is due to the fact that resource allocation is not tightly linked to their quantitative performance information in this professional environment. I made my point that quantitative forms of accountability have not transformed resource allocation in the prosecutorial workplace on two different levels.

Firstly, I showed that the way state courts are run in South Africa does not create an environment where prosecutors and courts can compete freely for cases, funds and clients. Resource allocation is need-based and not merit-based in this organisational field and follows strict legal principles enshrined in the Constitution and the Criminal Procedure Act of the country. Furthermore I also pointed out that the less sophisticated and established quantification chains in this organisational field, and the fact that much of the NPA's performance information is non-public or only publicized in aggregated form, are factors which explain why the authority of numbers cannot easily encroach on the authority of law in the prosecutorial workplace.

Secondly, I showed that the NPA's two attempts to allocate portions of their labour costs more competitively – connected to prosecutors' performance – never really materialised. While there were ideas to reward all employees when certain performance targets were met and subsequently to attract and retain skilful legal professionals with more flexible career paths and performance-based pay, these proposals were never properly implemented due to budgetary constraints and the NPA's and the DOJCD's failure to attract additional resources for these extra payments and salary increases (on top of the annual inflation increases). The NPA's attempts to create a more competitive work environment occurred at a time when prosecutors had been engaged in a nearly twenty-year struggle for improved remuneration. These negotiations were characterised by many dishonoured and/or delayed promises. I argued that this broader dispute, where the monetary advancement and recognition of all prosecutors was at stake, pushed the notion of competitive performance-based salaries into the background. Creating a more attractive work environment was more important in that context than rewarding 'hard workers' and sanctioning 'underperformers'.

The concept and the practice of performance-related rewards still currently exists in the NPA. However, I provided evidence that prosecutors do not believe there to be a close relationship between their performance statistics and their remuneration or their promotional prospects. While they certainly compete for higher paid positions or for bonuses with one another, this competitiveness is not tightly coupled to the numerical representations with which they account for their work and are held accountable.

I argued in the previous chapter that to accept prosecutors' 'stats talk' as evidence of their audit mentality and for their narrow or reduced understanding and practice of their accountability is to ignore that lower court prosecutors had some control and flexibility over how their reputations were defined and what good prosecutorial performance should entail. I would suggest that the loose coupling of resource allocation and quantitative performance information explored in this chapter is an important factor as to why court prosecutors are not severely intimidated and stressed by quantitative forms of accountability; why they feel their professional discretion is still intact; and why they practice their accountability in a wider sense, by that I mean with more deliberate and non-quantitative forms of accounts.

In the next two chapters I examine the working worlds of managerial prosecutors and seek to understand how they define performance and what role numerical representations and knowledge played in their everyday work. Chapter 5 is therefore a continuation of my deliberations in Chapter 3 in which I presented empirical data as to how quantitative performance measures affect legal professionals in the NPA, and where I argued that in this organisational field the relationship between quantification, accountability and professional work practices is less straightforward than many social studies of numbers assume.

5

AT THE TOP OF THE NPA

Managing with Numbers and Numerical Reflexivity

INTRODUCTION

Accountability always involves at least two parties ('A' and 'B'): A, who has been entrusted with authority, discretion and/or money and who has therefore the duty to take responsibility and explain and justify certain actions and decisions to B; and B, who has some form of authority to compel A to act in a particular way and who has the right to ask questions and to demand an account from A about what she did or did not do (Sinclair 1995; Mashaw 2006; Messner 2009). A crucial moment in this relationship is, according to various accountability scholars, that those to whom accountability is to be rendered, have to be convinced – after they received the accounts – that accountability has indeed been rendered. They state that while expectations of how accountability should be demonstrated are never static (Dowdle 2006), they often have a 'cultural stamp' (Strathern 2000a: 2). That means that there are often only certain forms of account-giving in a specific setting that A has at its disposal to persuade B that accountability has been rendered.

In Chapters 3 and 4, I focus on how quantitative forms of account-giving affects lower court prosecutors' understanding and practices of their accountability. I show that performance statistics, indicators, rates and targets were prominent in their work life, but that they were not exclusively indicative of prosecutorial performance and were not the only legitimate measure of it. These legal professionals felt that other forms of accountability indeed counted and that they perceived them as seminal for the execution of their prosecutorial work.

This chapter explores whether this wider and more nuanced understanding of prosecutorial performance and accountability was also shared in other parts of the organisation, where actors have to fulfil different tasks and responsibilities and where the pressure of 'numbers' might therefore unleash or encroach differently. In other words, I will ask whether prosecutorial managers accept and are convinced by lower court prosecutors' other non-quantitative forms of account-giving. I will commence this chapter by providing examples which demonstrate the role that quantified performance information plays in the way more senior prosecutors and members of the NPA executive conduct their work, namely, managing groups of court prosecutors and running the NPA on a provincial and national level. In the second section I will provide a case example, namely a summary of a series of management meetings I attended during the course of 2008 and 2009 at an NPA regional head office, which demonstrates that while quantitative performance information is central to how managers held their staff to account, they were also clearly aware of its limits. In the third and last part of this chapter I explore managers' numerical knowledge and competence, namely in relation to their staffs' career advancement and performance bonuses. I show that many perceived the performance statistics as an unreliable and insufficient source to make such important human resource management decisions. I will argue in this chapter that managers' wider and more nuanced understanding of accountability and performance can be attributed to their numerical knowledge and their awareness of the constructed-ness and constructiveness of quantifications.

NPA MANAGERS AT WORK WITH QUANTITATIVE PERFORMANCE INFORMATION

Amongst prosecutors with managerial functions[1] and with access to more aggregated performance rates and rankings, it was common, as I indicated in Chapter 3, to use the NPA statistics in the description of their work and their daily concerns. When talking about their work to me or to their colleagues, the managers would frequently refer to the NPA's different performance indicators to indicate how or what they and their staff members 'have been doing'; in a specific time period; or

[1] When I refer to NPA managerial prosecutors in this chapter I speak of senior public prosecutors (SPP), chief public prosecutors (CPP), deputy directors of public prosecution (DDPP) and directors of public prosecution (DPP). Senior public prosecutors, which are involved in 'advanced production' (meaning they are doing direct court work) or in a 'tutor' position (meaning they are training aspirant prosecutors) are not included in the discussion. Most of these managers do not do any direct court work. However, in 2010 when the NPA received a new NDPP, Adv. Menzi Simelane started his new job with a controversial instruction that experienced managerial prosecutors should be redeployed in order to have more prosecutorial skills in the lower courts ('NPA defends reshuffling of prosecutors' 2010; 'Simelane backs down on prosecutor demotions' 2010). How far that directive still applies is not known to me.

after they have introduced certain changes to the organisation. The use of vocabulary in the following quote, extracted from a one-hour interview with Adv. Lionel de Villiers, a director of public prosecution for the last fifteen years and in his early fifties, is characteristic of how various NPA managers spoke about their everyday tasks. So is the DPP's focus on outstanding court cases:

> we run it [NPA] like a business, with a strategic plan, objectives, goals, performance agreements and so forth [. . .] at the beginning of the financial year you have to do your planning and you need to look at what you are doing, how are you doing it and if you are effective. What other things can you do to increase your performance? [. . .] We told them [prosecutors] their job was to look at performance and how many cases they have. They can't have thousand cases and just sit there only doing one case. They must make a plan as to how you are going to get rid of those thousand cases and bring it down. If you don't bring those thousand cases down someone is suffering. [. . .] The court mustn't stop at one o'clock in the day and then they go home because there is no more work. They must manage it in such a way that they utilise all the court time. [. . .] You have a bigger responsibility other than just dealing with the one case.

In conversations and interviews where I asked managers specifically about the function and purpose of the NPA's performance measurement system for the execution of their everyday work, they often pointed out that the quantitative performance information assists them in accomplishing their job. The way the DPP, Adv. Lionel de Villiers, described performance measurement in the following three quotes as a useful planning and sense-making tool is again representative of what various other NPA managers said with regards to the purpose and function of numerical performance information. The three quotes are extracted from a three-hour interview and give a good indication that the quantified performance information has multiple tasks to fulfil in the work environment of prosecutorial managers. He stated:

> [w]ell the main thing around the [performance information] reports that we receive is how the courts are doing. At a glance [. . .] I will know exactly [. . .] all those things relevant to our work, I will know exactly each court in each province [. . .] So I will know at a glance the court hours, I'll have a daily indicator to say this is how long the court sits, what the reason were why the court didn't sit for the full hours, I'll know how many cases are finalised in a court, I'll know how many cases were

received outside of the court, so what we call the [decision] dockets,[2] the police dossiers.

So every prosecutor in a court must capture the number of cases that went through that court, what happened to the case, how the case was finalised, if the case was finalised, if the case was postponed, all of that information, then besides the case we also ask for information regarding the types of crimes. So if it's a sexual offence we want to know if it's a child, so the crime types are also captured you see, and that gets through every month and then it also goes up to our national head office every month. So that is why when you read our reports, you will get a sense of different things, finalisation, court hours, number of cases, crime types, number of sexual offences, conviction rates, you know, in terms of the cases we actually put through the court what is the conviction rate. [. . .]

A few minutes later DPP Adv. de Villiers added:

I think the focus with [performance] plans is, it helps you to identify exactly what you want to achieve and then you got to also say up front that this is what we are going to deliver at the end of each year, you know. So although you have got a five-year strategy which broadly sets out where you want to go over the five-year period, every year you have to have a specific plan, to say how you are going to then every year contribute to that five years, right.

The targets help you to focus to achieve and to deliver. Now that is a good thing, in the past perhaps if we didn't have the plans like that, people will be busy with many things but you're not sure if it's actually contributing to the specific mandate of that department, you know. So we must be sure that what our people are busy with is actually helping us as far as the prosecutions are concerned. Are the people spending their energies in the right way, you know? People can be busy with many things but are they busy with the right things, right, so if you say well everybody must be focused on prosecutions, getting cases into courts, doing cases and you start counting those things, and then it helps people to focus on what are the important things.

If you get cases allocated to you onto your table it's important that you get those cases done, to look at it, get the file, deal with it and move on

[2] Decision dockets are crime dockets in which the police opened a docket but did not yet detain anyone for the offence. Control or senior prosecutors who receive these dockets give either written directives to the police investigator in the investigation diary part of the docket as to what further investigation is needed, or, if they decide that sufficient evidence has been compiled to prove the case before a court they, will issue a summons, warning notice or warrant of arrest for the offender to appear in court.

> and move on and move on, you know. So it helps with productivity. It helps us to ensure that people are productive. [. . .]

About an hour later this DPP stated:

> So you know, people must understand what they are contributing towards, you know you need to make them know that there is a bigger picture. If I am sitting in Umhlazi[3] at court and I'm busy with these cases, what do I do? Do I just go to work every day, there is another file, no, people must be able to see well this is actually impacting on the bigger picture. This is what we are doing at provincial level, this is what we want to do at national level. Why are we doing all of that?
>
> Because we want to impact on reducing crime, or we want to impact on confidence of the public in the court system, so that's the strategy and they must know that, at a local level they must know that they can make sense. [. . .] a performance contract will give the context. These are our objectives, this is what we want to achieve and this is how you are going to make it work. [. . .] They have to think about that and that is why we explain to them what we get, how much money we get, how much money goes to payment of salaries and of other things. [. . .] We also want people to be aware that when you have court time available, it's expensive and you need to do as much as you can in the available court time and so that is really what those targets are about.

These three quotes show well that DPP Adv. Lionel de Villiers uses the performance information for different management tasks. Firstly, he uses them for internal management purposes. The numerical representations are central to the way he, who rarely does any direct court work, receives information about the people and courts and specific parts of the NPA he has to manage. With a quick look at the respective performance statistics, he says, he has access to perspectives and fields of vision in the organisation he would not have otherwise. Without visiting each court in his province he can 'know', as he says, how specific courts, clusters or his whole province 'is doing' and whether they are 'productive'.

Secondly, Adv. de Villiers indicated that the performance information is not only important for his daily and monthly tasks of monitoring the prosecutors and courts he has to oversee, but also for defining key priorities for the organisation which assist him to track whether what is happening every day at the courts is contributing to the organisation's

[3] The name of the geographical location mentioned by the DPP in this interview has been changed by the author of this book for anonymity and confidentiality reasons.

long term plans and goals. In that sense he uses performance indicators as attention-narrowing mechanisms but also as a planning and strategising tool.

Thirdly, he pointed out that the performance indicators help him to communicate to his staff members the 'bigger picture' of their and the NPA's work. He feels the performance information which tracks how each prosecutor, court and each province is performing assists people to 'make sense' of their work and to see the linkages between the work of individual courts, the province and the larger societal role the NPA has to play. Furthermore, this DPP indicated that he perceives the tracking of non-financial performance information as an activity, which assists him to be financially accountable and to create more economic awareness amongst his staff for court costs.

That interviewed and observed managers emphasised the internal management and economic control purpose of the NPA's performance measurement system was common. John Cloete, a senior prosecutor in his fifties who worked at the time I interviewed him for three hours at the NPA's national head office, said for example that the various 'baseline studies' which the NPA's strategic management office conducted since its establishment that looked at how many cases were been finalised in each court over the last years and how many court hours were used to finalise those cases helped them to get an idea of 'what is a "reasonable" number of cases which can be finalised by one court under "normal circumstances" during a specific amount of time'. He said that these numbers assisted the NPA to set a 'benchmark' from which its performance can be continuously improved and to ensure that 'target setting is more realistic' and 'based on past performance' and 'trends'.

Deputy director of public prosecution Adv. Elise van Jaarsfeld, who was at the time of the one-hour interview involved with the 'strategic management' of the NPA at national head office, stated for example in relation to how indicators created an economic awareness in the NPA:

> in the past [. . .] the focus was more on spending the money in the right way, rather than spending the money for the right things. [. . .] So if you've got R5 Million, a simple amount of money, and you spent it in terms of the guidelines, you were wonderful, that was great. So you spent the money in the right way, the way in which it was prescribed. So regardless of whether you paid R5 Million for a thing which you could have paid R2 Million for, as long as [. . .] you followed the process

> everyone was very happy with you. Stuff what you delivered with the money, no one was interested or people didn't understand that, [. . .] it was just as long as you can account for what you spent the money for, basically it was fine. The new government is far wiser. The shift has then gone to, 'That's not good enough anymore'. They now want to see, not only – because it still remains that you must spend the money within the prescripts, but they want to see whether you did as much as possible with that money and they want to see what you did with the money, and that's when the focus on the indicators became stronger and stronger and stronger.

DDPP Adv. van Jaarsfeld pointed out that it took prosecutors on all hierarchical levels in the NPA some time to understand the link between performance measurement and money. Her managerial tasks included for example the development of the NPA's strategic plan, its annual performance plan, the creation of new, or the adjustment of existing, performance indicators and communicating the NPA's 'strategy' in the wider organisational environment and to parliament. People 'finally understood', she said, but in the beginning people would come to her and ask:

> So why do you want to know this stuff? Why is it important that we measure it? Why are we measuring these things? Why don't we just measure something else and what is this anyway? It's not money. But the shift in government is, and how I explained it to them, I said, 'It is money. Your performance information is money. It tells you what you have done with your money. For government it's as equally important now to know what you did with the money as to know that you spent the money following the prescripts.' [. . .] There is nothing for nothing. [. . .] You don't get money and then you don't have to deliver something with it. So if you get money you've got to deliver.

DDPP Adv. van Jaarsfeld's quote also indicates lastly that the NPA's performance indicators and targets have an additional role to play in the working environment of managerial prosecutors. They are used when members of the NPA's highest level of organisational management have to adhere to external accountability demands, namely when they have to appear in front of parliament or in front of specific parliamentary committees and account for their work or when they address the media. During these encounters with members of the public the roles were reversed. While during encounters with journalists, managers would sometimes only announce specific 'NPA achievements' like a high conviction rate for the province for the last year, during parliamentary performance audits or specific parliamentary portfolio meetings where managers had to present their respective strategic plans and budgets for the following financial year, they had to give a more detailed account of their performance numbers. During those meetings the NPA's numerical representations were presented to the audience on hundreds of Powerpoint slides and the respective managers talked the present members of parliament through them, for example Deputy NDPP Adv. Nomgcobo Jiba presented on 7 October 2013 the following numbers to the Parliamentary Committee on Justice and Correctional Services. The meeting report notes:[4]

> Advocate Nomgcobo Jiba, Deputy NDPP, NPA, tabled the vision and mission and then proceeded to a list of the sub-programmes. The strategic objectives had not changed, and NPA was concentrating on increasing the successful prosecution of serious crime, improving collaboration with JCPS partners, reducing corruption and increasing prosecution of cyber crime. The NPA had not managed to reach all targets. 75% of the indicators showed improvements, but only 25% (or 10 indicators) did not show improvements. 66.7% of the core indicators improved compared to the previous year. The NPA set "stretch targets" for the year, indicating by how much it wished to improve. The full figures were shown in the annual report (AR) itself.
>
> The number of criminal cases finalised, including those finalised by alternative dispute resolution mechanisms (ADRM) increased by 4%, with 18 007 more cases finalised than in the previous year. The number of verdict cases finalised increased by 2.3%, or 7 292 more cases. A focused approach on ADRM, to reduce trials, resulted in 8.1% improvement in ADRM cases finalised.
>
> High conviction rates were maintained, at an average of 89.9%. This was broken down into the results for various courts (see presentation for full details). Ms Jiba reiterated that these were calculated according to the same formula as explained in the past. Slide 14 showed backlog, and outstanding cases. The number of outstanding cases was reduced by 5.3%, and the backlog by 11.1%. She noted that the regional backlog courts maintained a conviction rate of 73.7%, and district courts of 86%, which was particularly significant, given the difficulties in these cases.
>
> There had been a positive clearance ratio. 916 917 new cases were enrolled, and 942 792 were disposed of; the difference was the outstanding cases carried forward from the previous year, which was important in keeping the backlogs lower. There had been increases in the

[4] Available at: https://pmg.org.za/committee-meeting/16434/ [5 July 2018]

> number of dockets referred for decision. Much time was spent on the dockets, making decisions and it was important to recognise this as an important step of the process. The target was to finalised 1 683 appeals, but this was exceeded, with 2 068 finalised.
>
> There had been an increase in Thuthuzela Care Centres, of which there were now 35. No witnesses were harmed or threatened whilst on the Witness Protection Programme (WPP). 152 JCPS officials were convicted of corruption with a conviction rate of 82.3%. 42 people were convicted of corruption, where the amount involved exceeded R5 million.
>
> Ms Jiba tabled an input and output trend analysis covering the years 2008 to 2013. There were positive trends on the cases finalised (see slide 19). The court utilisation, showing cases finalised, verdicts, convictions and ADRM, was also tabled (see slide 20), and she noted that utilisation of courts and court time still posed a challenge – the hours spent in court had reduced, down to an average of 3.5 hours. If there was increase in the court utilisation time, this would increase the number of cases. However, this did not lie in the hands of the NPA alone. [. . .]
>
> The next objective was to improve the collaboration with the Justice, Crime Prevention and Security Cluster partners. Overall convictions was at 89.9% but 466 800 cases were finalised. She reiterated the need to finalise cases in courts, and reiterated also that reduced court utilisation was part of the problem. The number of appeals finalised was to do with the number of appeals received, but there were delays in transcription of records that led to backlogs. All unfunded prosecutorial posts were abolished. She emphasised that the posts were still needed, but that there were no funds to pay for vacancies to be filled.
>
> Slide 40 reflected on case management. There were 897 842 new cases, of which 448 793 were finalised, and 488 564 were removed. The following slide showed how the cases were dealt with and in what venue. A breakdown was also given on transfers, warrants, mental referrals and cases struck off the roll. There were numerous reasons why cases would be withdrawn, including insufficient evidence, or failure of accused to attend court. A summary was also given of cases finalised, including alternative dispute resolution methods.

After these presentations, discussions would begin revolving around the presented figures, and managers would have to answer the questions members of parliament were posing to them regarding the NPA's performance information. For example: 'Why are the conviction rates for sexual offences still so low?' (Parliament 16.12.2012);[5] '64,000 cases

[5] See also The Budgetary Review and Recommendation Report of the Portfolio Committee of Justice and Constitutional Development, 5 November 2013.

of sexual offences were reported annually and only about 10% was finalised. That was horrendous. What did the report mean by "finalised"?' (Parliamentary Committee on Justice and Correctional Services 15.10.2012);[6] 'how can it be that 55% of NPA's targets, you presented us with last year, have not been achieved this year?' (Parliament 16.09.2013; Hartley 2013); 'Ms Breytenbach noted that cases lost or withdrawn had increased from 33% to 53% and asked for more detail on this' (Parliamentary Committee on Justice and Correctional Services 21.10. 2014).[7]

It is important to mention that in these sessions, the performance information would, most of the time, be the focus of the discussions at the beginning of these day-long meetings, but members of the committee would then often briefly pose specific non-numerical related questions to the NPA representatives about the progress of specific high-profile matters (e.g. Jakob Zuma; Richard Mdluli; Oscar Pistorius); the handling of specific priority crimes (e.g. sexual offences, high-level corruption); cases being linked to events which received national news coverage (e.g. 'Marikana killings' during mining protests in 2012; arrests of students during '#FeesMustFall' protests at the country's universities in 2016); the appointment of controversial NPA members to the NPA executive; the image of the NPA and the morale amongst NPA employees at times when the NDPP was suspended or under attack; or questions relating to personal experiences of being a victim of crime (e.g. phishing, the electronic attack on banking institutions and how the NPA was dealing with these forms of internet fraud) or of their constituency (e.g. problem of South African accused being tried in a language (English) they do not understand).[8]

[6] NPA's Annual Report briefing in front of the Parliamentary Committee of Justice and Correctional Services 2011/2012, available at: https://pmg.org.za/committee-meeting/16434/; [5 July 2018].

[7] NPA's Annual Report briefing in front of the Parliamentary Committee of Justice and Correctional Services 2013/2014, available at: https://pmg.org.za/committee-meeting/17691/; [5 July 2018].

[8] See meeting reports of NPA's Annual Report briefing in front of the Parliamentary Committee of Justice and Correctional Services: 2015/2016, available at: https://pmg.org.za/committee-meeting/23382/; 2014/2015, available at: https://pmg.org.za/committee-meeting/21639/; 2013/2014, available at: https://pmg.org.za/committee-meeting/17691/; 2012/2013, available at: https://pmg.org.za/committee-meeting/16434/; 2011/2012, available at: https://pmg.org.za/committee-meeting/15032/; 2010/2011, available at: https://pmg.org.za/committee-meeting/13485/; 2009/2010, available at: https://pmg.org.za/committee-meeting/12112/; 2008/2009, available at: https://pmg.org.za/committee-meeting/11127/; 2007/2008; available at:https://pmg.org.za/committee-meeting/8830/ [18 May 2018].

The quotes and examples presented above demonstrate that quantitative performance information plays a central role in managers' everyday working life and that they are at ease and familiar with the pertaining vocabulary. They use performance reports for managing their staff, thus for internal management accounting, for creating economic awareness and for adhering to external accountability demands. However, to interpret managers' everyday reliance on the performance information to do their job as a sign that their understanding of prosecutorial performance and accountability is predominantly linked to 'bringing the numbers up' or 'down' would be wrong. While managers, as I showed, frequently emphasised the helpful qualities of numerical representations, they were also clearly aware of their shortcomings. In the following section I will present NPA senior and executive managers' more nuanced viewpoints about accountability and what good prosecutorial performance means.

OVERSEEING PROSECUTORIAL COURT PERFORMANCE IN PRACTICE

Management Meetings

While prosecutorial managers frequently pointed out that the NPA performance information tells them 'exactly how they are doing', when observing them in practice, for example at management meetings or when talking informally to their colleagues during tea breaks, it was clear that they relied on additional forms of information to find out what was going on in the parts of the NPA which were under their supervision.

The following example, where I describe the course of events at a series of management meetings chaired by DPP Adv. de Villiers and which I attended during the course of 2009 and 2010 at a regional NPA head office, is illustrative of this more complicated relationship between numerical performance information and managerial knowledge and decision-making. It is important to mention that the following summary of the meetings also contains additional data I collected. To make sense of what people said (or did not say) and did (or did not do) at the meetings, I interviewed a large number of members of the meetings in person (social workers, policemen, magistrates, interpreters, clerks, security guards); I did around 350 hours of participant observation at the three respective courts whose performance the participants of the meeting were discussing; I attended several local management meetings at these respective courts; and I shadowed on a regular basis the senior prosecutor and the control prosecutor responsible for one of the courts. Let me start with the summary.

DPP Adv. de Villiers, three of his chief prosecutors and one to two of his senior prosecutors would come together at these bi-monthly management meetings with police station commanders, representatives of the DOJCD, the city and NGOs to talk about the working of three specific magistrate courts ('Court A'; 'B'; and 'C'). These courts were located in the metropolitan area of a major South African city in three different NPA clusters. Each cluster contains a number of district and regional courts and is headed by one of the present chief prosecutors.

The three courts had the jurisdiction of an ordinary South African magistrate's court, but they were specially monitored at these meetings because they formed part of a DOJCD- and NPA-led 'justice innovation' project. The aim of these courts was firstly to provide communities with a state forum where cases which other magistrate courts often perceive as 'petty offences' could be heard; and secondly, where restorative and community justice approaches, mainly in the form of diversion, mediation and community service programmes, could be applied. The underlying idea of the project was that the court should, together with the 'community' and 'civil society', address the 'root causes' of offenders' criminal behaviour instead of criminalising it. It formed part of the NPA's (at the time) stronger 'commitment to crime prevention'.

The meeting would start at 10:00 AM in the spacious boardroom of the DPP, located at the top floor of a high office building, overlooking the CBD of a large South African city. While everyone was arriving, the chief prosecutors were often already sitting at the huge wooden oval table and were busy with their court's statistics. Sometimes they would calculate and scribble down numbers on the statistical sheets they had printed out, either by themselves or by putting their heads together with their respective senior prosecutors.

At around 10:00 AM, after everyone was sitting down and after the DPP opened the meeting with a short and friendly greeting, it usually started with the three chief prosecutors, who were each responsible for a cluster in the province, reading out loud the monthly statistics of one of these specific courts. After that a discussion started in which the respective chief prosecutors, but also the senior prosecutors and other participants of the meeting, explained the performance statistics in more detail to the DPP.

At each meeting, two courts (Court B and C) received specific attention. Court B often had very bad statistics: In other words it was not finalising many cases, did not utilise its court hours well and had a low diversion rate. It was clear to the DPP and all present that things had to be changed, but the court did not receive much attention in the meeting because a senior prosecutor, one who was trusted and respected by the DPP and the chief prosecutor for her insights into the working of the specific court and for her expertise in the restorative and community justice field, was assigned to the issue. Those bad numbers were not perceived as a major concern.

The senior prosecutor in charge had some twenty years of prosecutorial experience and excellent interpersonal skills and a good working relationship with the court personnel and other role-players, like those at the three police stations in the jurisdiction of the court. The underlying expectation and understanding at the meeting was that the senior prosecutor would be able to 'bring the court back on track' because she was energetic and very persuasive, and was known amongst different role-players at the meeting as someone who did not take 'no' for an answer. It was believed that she would be able to sort out the problems that arose when the three police stations did not send enough cases or sent the wrong cases to this specific court and the court roll nearly collapsed, which means the court did not have enough work to sit for a full day. Or the assumption was that she would be able to rectify the tense situation with the current magistrate who had his own understanding of what restorative justice meant and how diversions should work – an understanding which was not always in line with the official framework the court's prosecutors were trying to follow. Despite the court's unsatisfactory performance, the DPP, after considering the reasons the chief and the senior prosecutors had given him for the court's bad statistics, was satisfied that this court's problems were under control and did not need further attention or instructions from his side. The meeting would then often move quickly to Court C.

Court C had very good statistics every month, meaning the court finalised many cases, utilised court hours well and had a high diversion rate. It was however also clear to most committee members present that these great numbers were a success only on paper. While the court's prosecutor did exactly what she was supposed to do – divert petty offenders instead of giving them a criminal record – the programs the offenders were sent on were not very effective in rehabilitating the respective offenders. Almost all cases were diverted on the condition that the offenders would do community service. The community service program most people were sent on was administered by a faith-based NGO and required offenders to do two to three hours of street sweeping wearing bright orange vests printed with the words 'Jesus saves you'.

Many of the offenders were neglected, homeless and alcoholic who had been arrested for offences like drinking in public, being a public nuisance, riotous behaviour or urinating in public, and they returned to the court on a regular basis. The court's staff members referred to some offenders as 'regulars' because they reappeared so often that they knew them by name. One of the judicial officers who worked at this court started to compile his own personal statistics in addition to the official court statistics, which did not contain the same information, to document how often specific offenders re-offended.

The performance information was excellent on paper for the NPA, but Court C was the problem child of this meeting. Adv. de Villiers was giving instructions to his team to bring this court in line with official restorative and community justice ideas. While policemen at the court were telling me 'this is restorative justice because these people are cleaning up their own shit', to my observation the unspoken consensus at the management meeting was that the court's current practice 'criminalises the poor' and was therefore ethically questionable.

The plan at the meeting was that other social development programs needed to be found which would come up with better monitored and planned 'long-term solutions' for alcoholic homeless people and which were more 'restorative', 'just' or 'effective', and which would also help to reduce the court's unofficial, but known to everyone, high recidivism rate. That the task of finding suitable diversion programmes for seasoned homeless alcoholics is a tedious or even never-ending task and does not fall into the mandate of the NPA was clear to Adv. de Villiers and the prosecutors working on this project. He saw his job therefore more in bringing his weight as a high-ranked government employee to the table to ensure that the other involved government departments were taking the recidivism rate problem seriously. The above-mentioned trusted senior prosecutor was assigned to the matter and she started to meet with representatives of the city, NGOs, the Department of Social Development and of the Department of Correctional Services to 'push' and 'lobby' for more sustainable solutions. After a while she managed to get the respective role-player to assign a permanent social worker and probation officer to the court so that the court would be able to send seasoned homeless alcoholics to state-funded drug and alcohol rehabilitation centres. In addition, she was negotiating with a shelter for homeless people in the city to receive a guarantee that the homeless people would be taken into the shelters once they get discharged from the rehabilitation clinic and until they find an alternative place to stay.

This summary of the course of events of several management meetings during 2009 and 2010 chaired by the DPP Adv. de Villiers demonstrates aspects of the numerical knowledge and reflexivity which many prosecutorial managers exhibit when dealing with performance measurement information. It gives firstly an impression of managers' awareness that good prosecutorial work does not necessarily translate into high court hours or finalisation rates, and alternatively that high performance statistics in these categories do not always indicate excellent performance. The DPP did not treat the presented 'stats' at the meeting as self-evident. He relied instead on certain experienced prosecutors' views on the data to decide how the statistics should be read and interpreted. Court C with good-looking statistics was, as I showed, determined to require further managerial attention and interventions and vice versa. The one with the negative-appearing statistics was declared unproblematic after the numbers were accounted for and explained by a practised prosecutor.

Secondly, the above-presented case example gives insight into managers' awareness that the performance information did not necessarily tell them whether a desirable outcome had been achieved. The performance information of Court C was excellent, but it was clear to the DPP and the respective chief prosecutors that it was only so on paper. The court's unofficial recidivism rate and the criticism that the court was criminalising poor people was not in line with the conception of this new court, which was to prevent crime in the respective communities and to deliver 'restorative' and 'community justice'. The participants of the management meeting knew that offenders were clearly not assisted with their problems that potentially lead to their unlawful activities, and that it was 'unjust' and 'useless' to send homeless people who are completely neglected to prison because they had repeatedly not complied with their community service conditions. Furthermore, the NPA's overall aim to increase the public's trust and confidence in the South African court system, something various managers often pointed out was an important larger aim of the organisation's current work so that South Africans can feel safe, was also not achieved with such a high recidivism rate.

That the outcome and impact of prosecutorial work was not always straightforward and certainly not easily measurable, a managerial numerical awareness that I could observe in practice at the summarised management meetings was explicitly expressed by a high-ranked prosecutor in an hour-long interview. Adv. Irene du Toit, in her early forties, who had worked for the last twenty years for the prosecution authority and who belonged to the national executive management of the NPA, said that the Public Finance Management Act of 1999 and the respective guidelines on how to manage performance information differentiate between:

> input-, output-, outcome and impact- indicators [...] we have mainly output indicators. Of course you want to get to the stage where you get to outcome indicators. None of us [justice role-players] are there by outcome indicators yet. [...] The only thing that we can really be held responsible for is quality prosecution, but the problem is, to measure a quality prosecution there are so many variables within it, that you would to have a full time staff complement of 3000 people to measure it, so therefore—and any rule to measuring is, if it is so cumbersome or so costly to measure, it's the wrong thing to measure and therefore—we measure things which are far easier to measure. They are not 100% correct things.

An important impact indicator for the NPA's work would be for example, according to DDPP Adv. du Toit, one that measures 'Whether people feel safe walking at night in their neighbourhood?'. 'But they are not measuring it', as she said because they could only measure it, like quality prosecution, through large sample surveys. She emphasised again that conducting surveys is more time- and staff-intensive than drawing on already collected administrative data to compile in- and output indicators, for example, on how many cases are 'coming into the courts' and how many cases are 'being put out'.

The summarised meeting and DDPP Adv. du Toit's statements evidence that while prosecutorial managers rely on the performance information to see things they cannot see without the respective statistics, rates and targets, they are clearly aware of the constructedness and constructiveness of numerical representations. Although the observed and interviewed NPA managers work day in and day out with performance indicators which they use to 'improve' or 'drive' the NPA's overall performance, the examples show that they nevertheless held the opinion that their main task, namely delivering 'justice' and 'quality prosecution', was due to its complexity difficult to capture with a few selected indicators. Although they used the performance indicators to understand, to see and know 'what's going on', they often described them to me as good thinking tools to plan, strategise and prioritise the activities of the NPA.

However, as I mentioned in the first part of this chapter, they still referred to the performance indicators as 'not 100% correct' in capturing their main functions and responsibilities. I argue that this form of numerical reflexivity makes them more cautious when interpreting quantified information. As I showed with Adv. de Villiers, the manager who said in an interview that he is able to know 'exactly' what is happening at each court in his province by looking at the performance reports, he (re-)checked the performance data he received at the meeting in light of other additional forms of accounts, in this case with a personal report of a trusted and experienced employee, before he gave instructions on what needs to be done. Good prosecutorial performance or a desirable just outcome was for him, as for DDPP Adv. du Toit, not to be automatically equated with high performance statistics.

In the next section I want to show that managers' numerical knowledge, and related to that, their more nuanced understanding of prosecutorial performance, also has an impact on why performance related pay mechanisms are less established in the NPA then initially intended.

Managing Career Advancement

One factor which can explain lower court prosecutors' more positive and conciliatory attitude towards the quantification of their work, as I argued in Chapter 4, was the decoupling of financial resource allocation and prosecutors' performance information in the NPA. The observed and interviewed court prosecutors were not afraid of being sanctioned by receiving a reduced salary at the end of the year or even losing their job when they did not achieve their respective performance targets. Furthermore, they did not express concern that they might not get the desired promotion due to unsatisfactory performance statistics.[9] It was more common that prosecutors were

[9] There was one prosecutor with two years' experience in the NPA, Reesha Naidoo in her mid-twenties, who hoped that by achieving outstanding statistics she might qualify for one of the rare

concerned that other accountability dimensions guiding their work might lead to the loss of their position or to a failure in receiving a promotion. Various prosecutors mentioned that they might lose their job if they act negligently and were held liable by a South African court for their misconduct. It was common that court prosecutors discussed the country's Employment Equity Act of 1999 and the NPA's respective affirmative action practices as hindrances to their personal career advancement.

While the unavailability of funds in the NPA to meet the performance-related pay mechanism and a twenty-year-old conflict over more recognition and higher base salaries for all prosecutors are important factors for this current less 'competitive' situation, I suggest that managers' numerical knowledge and competence play an additional role in why court prosecutors do not feel pressurised and stressed by the quantification of their work. In the following I provide several examples in which managerial prosecutors reflect on the shortcomings of specific NPA performance indicators and on what additional information they need to make a decision.

Jonas Dlomo, a senior prosecutor in his early forties who was about to become a magistrate, explained in an hour interview in his office why the NPA performance indicator conviction rate was not decisive when he looks at whether a prosecutor receives a promotion. He stated:

> You see you might achieve the 85% target for example in the District Court but again you might just have been able to achieve 90%, but you were not so good technically in what you did. What I am saying is some of the cases are guilty pleas and they do not go to trial so you might be achieving 85% where 70% of those were guilty pleas because they were so well investigated by the police and you as a prosecutor in the trial cases may be achieved 15% but that you should have achieved 20% or 25% to get 95%. So it's not only convictions that we look at before we can promote you.

performance bonuses of her cluster, but as I pointed out this prosecutor's rationale was exceptional. She told me that she tried to get the bonus by 'doing many cases'. The presiding magistrate at the courtroom where she was stationed was on contract, meaning he did not have a permanent position as a magistrate, and he was also hoping that if he had good court statistics he might have a better chance of receiving a permanent position. When I observed them at work, 'working hard' meant working faster, concentrating more, having less court breaks and preparing better in order to 'do more cases'. Neither of them received a bonus. I was unable to follow up how far the 'good court stats' played a role in the magistrate's success to secure a permanent magistrate position in another cluster a few months later.

SPP Teresa Williams, in her forties, also perceived the conviction rate as an insufficient indicator of prosecutorial performance. She said in an hour interview when I interviewed her in her office at court:

> So there are multiple questions that we need to ask and what the 83% conviction rate doesn't tell us, if somebody else looks at the matter would that percentage have changed? Maybe the conviction rate is then 100%; or the two cases we based that 100% conviction rate on, because there was only two cases that he had to deal with, were set aside for review then the percentage is 0%.

DDPP Adv. Daniel Jacob, in his mid-sixties, who has been a prosecutor for over thirty-five years and who was, amongst many other things, responsible for compiling the performance statistics of a whole province, emphasised in an hour-long interview in his office at a regional head office, that the legal, technical and organisational skills of a prosecutor cannot be easily read from a person's quantified performance report. While we go through the performance statistics of his region he stated:

> You get the guys who are good at handling many cases fast and the ones which thrive when they through themselves into more lengthy and complicated ones. The stats won't tell me their capacity to prosecute. That's my job to find that out and post them accordingly.

DDPP Adv. Elise van Jaarsfeld, who is involved in the (re-)design of NPA performance indicators at the NPA head office, explained why the court hours performance indicator was not decisive when evaluating prosecutors' performance. She said 'court hours' refers to the time when a court is actually sitting and cases are being heard and processed, not to the amount of working time a prosecutor spends inside his or her working environment, namely the court. Many prosecutors complained, she said, that they are not the role-player at court who can control the court's proceedings, since opening and closing court forms part of the power and responsibility of the presiding judicial officer and that the indicator misrepresents their everyday work. While being 'at' court is a central task of prosecutors, their preparation time is usually done in their offices, at home or in court while the court is not running, and this forms an equally important part of their daily workload. She said that the 'court hours' indicator caused some frustration amongst prosecutors during those first years when the NPA financial department and not her office created the measurements. Van Jaarsfeld explained that her office is still measuring and monitoring court hours because it still gives them an important indication of how the available court hours are utilized, and since they have been measuring it for some time, they now have a useful 'ten year trend'.[10] But the indicator no longer forms part of prosecutors' individual performance agreements.

DPP Adv. de Villiers also pointed out that prosecutorial performance and skills cannot so easily be translated into neat amounts of court hours and production units. Although he was the manager who stated that they 'run the NPA like a business' in this quote extracted from a three-hour interview with him, he emphasised the difference between justice and industrial work. He stated:

> You will have a baseline, you will look back and you will say okay, over the past few years how many [cases] have we finalised and then you will sort of get an idea of what is a reasonable amount of what should be finalised under normal circumstances, so you work it out like that. [. . .] If it's 40, then how many do you have to do per day and then you get a target per day, you need to at least produce so many, but of course we are busy with justice so it's really just there designed to make people work towards something. We understand that sometimes a court can do one case for a month, because that's how justice works, we are not in a factory producing bottles [. . .]
>
> You know, we are busy with people's lives, we are busy with justice, when you become too focused on numbers in this game, you might lose sight of what we are busy with. [. . .] It can never be, oh, you were supposed to have that amount therefore you didn't achieve it, therefore you failed, it's not about that and then you're fired. It can't be about that you know, and that's the difference.
>
> In a factory you can do that, you can say this machine and this machinery can deliver 100 000 stuff every month or every week of this and these people should be able to produce that etc. Now under ideal conditions they should be able to produce 100 000 and if they deliver because they are working harder, they deliver 120 000, it's easy to quantify, you can say, well they delivered 20 000 more than their target and then normally what happens in business world, well because you delivered 20 000 more, we sold so much more and we made more profit and therefore you get a bonus based on that. So sales department sold

[10] For a discussion between NPA representatives and members of the Portfolio Committee on Justice and Correctional Services in 2008 on the relevance of court hours for the measurement of NPA performance see meeting report, available at: https://pmg.org.za/committee-meeting/8830/ [18 May 2018].

> 20 000 more, right, but in the factory the machinery may break down for a month or there may be, I don't know, an explosion or something and they can't function so they can't deliver. So nobody can then blame the operators because they couldn't deliver and similarly in this environment you may say your target is X amount in a court to finalise but we know that depends on lots of different things.

These five examples do not evidence the basis upon which senior and executive managers actually promote their staff members in practice or distribute performance bonuses.[11] They do, however, indicate their awareness that it is difficult to capture the actual complexity of a specific case, court prosecutors' skill levels or the unpredictable and uncertain multi-actor environment in which they are managing with performance indicators, and their hesitation to rely on this form of information to make far-reaching human resource decisions. I observed that it was generally accepted that it is seldom clear whose problem or fault it was that a court case had to be postponed and could not be finalised and that circumstances beyond the court prosecutors' control could, and often did, affect the results. Managers often listed all the actors which need to be at court in order for it to start timeously and that it only takes one of those actors not to play their role for the case not to proceed. They often aired frustration about their own dependence on the performance of other role-players, but they also perceived this time-consuming interplay between police, prosecution, judiciary, defence (legal aid and private), interpreters, accused and witnesses as an intrinsic element of justice and of working at courts.

Therefore, I argue that there was no clear automatic connection between bad performance statistics and reprimands or sanctions in the NPA, and between good statistical performance and financial rewards. If one recalls the management meeting described earlier, it was interesting to notice that the performance statistics of the prosecutor working at Court B were bad, but her work was never discussed as unsatisfactory at any of the meetings or at other occasions. The same applies for the opposite. The prosecutor at Court C had exceptionally good performance statistics – on paper she finalised a large number of cases – but they were never noted as such, because managerial prosecutors differentiated between finalised cases though trial work from finalised cases through diversion. The latter requires, according to

[11] I tried to get access to NPA job and promotion interviews, however the access was declined by the DDPP of the respective province. See also Chapter 4 for a brief summary about what constitutes, according to court prosecutors, the NPA 'pecking order'.

them, less prosecutorial skills because the prosecutor does not have to prove the guilt of the accused 'beyond reasonable doubt' and obviously then has a higher performance statistic than a prosecutor who does mostly trials.

CONCLUSION

This chapter has shown that the NPA's quantitative performance information was central for managers' execution and accounting of their work, but that their understanding of prosecutorial performance and accountability was also not exclusively linked to 'bringing the numbers up' or 'down'. While managers frequently emphasised the helpful qualities of numerical representations and had throughout conciliatory attitudes towards them, they were also clearly aware of their limits and shortcomings. They did not treat the quantified information as something with completely objective, precise and accurate meanings. In other words, they did not perceive them as simple and straightforward facts. They viewed indicators just as indicators of the central issues in question, as something that hints at some, but does not represent all, aspects of their working reality. Managers accepted, insisted and relied on other non-quantitative and deliberative forms of knowledge and accountability, as I showed, to determine 'what is going on' and 'what needs to be done' in the parts of the NPA they were responsible for. For them being accountable was not synonymous with using quantitative measures, and good prosecutorial performance was not to be equated with high performance statistics. I argued that managers' numerical reflexivity, their more prudent, considered and ambiguous approach to dealing with numbers, gives firstly lower court prosecutors greater reputational control and flexibility in how they account for their work, and secondly contributes to the decoupling of resource allocations and performance statistics in this organisational setting.

Now that what court and managerial prosecutors do with numbers at work and what these numbers do (or do not do) with these professionals has been explored in the last three chapters, the final chapter will ask: So what does it all mean for the South African public? I will be focusing on the discussion around the NPA's conviction rate counting standard. Various public representative bodies criticise the NPA's conviction rate as 'misleading', 'creative' and 'inflated'. In other words, the NPA is accused of manipulating their performance and for creating public confusion and obscurity instead of public accountability and transparency. This chapter will discuss this criticism and by doing so continue with the exploration of managerial prosecutors' numerical reflexivity. I will argue that these 'misleading' numbers might contribute more to the NPA's public accountability and the public's knowledge about the NPA than critics suggest.

6

LIES, DAMNED LIES AND STATISTICS

Making Sense of Misleading or Imperfect NPA Conviction Rates

INTRODUCTION

When the old apartheid prosecuting authority was transformed and the first new National Prosecuting Authority was established in 1998, one of the main objectives of the new NPA leadership was to legitimise the power of prosecutors in the eyes of those they had until recently suppressed. They envisioned prosecutors, as I mentioned before, as 'lawyers for the people' (Barrell and Soggott 1998; Schönteich 2001: 1). To be accountable became an important and desirable good in that transformation process.

Are the NPA and the prosecutorial profession accountable today? Are they more accountable than before 1994? While I showed in Chapter 1 that the accountability mechanism governing the NPA and its employees has been clearly diversified and intensified since 1998, I also argued at various stages of this book that whether accountability has been rendered depends to a large extent on the involved actors' understandings of the concept. The South African Black Lawyers Association, a crime victim, a constitutional lawyer or an opposition politician would potentially answer the question of NPA accountability very differently.

The Black Lawyers Association might, for example, perceive the change of the demographic composition of the NPA – unlike the country's legal profession, its demographic has changed markedly since 1998, despite the new requirement that prosecutors be qualified with a law degree – as a sign of the organisations' greater accountability (Redpath 2012: 78–83). In contrast, a woman whose sister had been murdered with a bread knife by her ex-boyfriend and whose case has been going on 'forever' and was finally withdrawn by the prosecutor in charge due to 'insufficient evidence' might not feel that prosecutors are more accountable today based on her experience of 'lack of justice'.

A constitutional lawyer or judge might perceive the fact that the NPA has been held liable for their employees' wrongdoings and the option of judicial review as a sign of improved legal accountability in the new South Africa (Davis and le Roux 2009). In contrast, members of the opposition party might interpret the 2008 NPA's decision to withdraw the criminal charges against Jacob Zuma, who was to go on to be the country's president, and against various other politically connected individuals, as a sign of an encroaching lack of prosecutorial accountability and independence which undermines the NPA's public credibility and legitimacy. Or, they could welcome the announcement of the decision of NDPP Adv. Shaun Abrahams to reinstate the charges against Zuma in March 2018, after the Supreme Court of Appeal had upheld an appeal in October 2017 against an earlier High Court ruling that the NPA's decision of 2008 to withdraw the charges was 'irrational', as a sign that the tide is finally turning again towards a more accountable NPA.

This book concentrates on quantitative accountability and prosecutorial work practices. That is why I focus in this last chapter on the question of whether the NPA's performance measurement practices make the organisation more accountable to the public. Although it is a well-asked, important and a seemingly straight-forward question, it is difficult to answer it since my research has not aimed at exploring the 'people's' perspective on the NPA's performance measurement system. Therefore, I focus on the criticism from public representative bodies which question whether the NPA's performance indicator conviction rate makes the organisation more accountable. The South African Law Commission and the Democratic Alliance (the 'DA'), South Africa's largest opposition party, argue that this performance indicator actually 'misleads' the public as it is 'creatively' calculated. In other words, the critics accuse the NPA of gaming the numbers.

In the first section of this chapter I describe the criticism of the NPA's conviction rate in more detail and show that there are currently at least four different calculation standards in public circulation. I then move on to engage with Kevin Haggerty's study 'Making Crime Count' (2001a), in which he argues that actors often have (micro-)political and economic reasons, which are beyond accuracy, for counting things differently. By presenting examples in which NPA managers reflect themselves on their conviction rate standard, I argue that this interpretation ignores other reasons why people choose different counting rules, in this case: when managers want to make sense. I end the chapter by showing that these 'misleading' numbers might contribute more to the NPA's public accountability and the public's knowledge about the NPA than these critics allow.

HOW TO MEASURE CONVICTION RATES?

The NPA's conviction rates are its performance figures, which the media and the wider public pay most attention to (see for example: 'Alarm over rape conviction rate' Mposo 2012; 'High conviction rate for Cape courts: NPA' 2012; Newham 2013; 'NPA secures 88% conviction rate in High Courts' 2013; 'NPA records 93.8 conviction rate' 2016; 'The 8% percent conviction rate is disturbing' Hosken 2017). This is so especially when studies which indicate that the conviction rates for specific offences are particularly low are released.[1] The conviction rate is not a descriptive number like many of the other NPA's performance indicators. The finalisation rate is, for example, a descriptive indicator which no clear indication of reference: it counts all the cases the NPA finalizes, whether through alternative dispute resolution mechanisms or through a trial ending in an acquittal or a conviction of the accused. Thus, the finalisation rate does not differentiate or value the different ways of finalising a case. By contrast, the conviction rate values the result. It exclusively measures the number of convictions prosecutors achieve in court and has a clear reference, namely the number of convictions as compared to the number of cases the NPA takes to trial. This approach to calculating conviction rates is also called 'trial-to-conviction rate' (see Artz and Smythe 2007a; 2007b).

The South African Police Service (SAPS) also measures conviction rates, but they use the 'report-to-conviction rate', which measures the proportion of cases which end in a conviction compared to the total numbers of cases which have been reported at the respective police stations. Thus, there are currently two different official approaches used

[1] For example Rudolph Zinn (2010) conducted a qualitative study on what kind of crime intelligence information on their *modus operandi* the police could obtain from convicted and incarcerated house robbers. When his results were published, his finding that the thirty interviewed house robbers had committed on average 103 criminal offences (including crimes other than robbery) over a seven-year period before they were arrested and convicted for the first time was particularly discussed and focused on in the news (Smillie 2008; 'Households under siege by armed robbers' 2009; Bateman 2010). Similar attention was given to studies which emphasise that in South Africa rape has one of the lowest conviction rates of all crimes classified, in a country which has one of the highest reported rape rates in the world (Broughton 2002; Mposo 2012).

within the South African criminal justice system to calculate conviction rates. Although the NPA's conviction rate will always be considerably higher than SAPS's, both rates are referred to in everyday language and official documents as the 'conviction rate'.

A third way to calculate conviction rates is used by NGOs. For example, CIET, an NGO raising awareness about violence against women and advocates shifts in how specifically rape cases are treated by the police and the courts, measures the number of court convictions both against reported rape cases and against the estimated number of unreported rape cases (see e.g. CIETafrica 1998). The number of estimated rape victims was calculated on the basis of house-to-house surveys CIET conducted in specific areas in South Africa. As a result of these different measuring standards, conviction rates – for example of rape cases – commence from completely different base lines and rely on different counting procedures, and as a result can look very different:

- from 4% to 8% for the police (Vetten et al 2008; Smythe 2015);
- 45% to 67% for the NPA (NPA Performance Plan 2012; NPA Annual Report 2010/2011: 17); and
- 0.28% for the non-governmental organisation like CIET (CIETafrica 1998; see also Mposo 2012).[2]

Besides national aggregated conviction rates for specific offences (besides rape, serious corruption, complex commercial crimes and trio crimes), the NPA also publishes annually in its performance reports national aggregate conviction rates for district courts (87%–93%), regional courts (73.4%–74%) and High Courts (86%–88%). A so-

[2] In my example mentioned above, the NPA's conviction rate fluctuates the most, since from 2006 till 2010 the NPA reported conviction rates of so-called 'Dedicated Sexual Offences Courts' in their annual reports. The rate of these specialised courts was around 65% to 67%. After the NPA commissioned research into the performance information of these courts, it emerged that these courts were not only dealing exclusively with sexual offences but were also hearing other types of offences. The NPA announced that it would not publish conviction rates for the 'dedicated sexual offences courts' until they found a reliable reporting mechanism. The 2011/2012 NPA Annual Report states that those specialised courts do not exist any longer and therefore they are only publishing the average conviction rates of sexual offences in all courts which was 47% (NPA Performance Report 2011/2012: 22). In 2012 the Sexual Offences and Related Matters Act was amended to make special provisions for these courts, however the DOJCD is failing to re-establish these worldwide applauded victim-centred courts all over the country. Despite the fact that the NPA developed the blueprint for these courts in 1999 and that other jurisdictions internationally are copying the model. However, the focus of the NPA since 2010 on the prosecution of priority crimes, which include corruption and contact crimes (especially sexual offences and trio crimes) and the availability of specialised prosecution units such as the Sexual Offence and Community Affair Unit ('SOCA'), assisted to improve the conviction rate for sexual offences at least in the meantime to around 70% (see NPA Annual Report 2016/2017: 24–25; 46–47; see also DOJCD 2013; Thamm 2016).

called 'overall conviction rate' (between 81.5% and 88.77% for the period 2002 until 2013) is also included in these publications (see NPA Annual Report 2009/2010; 2010/2011; 2011/2012; 2012/2013; 2013/2014; 2014/2015; 2015/2016; 2016/2017; NPA Performance Plan 2012/2013).

The NPA has been, as I mentioned in the Introduction, repeatedly criticised for counting convictions in relation to cases they decide to send on trial. The South African Law Commission (SALC) in their research paper 'Conviction rates and other outcomes of crimes reported in eight South African police areas' (2000: 9) criticised the NPA's approach to measuring the conviction rate for producing an 'inflated' conviction rate, which in turn creates a potentially 'misleading impression' of the extent to which offenders of criminal offences are held accountable for their actions by the state's criminal justice system. They argued that it is irrelevant to the victims of crime to know precisely where and when the criminal justice system has failed them: at the stage of the police investigation; or the prosecution in court; or when there is a disjointed interaction between the two role-players. SALC suggested that it is therefore important to:

> measure the effectiveness of the criminal justice system as a whole rather than artificially isolate its constituent elements [...] This approach recognizes that the criminal justice system is an integrated system and holds the police and prosecution authority jointly responsible for ensuring that criminals are brought to book.
>
> (2000: 9)

Twelve years later the points of criticism raised by the DA regarding the NPA's conviction rate mirrors that of the South African Law Commission from 2000. In June 2012, Debbie Schafer, DA Member of Parliament and DA Shadow Deputy Minister of Justice and Constitutional Development, released two statements arguing that the NPA's conviction rates

> reveal a gross distortion of the conviction rates in our courts. The [NPA] indicators claim a conviction rate of almost 90% for the period from 2006/7 to 2010/11. Using quite a 'creative method' – lending credence to the expression 'lies, damned lies and statistics' – the Department takes the number of convictions as a percentage of the number of cases finalised with a verdict. This is completely disingenuous given the number of cases disposed of in each year.

> The conviction rate should in fact be calculated by using the number of convictions as a percentage of the total number of cases disposed of in court. Calculated in this manner, fewer than one in three cases before South African courts lead to conviction. [. . .] South Africa has an unacceptably high level of contact and violent crime, with approximately 2.1 million incidents of crime reported last year alone. To grossly misrepresent the conviction rate in this manner is not only an insult to the victims of crime, but also undermines the efforts of the criminal justice system as a whole to effectively and efficiently deal with crime.
>
> (Schafer 2012a) [. . .]
>
> The DA accepts that it is possible to calculate conviction rates by employing various methods, creative or otherwise. However, claiming that there is a 90% conviction rate, in a society such as ours which is marred by violent contact crime, is not a reflection of the reality and untruthfully creates the impression that we are winning the fight against crime. [. . .] For the NPA to pat itself on the back for a 'real' conviction rate of less than 30% is simply unacceptable. Instead of defending their methodology the NPA should admit that their approach is flawed and undermines the fight against crime. [. . .] It does not give a realistic view of what is really happening.
>
> (Schafer 2012b)

Both the South African Law Commission and the DA criticise the NPA's trial-to-conviction rate for giving South Africans the impression that the criminal justice system is 'effectively and efficiently' dealing with criminal offences meanwhile the chances are high that a complainant's case will never be sent to the court by the police or will be withdrawn by the prosecution despite the police classifying the case as 'investigation complete' and 'ready for court'. So the chance that a criminal offence is punished by the state is, according to the DA and SALC, much lower than the NPA's high conviction rate suggests. In other words, they criticise the degree of correspondence between the official NPA conviction rate and what they perceive as the appropriate, right or 'real' conviction rate. SALC suggests that the standard for calculating a conviction rate within criminal justice institutions should be the 'report-to-conviction rate' used by SAPS. The DA, in contrast, is of a different opinion about how 'real' rates should be measured. It argues that counting the convictions in relation to reported cases is not helpful since not all reported cases are ready for prosecution in the year that they get reported at a police station. Therefore, the DA proposes a conviction rate for the NPA which should be measured against cases which the police deem 'ready-for-court'. Despite these stark accusations that the organisation is gaming its numbers, that they are more concerned about presenting favourable figures to the public than about taking responsibility for their actual performance and for the working of the country's whole criminal justice system, the NPA insists on its own counting standards. In the following section I am exploring managerial prosecutors' reasons and motivations for counting things differently in a climate where there is pressure to count things in a uniform manner.

PROSECUTORIAL MANAGERS' ATTITUDE TOWARDS THE NPA'S CONVICTION RATE

Quantification scholars have for some time shown and (raised awareness where necessary) that there are often numerous ways to standardise, count and calculate social phenomena, and that using slightly different counting standards changes the measured object since these standards are constitutive of the objects they are attempting to represent (Porter 1995; Power 1997; Bowker and Star 2000; Kalthoff et al. 2000; Desrosières 2001; 2009; Mennicken and Volmer 2007). In other words, something like a conviction rate does not exist independently of the specific criteria and rules actors use to measure convictions. SAPS, the NPA, SALC, the DA and the NGOs are not simply using different approaches to measure the same thing, but their different calculation practices constitute to some extent very different phenomena under the same label.

The NPA managers, whose numerical knowledge and competences I described in Chapter 5, did not need an anthropologist to tell them that social phenomena can be measured differently. This was nothing new to them. In many of the conversations and interviews I conducted with them, they talked about the different conviction rates' counting standards and they were aware that the NPA's approach to calculating its conviction rate was controversial and criticised from numerous sides for different reasons.

DDPP Adv. Irene du Toit (the executive manager who emphasised that 'the only thing that we really can be held responsible for is quality prosecution' but because of the costs involved in measuring something as complex as 'quality', the NPA measures easy-to-quantify aspects of prosecutorial work, even if '[t]hey are not the 100% correct things') was outspoken and straightforward about the fact that she perceived the critics' emphasis on the numerical discrepancies between the different ways of calculating the conviction rate as rather predictable and trivial. She felt that the accusations that the NPA tries to mislead the public about its conviction rate by producing inflated performance numbers were far-fetched and removed from her daily, pressing managerial concerns and from what it means for an organisation like the NPA to be held quantitatively accountable. Additionally, she noted that it was a sign that people still did not really understand the work of the NPA's strategic management unit and the role of indicators in the NPA or why government demanded them.

For her, who is amongst other things responsible for the design of performance indicators, it was obvious that the different ways in which phenomena can be calculated can effect the results in different ways. She pointed out several times that she did not perceive the differing figures as a problem as long as one was 'transparent' about one's measuring standards. By making public the organisation's measuring criteria in various NPA publications, amongst them the widely circulated annual reports of the NPA – 'So anyone can see. We are not denying how we are measuring our conviction rate,' as she said to me – the NPA was in her opinion 'transparent'. When she explained the reasons, in an hour-long interview, for not using the SAPS's report-to-conviction rate or DA's suggested methods, she stated: 'we are in the middle of the [justice] value chain. As prosecutors we cannot influence what kind of cases are coming to court, the quality of the investigation and we also have no control on how cases get finalised since this is at the discretion of the judiciary'.

That means that the NPA, according to Adv. du Toit, has no direct control over the number of reported cases in relation to the number of referred cases, because firstly the police are the role-players who filter out cases where investigators, for instance, cannot link a suspect to a specific offence, and secondly the NPA has no control over whether the police investigated cases are fit for trial at the time of referral. Obviously, the third reason she mentioned is accounted for within all three conviction rate counting standards. So to use a conviction rate, which is measured in relation to the number of reported cases, would not, as du Toit argued, reflect the responsibilities of the NPA.

To use a conviction rate which is related to the number of referred cases from SAPS is, in du Toit's opinion, also not an adequate 'reflection on ourselves' because a prosecutor can only start criminal proceedings against a suspect if the police have identified the suspect and have gathered sufficient evidence to enable the prosecutor to convince the court of the suspect's guilt. She said that this is not always the case: Not all the cases SAPS declares as 'ready for court' contain sufficient evidence. She also includes the danger of insufficient evidence for the respective court prosecutor: 'you can ruin a person's life if I prosecute you for rape and I have no evidence. I cannot willy-nilly prosecute, because we have the power to ruin a person financially and emotionally'. Therefore, she said, the current NPA conviction rate only measures the number of convictions against the number of cases in which the responsible court prosecutor has decided that there is a 'reasonable chance of success'. Du Toit explained that with the conviction rate the NPA is interested in measuring 'how good our decision-making is', not how good the decision-making of other criminal justice role-players is. She emphasised that according to their own rate their decision-making is 'quite [. . .] good', but if one measures it according to the overall reported figures 'we are aware, it's poor'.

Adv. du Toit said that the NPA's performance is poor because the country's criminal justice role-players are not performing well in terms of the combined performance indicator government has given them. She said all the criminal justice role-players are working towards 'feelings of safety [. . .] Do you feel safe to walk after dark near your home? Our main goal is that people feel and are safe. We agreed that is what we want'. She explained that the police, the NPA, the Department of Justice and Constitutional Development, the Department of Correctional Services and the Department of Social Development

> we all contribute, we are in this value chain. [. . .] if each of us just did our job, people would feel safe to walk in South Africa. [. . .] But we are not doing our job, and that's why people don't feel safe. [. . .] Our role as the prosecution is, basically you get feeling of safety if you bring back predictability within the system. That is what it's all based on, is predictability. Predictability means that I must know that if I commit a crime it will be detected, it will be prosecuted, there will be a proper sentence. That's the only way you will address it, but at the moment crime pays and while crime pays, no one will ever feel safe in this country.

The reasons Adv. du Toit mentioned as to why the NPA insists on its own conviction rate standard and against using the SAPS's report-to-conviction rate or DA's suggested methods were representative for what other managers said on the topic. DPP Adv. Lionel de Villiers also stresses that an important goal of the NPA's conviction rate is to differentiate NPA specific tasks and responsibilities from those which, in his opinion, need to be addressed by a wider circle of people and institutions. He stated:

> we recognise that there are these cases and let's say it's a third because there are two-thirds that may not have gone to court, but that's a different question, that question relates to everybody, the police and everyone else, this broader society, so how do we deal with this? But as the prosecution we say, these are the cases that we decided we have sufficient evidence and we proceed and those are the ones that we measure against the conviction rate. The conviction rate is really to tell us how we are doing, you know.

A few minutes later in the interview, while talking about why there is no clear target attached to the indicator conviction rate, Adv. de Villiers stressed, similarly to Adv. van Jaarsfeld, the importance of the conviction rate for internal management purposes. The passage is worth quoting at length:

> Do you really want 100%, is that what you want to achieve? It's not realistic, besides that, we don't really want a 100% conviction rate [. . .]. There must always be room for acquittals. We are not in the business of getting convictions, so it's a strange indicator, because all we have to do really is to place all the evidence before court, the court must decide. Of course you place that evidence before the court in the hope that you are going to get a conviction but our primary focus is not to get a conviction, you know. [. . .] The work that you do in a court is designed to achieve a conviction [. . .] but it's not the overriding thing and many prosecutors don't understand, they actually want a conviction, [. . .] but it's fine, as long as they do things correctly. So you don't do things at all cost to get a conviction. So in other words if you know there is evidence in favour of the accused, you don't hide it away, it's unethical. So that is part of the role, you must put it there even if it's going to damage your case and the court may say, well this person is going to be acquitted now, that's your role, that's your duty as a prosecutor, so your duty is not to get a conviction at all costs, that's the point. So why we have conviction rates, why do we measure convictions? It's simply an indicator to say alright, it's like a quality measure, although it's not really a quality measure, but it's really to say, so how are we doing? If the conviction is 30%, then there is something wrong, it may be an indicator that there is something wrong. [. . .] So that's really the role of the conviction rate, for us internally. [. . .] Why do we measure that? Because we say, well, if we say there is a case then at least we should be able to achieve a conviction because otherwise why did we take it to the court in the first place?

What can be seen from the passages I quoted is that managerial prosecutors insist on their organisation's own counting standard for two reasons. The first reason refers to the external use of the conviction rate or one could say to managers' external accountability relationships. The numerical data, collected all over the country every day and published in aggregated form in the NPA annual reports is used, as I mentioned Chapter 5, by parliamentary members to question members of the executive management of the NPA about what they have achieved during the course of the last financial year.[3] While the NPA forms part of the 'justice cluster', when standing in front of Parliament it is the NPA who has to account to the MPs for what it has done or has not done, and not the whole justice cluster which is being questioned and pressed for answers. A distinct conviction rate, I suggest, assists the NPA managers in this moment to assert the NPA's specific identity, so the organisation can be seen and judged as an independent role-player in the criminal justice cluster and does not get muddled up with other role-players and their tasks. In other words, van Jaarsfeld and de Villiers insist on their own measuring method to ensure, as they both stated, that they are not made accountable for the responsibilities of other justice role-players like the South African Police Service.

The second aspect which both managers mention to explain their insistence on a specific counting standard for the NPA refers to the internal use of the conviction rate and internal accountability relationships. As managers of the NPA they pointed out that they want to know 'how we are doing', 'how good is our decision-making?' and want a figure which is a good 'reflection of ourselves'. As managers they are interested in knowing how the people who they oversee are performing – the employees who report to them and who they are in charge of and who have a mandate to act upon – and not how everyone else in the justice cluster is performing. While NPA managers and prosecutors in general work closely with the judiciary and more so with the police on various levels of the organisation, the constitutionally defined separation of powers

[3] See for example meeting reports of NPA's Annual Report briefing in front of the Parliamentary Committee of Justice and Correctional Services: 2015/2016, available at: https://pmg.org.za/committee-meeting/23382/; 2014/2015, available at: https://pmg.org.za/committee-meeting/21639/; 2014/13, available at: https://pmg.org.za/committee-meeting/17691/; 2012/2013, available at: https://pmg.org.za/committee-meeting/16434/; 2011/2012, available at: https://pmg.org.za/committee-meeting/15032/; 2010/2011, available at: https://pmg.org.za/committee-meeting/13485/; 2009/2010, available at: https://pmg.org.za/committee-meeting/12112/; 2008/2009, available at: https://pmg.org.za/committee-meeting/11127/ [18 May 2018].

and the legislative separation of authority restricts them (for good reasons) from giving binding instructions to a member of SAPS or the magistracy/judiciary about how they should go about their job. Therefore they want to measure something that they feel, as they said, 'in control of'.

Confronted with the statements of these NPA managers who say that a distinct and restricted definition of conviction rate assists them to limit external performance and accountability expectations and increases their managerial knowledge of what is happening at the country's courts, one could easily explain them as typical examples of 'management speak' or 'mere rhetoric'. What else should they say? As high-ranked powerful NPA managers they are supposed to speak for the NPA and defend their organisation's practices. Of course it suits them that their performance information looks good on paper and that they are not held accountable for the country's police service's lower conviction rates.

Some quantification scholars (e.g. Shore and Wright 2011: 20ff.) would explain these statements possibly as fine examples of the spread of 'neoliberalism', which is accompanied by ever-encompassing 'audit practices', which 'encourage cynical reporting that bears scant resemblance to what people actually do in their everyday practice' (21). While the chances of criminal offenders getting punished by the state are low in South Africa the country's prosecution service reports and celebrates high conviction rates. This line of thinking would probably agree with the above-mentioned South African critics, the South African Law Commission and the political opposition party the DA, that the NPA 'creatively misleads' the public with its trial-to-conviction rate standard, that these numbers are 'a gross distortion' and, as the DA says, an 'insult' to victims of crime. They may agree that the NPA's current conviction rates undermine the working of the country's criminal justice system, because a rate which only takes the work of one criminal justice actor into consideration 'disunite' and 'fragment' the various criminal justice institutions which need to 'work together closely' in order to be effective in their 'fight against crime'. These critics would only differ in respect to who they blame: whether they blame rational individuals and political parties for these serious deficiencies in the South African criminal justice system, or larger globally circulating ideas and concepts like 'neoliberalism' or 'new public management' which encourage such unproductive thinking amongst actors.

In the next section I show that, on the contrary, it might not make much sense to speak of 'misleading', 'creative' and 'disuniting' numbers in this context. While it can certainly make political sense for an opposition party to speak of 'misleading', 'distorted' and 'disuniting' numbers in a context where another party is in power, I would like to raise the question as to whether it makes sense from an anthropological view – which is interested in the anthropology of numbers and quantification, and what numbers do in organisations and what organisations do with numbers – but also from a more applied analytical view, such as that taken to some extent by the South African Law Commission. Its political interests are much more diffused than those of an opposition party due to the diverse academic, political and practical backgrounds of its members who act upon its mandate to do research in order to make recommendations to Government how to best develop, 'improve, modernize or reform' the South African legal system (South African Law Commission 2014).

MISLEADING NUMBERS – MISLEADING FOR WHOM?

Criminologist and sociologist Kevin Haggerty, who conducted a fascinating study on the production and communication of crime statistics within the Canadian Centre for Justice Statistics, states that while different actors in his field sites 'generally have an honest desire to create the best possible standard, they are also acting as representatives of their particular program and/or jurisdiction and have interests in the standards that extend beyond their accuracy' (2001b: 711).

Haggerty (2001a: 154ff.; 2001b: 712ff.) describes these interests in his field-sites for counting things differently as '(micro-) political and economic'. One Canadian province, for example, had a much higher inmate rate than the other provinces. The reason for that was that this province counted the number of inmates differently. Every time inmates were released from a correctional institution on a temporary basis – for example to go to hospital or to return to work during the week – they were re-counted as 'a separate admission' the moment they re-entered the correctional facility (2001b: 712). Other provinces, which had considerably lower inmate rates, only counted an inmate at first admission. While the province did not look good in terms of its incarceration rates, the representatives were hesitant to adopt the more common counting rules of other provinces due to budgetary concerns;

they feared, as Haggerty pointed out, they would receive fewer resources with a reduced inmate rate.

Another example Haggerty mentions to show how micro-(political) and economic considerations shape the way different actors prefer to count certain phenomena in a certain way is the attempt by the Canadian Centre for Justice Statistics to develop a 'cost per case' indicator to document the comparative costs of processing a single case through the courts (Haggerty 2001b: 713). One province again had its own ideas. It refused to provide the Centre with detailed information 'for the courts' "resources, expenditures and personnel" (REP) survey'. It was suggested by the Centre's staff members that one main reason why province X refused to participate in the survey was because its courts' costs were considerably higher than those of other provinces, 'a fact they did not want to publicize any more than was necessary' (Haggerty 2001b: 713).

Such (micro-political and) economic factors can to some extent explain why different actors in the South African justice sector measure conviction rates differently. While the DA might have a valuable point that the NPA conviction rate is misleading for victims of crime as the wider public might get the impression that 90% of all criminal offenders are convicted, there is probably also political capital to be gained by an opposition party in promoting a different standard. Firstly, a 30% conviction rate makes the current ANC-led government appear much less committed and effective in their crime fighting efforts; and secondly, the suggestion by the DA that the NPA calculates the conviction rate 'creatively' by calculating it in a manner which makes them look as though they are doing better than they actually are makes the NPA appear less trustworthy. This suggestion is particularly provocative in a political climate in which, for example, the legitimacy of the police was harmed when a moratorium on certain crime statistics in 2000 limited the flow of information between the national police commissioner and the public, and fear was widespread that government was trying to suppress and deny the country's high violent crime rates (Leggett 2000; Shaw 2002; Schönteich 2009).

In a similar way the NGO, whose aim it is to draw the public's attention to violence against women and to advocate a shift in how state criminal justice actors deal with rape and domestic violence cases, might consider possible (dis)advantages of employing one calculation standard over another. In their 1998 study CIET used as a baseline all women who stated in the household survey they conducted in that specific metropolitan area that they had been raped. In that way they arrived at a conviction rate of one in 394 rapists or 0.25%: a much more dramatic statistic, at least to a layperson, than if they had applied the countrywide report-to-conviction rate of the SAPS which, as mentioned earlier, lies between 7% and 8.9%; or the countrywide trial-to-conviction rate used by the NPA which lies between 45% and 67%. Artz and Smythe state that high attrition rates in rape cases through the criminal justice system were identified as a serious concern by government and criminal justice actors around the time CIET published its study (2007a: 168). The NGO was probably aware that low numbers would put the government under more pressure to address the problem at hand by changing their future budget and policy considerations in order to create more specialised sexual offence courts and so-called 'Thuthuzela Care Centres'[4] which aim to offer a more victim-friendly and sensitive environment than ordinary police stations and courts.

Lastly, those kinds of '(micro)-political' and 'economic' interests can probably also be found in the NPA. Victoria Whitehouse, a South African public lawyer and human rights activist in her late thirties, explained to me in a one-hour interview that the above-mentioned Thuthuzela Care Centres are partly financed by UNICEF. Since one of the expressed objectives of these centres was to improve the conviction rate for sexual offences in South Africa, the Department of Justice and Constitutional Development and the NPA found it important to show that these centres are indeed fulfilling that expectation. The reports compiled for the donor included, according to Whitehouse, the police service's naturally lower report-to-conviction rate as a baseline figure for ordinary courts processing sexual offence cases and the NPA's trial-to-conviction rate counting standard, which is always higher than the SAPS's figures, was used to report on the performance of the sexual offence courts connected to the Thuthuzela Care Centres. Although the new operational procedure for sexual offences was indeed successful in improving conviction rates, due to the (ab)use of the two different counting standards the performance looked even better.

[4] *Thuthuzela Care Centres* are one-stop facilities that have been introduced as a critical part of South Africa's anti-rape strategy, aiming to reduce secondary trauma for the victim, improve conviction rates and reduce the cycle time for finalising cases. The idea is that all necessary role-players are either on site, or visits to medical services and police officers are organised and accompanied by staff members of the Care Centre. NPA Brochure available at: https://www.npa.gov.za/sites/default/files/resources/public_awareness/TCC_brochure_august_2009.pdf [5 July 2018].

I find Haggerty's line of thinking helpful since it allows one to get away from the strict distinctions between numbers which are accurate and real and numbers which are incorrect and misleading and makes space for a more nuanced understanding of actor's considerations for counting things differently. However, I do think his reasoning does not go far enough in explaining the numerical discrepancies found in the South African criminal justice sector and the NPA's managers' insistence on their own counting standards. The prosecutorial managers I observed and interviewed at work in the NPA were not constantly involved in a scramble for financial resources and political positions, especially the ones who occupied permanent NPA positions which were not politically appointed. Numerical representations were in these contexts not exclusively the means to improve one's political profile or to gain a favourable budgetary position. I suggest that it is important to consider that in the NPA divisions I have explored extensively numerical representations were used for more mundane or genuine work activities, namely for making sense.

When describing the function and purpose of the conviction rate performance indicator, most managers stated that it tells them 'how we are doing' and 'what is happening, what is going on at court'. These kinds of questions are typical queries that people raise, according to organisational scholars Karl Weick, Kathleen Sutcliffe and David Obstfeld when they try to make sense of a situation (2005: 410). They state further (2005: 410) that '[a] central theme in both organizing and sensemaking is that people organize to make sense of equivocal inputs and enact this sense back into the world to make that world more orderly'. In other words sensemaking starts with 'chaos' as there is an indefinite 'flux' of events and human action that surround any organisational actor (Weick et al. 2005: 411). One of the first steps in the sensemaking process is – Weick et al. (2005: 411) quoting organisational scholar Chia (2000: 517) – that the phenomena actors try to control must be 'forcibly carved out of the undifferentiated flux of raw experience and conceptually fixed and labelled, so that they can become the common currency for communicational exchanges'.

I suggest following Weick et al. (2005) here that the NPA trial-to-conviction rate 'carves out' for the managers a specific portion of the flux of all actions which occur before or when an offender is convicted within the criminal justice system. It brackets off all the offences which have not been reported to the police stations but are nevertheless occurring and to some extent documented in victimisation surveys.

It ignores cases where victims have reported the incident but where the police are unable to collect sufficient evidence to sustain a charge, and cases in which the opinion of police is that they are 'ready for court' but where court prosecutors determine otherwise. The object of this bracketing action is, I suggest, to focus managerial attention on that part of the conviction process which prosecutors are involved in, in order to reduce the high level of ambiguity and equivocality associated with the non-differentiation of the roles the different actors play in the criminal justice process, inherent in a report-to-conviction rate or a referred-to-conviction rate.

According to Weick et al. (2005: 414) the next step in the sense-making process is that a 'locally plausible story' is then generated based on the bracketed raw data to interpret, explain and order what has occurred. So when the conviction rate is suddenly considerably higher or lower than the planned and expected figure, 'when things don't add up' as some phrased it, managerial prosecutors use these figures as a cue that something is or might be wrong and needs further attention. They are the starting point for making presumptions about what is wrong and what went wrong, for asking for further information and explanations and for thinking about possible actions, while considering the available resources the NPA can use to address the identified problem.

DPP Adv. de Villiers mentioned that when encountering low conviction rates in his unit they begin with the following questions: What kind of case was the prosecutor working on; is the prosecutor sufficiently trained for the cases he or she is handling; did the prosecutor misjudge the quality of the evidence; is insufficient police investigation the problem; do we need to speak to the investigators and the police station commanders; was the prosecutor negligent; was it a mistake; and, do we have resources for more training; is the workload too high; can we afford to have another court running; and, if we can't, how can we spread the workload amongst the available prosecutors?

While they could of course also ask these questions with the other suggested or used conviction rates, the equivocality of these rates would be higher. For example, any unilateral changes in police activities would have a greater impact on a conviction rate measured against referred cases rather than against trial cases, as with the later the point of departure for measurement is a prosecutor who is trained to determine whether the case is trial ready and should be sent to court. To further illustrate this impact, should the police send more cases to court (as it was the case in one of my court field sites) because police stations have been told by their senior managers to improve their referral rate and pick up the speed of investigation, the referral rate could drop as prosecutors might be unable to deal with the sudden increase in volume of referred cases. The rate could even drop if the NPA had the necessary capacity and skills to prosecute a higher volume. This would occur when the police send more cases without necessarily receiving more resources to investigate these increased cases thoroughly. Prosecutors would then return improperly investigated matters, which would result in a drop in the referred-to-conviction rate (see for example Leggett et al. 2003 for discussion around the drop of report-to-conviction rate after SAPS's 2001/2002 'Operation Crackdown').

My aim is to emphasise here that these numbers critics called 'misleading' and 'creatively calculated' had a specific purpose in this organisational setting which goes beyond 'looking good', 'cooking the books' and 'lies, damned lies, and statistics'. They are used to make sense, to manage and to think. The trial-to-conviction rate helped the managers, as they said, to focus and to narrow their attention to specific aspects of their own organisation. They could see something with their own counting standard which they would not see with a less narrow one. As mentioned before, the counting rules and standards are constitutive of the object they are trying to represent.

My deliberations are shaped and inspired by Martha Lampland's work (2010). She emphasises that in order to 'grasp the meaning of any set of numbers it is crucial to appreciate who created those numbers, for whom and why' (Lampland 2010: 383) because as she writes, '[t]he purpose of numbers varies, as does their meaning' (2010: 377). Lampland is interested in the role numbers play in 'formalizing practices'. She suggests that term because it captures, as she says, 'a wide range of social practices, which are usually treated separately: quantification, standardization, rationalization' (Lampland 2010: 379). It brings our attention to the 'doing of quantification', to all the activities and actions which actors need to take in order to 'institute standard protocols or rationalized procedures'. She argues that the doing of quantification can look substantially different from 'the final form of a rationalized organization or standardized process' (2010: 379).

Lampland pays specific attention to numbers which she calls 'provisional' or 'false'. She argues that 'provisional' or 'false' numbers do not have the same meaning and purpose as numbers in other settings, where they are usually understood as 'referents to stable entities that carry the same meaning no matter what their context' (2010: 378). She defines provisional numbers as numbers that are used by people who need to plan and strategise. They 'assist groups in setting the parameters for tasks at hand and debating their relative merit' (Lampland 2010: 378). She says provisional numbers can be used as a 'stable and fixed indicator' in some settings, but the people who are responsible for making them are aware of their 'provisional status' (2010: 378). False numbers in contrast are numerical representations in which the accuracy of numerical representations is less important than the aim that actors learn how to deploy numbers and become familiar with 'the logic of formal procedures' (Lampland 2010: 378).[5] Lampland's thinking is inspiring for me as she suggests that it is useful to identify the thinking and planning tools actors use when they make sense and organise because identifying them allows us to 'track the means' by which a variety of complex social projects are managed and accomplished. She argues for the divorce of

> the study of everyday formalizing practices from criteria inherited from modernist paradigms that evaluate social practices in terms of idealized representations in which approximations to elegant structures serve as evidence of increasing formalization. Attending merely to the spare features of formalized procedures means we overlook the dynamic social processes by which rationalization actually occurs. In other words, assuming that the effective use of numbers depends upon their veracity obscures crucial social processes at the heart of modernizing practices.

Her argument, that false and provisional numbers do not necessarily undermine rationalisation but can play a stabilising and fixing role in formalising practices and enable them in a range of projects in the first place, is useful when one considers NPA managers' approach to numerical representations. The managers depicted in Chapter 5 and in this chapter do not speak of false or provisional numbers, but various managers refer to the performance indicators in general and the conviction rate specifically as 'strange', 'not perfect' or 'not 100% correct', all attributes which would not count in a 'modernist paradigm' as

[5] Lampland uses the example of Hungarian accountants in the agricultural sector in the 1950s who were praised by the Stalinist state for their accounting work despite their books lacking the necessary accuracy and meticulousness usually required by this profession. She shows that it was more important for the state to finally establish some accounting procedures in agricultural plants, whose workers, to the disappointment of the state, had successfully resisted the introduction of bookkeeping and time measures for a while than to receive no figures whatsoever (387ff.).

evidence of increased rationalisation – as a sign that something makes sense and is organised.

The reasons the managers called the conviction rate indicator 'strange' or 'not correct' differed from the points of critique that the above-mentioned SALC and the opposition politician raised. These reasons were not related to how one measures 'real' convictions in the most correct or meaningful way, but rather to the certain and simultaneously uncertain knowledge the conviction rate indicator made available to them for purposes of managerial sensemaking. They were aware that the conviction rate told them something but they also pointed out that they knew that it did not tell them or others everything they needed to know about their work environment as it is difficult to capture with such numerical representations.

First of all the conviction rate was described as a strange indicator because on the one hand it was measured for district, regional and High Courts and specific crime categories, but on the other hand it was not attached to a specific target like other NPA performance measuring indicators.[6] While politicians, for example ex-President Thabo Mbeki in his State of the Nation address in 2004, or ex-Deputy Minister of Justice and Constitutional Development Johnny de Lange at a launch of a new court model[7] sometimes treated a court's 100 per cent conviction rate in their public speeches as something particularly laudable and a sign that the justice system is working well, the aim of the NPA, as various managers have pointed out, is not to increase the target every year, but to have a more 'static' rate. Success is here not equated with a rate of 100 per cent since this high figure would mirror the apartheid courts where people were convicted without the opportunity of a fair trial. There must always be room for 'error' and 'acquittals', as DPP Adv. de Villiers emphasised. Furthermore managers explained that conviction rates by themselves do not tell much about the success of the NPA; only in relation to counter indicators like finalisation rate, withdrawal rate and outstanding cases rate do they become meaningful (see also Chapter 5: 21ff.).

Secondly, measuring conviction is 'a strange quality indicator' because, as de Villiers said, the NPA is on the one hand 'not in the

[6] Counter-examples or exceptions attest to the complexity of the indicator conviction rate. For example, for specific offences like rape where conviction rates are publicly criticised as particularly low, the NPA announced unspecific targets like the 'performance goal is to increase the conviction rate' or lately more specific ones like 'raising the conviction rate by 2%'.

[7] See for example: http://www.info.gov.za/speeches/2004/04121010151002.htm [23.3.2018].

business of getting convictions', but on the other hand, if too few accused are convicted, 'then there is something wrong'. In other words, it is also clearly expected of the NPA to secure convictions. While the prosecutor has to convince the court of the accused's guilt 'beyond any reasonable doubt', prosecutors are instructed to only bring cases to court where they find a *prima facie* case and not every single case they receive from the police. A low conviction rate might therefore indicate to the manager that, for example, the respective control prosecutor is too inexperienced to exercise that discretion and is misjudging the evidence he or she receives from the police because cases which are insufficiently investigated are sent to court and that is why the respective court prosecutor loses the case. It could also be a sign that the case has been sufficiently investigated but that the respective court prosecutor is not sufficiently well trained, so he or she presents the wrong or insufficient evidence to the court or makes procedural mistakes which lead to an acquittal of the accused. However, while a low conviction rate can say something about the quality of prosecution, a well-prepared prosecutor has a better chance of getting a conviction than someone who is, for whatever personal or institutional reasons, unable to convincingly argue the case. It might not, as the managers I described in Chapter 5 pointed out, always say something about the quality of the prosecutor and his skills when other factors like a lack of police and witness cooperation during the trial, the general complexity of the case, the overall work load, the strength of the defence lawyer or the judge's or magistrate's understanding of the law or even his or her political standing might be the determining factors on whether or not an accused is convicted.

Thirdly, the conviction rate was described as 'not 100% correct' when one is interested in controlling and accounting for 'quality prosecution', because quality of prosecution can be defined in many ways and can mean many different things to different people, as Adv. du Toit and other prosecutors mentioned. For example, various prosecutors frequently used the words 'tough' or 'technical' to describe their prosecuting style. The tough ones would use phrases like 'this mother fucker must be brought behind bars' when referring to the accused and would grill accused in the witness box, whereas for others it was a sign of their prosecution quality to be seen as an even-tempered and technical prosecutor who knows the law and uses sophisticated legal arguments to make his case. I observed at court that these tough prosecutors were often more popular amongst the complainants than the technical prosecutors. It was secondary to these victims of crime whether the prosecutor was respectful or knew the law well, as long as he or she gets a conviction in the case. In contrast, when talking to victim support or human rights organisations concerned with the fair and equal treatment of victims or accused, this aspect was indeed central for their understanding of quality prosecution. The same applied for some defence lawyers I spoke to. When they were intending to use a very legal and technical argument it was also important to them that the prosecutor and the magistrate know 'the law', otherwise they had difficulty communicating effectively at the same legal level in court. While many managerial prosecutors were concerned about the quality of prosecution and the outcome and impact of the NPA's work, they were aware that this is much more difficult and costly to measure than counting convictions.

The fact that managers repeatedly call the conviction rate 'strange' and 'imperfect' is an indication of their ambiguity towards this performance indicator. I argue that this ambiguity should not be necessarily interpreted as a sign that they have something to hide, because they are cheating, but that it can be read as an additional dimension of their numerical competence and reflexivity. What I want to stress here with Lampland's deliberations is that a numerical representation described as 'misleading', 'creative' or as an 'insult' in contexts outside the NPA can nevertheless be experienced as a good thinking device in specific managerial contexts within the NPA. While NPA managers themselves described the conviction rates as imperfect and flawed, they perceived them at the same time as good working tools to plan, strategise and organise the activities of the NPA and to accomplish a complex social task: 'justice'. The NPA managers expressed pragmatism when it came to the conviction rates. They were thankful to have these strange and imperfect numbers as clues and reference points for their daily work instead of having no numbers whatsoever. So, while the political opposition party might call the NPA's conviction rate 'inflated' and 'creative', scholars of the social studies of numbers and other academics should be slow to label these numbers as 'misleading' or 'wrong' without taking into consideration the varying meaning and purpose of specific numbers in specific settings.

CONCLUSION

I showed in this chapter that there are 'good' organisational reasons for these 'misleading' NPA conviction rates. These numbers might not make sense for external accountability audiences. But they do make sense to internal users, namely to the managers who insist on them, not only for economic or political reasons, but also because they rely on them to manage, organise and get things done. I want to question in this last part of this chapter whether there might also be good reasons for having various conviction rates when it comes to the wider public instead of having one universal rate as the critics suggest. Would members of the public be better informed about the working of the NPA and the criminal justice system with one rate?

For example, the South African Law Commission (2000) argued that it is irrelevant from the perspective of the victims of crime to know precisely when the criminal justice system had failed them: at the stage of the police investigation; or the prosecution in court; or when there is a disjointed interaction between the different role-players. I would contrarily emphasise that this is an empirical question. It might be indeed very satisfying and central for victims to know who is to blame for the delays and hindrances in their case and who can be made responsible or potentially liable. The competing rates can increase outsiders' awareness that the criminal justice system is not 'a system' as it is commonly often called, but that there are distinct state organisations involved and responsible for different parts of the processing of a criminal offence. It can make a difference, for example, for a rape victim's personal wellbeing or for her accountability demand to know whether her case never ended in a conviction of the perpetrator because the police officers did not know how to secure court-relevant evidence at the respective crime scene; or because the prosecutor failed to inform himself about the previous convictions of the accused and as a result the accused was released on bail and is since then on the run; or because the judge does not consider forced sexual intercourse within a long-term intimate relationship as rape. In other words, I suggest it is worth considering that differing rates cannot only be confusing and lead to less accountability for the public, but can be informative and enable more specific, less vague and therefore more realistic accountability demands and relationships.

While I am not trying to suggest that with differing conviction rates one can easily identify and explain who is at 'fault' when a rapist or murderer is not convicted, these different rates can make it more obvious to members of the public that firstly interdependent but distinct state parties with different tasks and responsibilities are involved in the conviction process. Distinct conviction rates highlight important aspects and subtleties which in turn enable one to situate shortcoming in 'the' system more clearly and thereby debate or negotiate division of labour and accountability attributions between the SAPS and the NPA.

And secondly, although it is something which requires further research, I suggest that the ambiguity created through the competing rates could help to increase ordinary peoples' numeracy with regards to the criminal justice figures. By numeracy I mean peoples' general ease of entry to and handling of numbers, as well as their ability to read numerical representations' specific meaning, purpose and value – whether it is numbers produced by the state's criminal justice institutions or by other non-state organisations. For example, being confronted by different conviction rates can potentially create more awareness amongst users that there are many possible and equally justifiable ways to conceptualise conviction rates and that there is not one 'objective', 'neutral' or 'scientific' standard of counting, but multiple appropriate criteria can be applied. In other words, the work, assumptions and debates which go into the social construction of something like a conviction rate, something which quantification scholars often warn can become invisible and pushed into the background when one measuring standard dominates the field, become more able to be seen or even obvious when different rates circulate in public discourses. In that sense the confusion these different conviction rates produce are important for keeping the power of numbers in check.

While my point that the various conviction rates could be beneficial for increasing peoples' numerical knowledge needs to be tested with further research, Sauder and Espeland (2006) indicate in their work that ambiguity created through the existence of multiple numbers can be helpful in counteracting the worrying effects of quantified information. They argue that due to the fact that *US News* holds virtually a monopoly over the rankings of US law schools, the effects are much more severe and palpable. In other fields where multiple rankings exist, for example in the business school sector in the USA five to six rankings predominate and a few more receive attention, the effects of public rankings are less harmful. The different methodologies and criteria used by the rankings to evaluate the schools produce ambiguity about the relative standing of each business school. While a few of them do well in all rankings, most schools receive quite a variety of scores in different rankings. Sauder and Espeland argue that the ambiguity created through the multiple rankings weakens the effect of performance indicators and therefore gives these institutions greater freedom and control in how they define and account for quality education and their specific mission. They state that they are an effective way to combat the 'taken-for-granted validity' which comes with powerful rankings as the availability of multiple numbers encourage users to be more cautious when interpreting quantified information (2006: 224).

I mentioned in Chapter 4 that the institutional and legal set up of the NPA tames the power of numbers' ability to be used to reallocate resources in the prosecutorial work environment. Therefore, even if their argument is based on quantification research in a different organisational setting, Sauder's and Espeland's example may be fruitful in getting an idea about how multiple numerical representations of the 'same thing' can be beneficial and not only confusing or even misleading as the critics of the NPA's conviction rate suggested. However, Sauder and Espeland also warn that relying on this tactic in the long-term reinforces 'rankings as the legitimate mode of accountability' and marginalises other very valuable forms of more 'deliberative, non-quantitative methods of evaluation' (2006: 207; 226). In other words, as they say, 'more of a bad thing cannot lead to a good thing' (Sauder and Espeland 2006: 225). It is true that quantification of complex social phenomena is always attended by radical simplification and editing processes, no matter whether there is now one rate or multiple rates, one indicator or multiple indicators or one ranking or multiple rankings. In my opinion this point neglects the argument this chapter has made, namely that numbers need not only have obscuring, annoying and harmful effects but also enlightening, helpful and productive ones.

CONCLUDING REMARKS

Accountability, or the way people explain and justify specific social situations, 'is part of the general fabric of human interchange' (Strathern 2000a: 4). It is a concept of central importance to the understanding of social action (Garfinkel 1967: 1). Futhermore, public accountability is evidently required for good governance, redistributive justice and fair resource allocation as it can minimise unpredictability and arbitrariness and can control discretion (Dowdle 2006; Mashaw 2006). How quantitative forms of accountability shape the way people work and experience their accountability in different organisational fields is therefore an important social question worthy of (more) sustained investigation. This is especially the case when one considers that the pressure for quantitative evaluation and demands for quantitative accountability have been on the rise over the past two decades. Our knowledge about the effects and consequences of the increased importance of numbers in accountability relationships, and organisational life more generally, is limited and/or often based on generalisations.

When I completed the initial period of fieldwork for this study in late 2009 and began to present initial ideas to colleagues from across the social sciences, I was repeatedly surprised at how quickly discussions around quantitative forms of accountability resulted in debates about how 'powerful people' and 'institutions' use statistics to 'lie', 'cheat' and 'game' and how 'statistics don't tell us what is going on on the ground'.[1] While I carefully listened and took notes of empirically grounded experiences and concerns, it was often astonishing how confident colleagues were in their assumptions about the serious and harmful effects of performance measurement systems, although many of them

[1] First ideas were presented in October 2009 at the Annual Conference of the German Anthropological Association (GAA) in Frankfurt am Main; in January 2010 and July 2011 at the Max Planck Institute for Social Anthropology in Halle an der Saale; Germany, in February 2010 at the International Max Planck Research School 'Retaliation, Mediation and Punishment' (IMPRS-REMEP); in Alsace, France, in September 2010 at the CRESC conference at the University of Oxford, UK; and in November 2010 at the Annual Meeting of the African Studies Association in San Francisco, USA.

had never put a foot inside of this kind of organisational setting during their own research. This did not seem to matter. Colleagues repeatedly referred to their own experiences of performance measurement in the academic world and the much-celebrated American TV crime drama series 'The Wire' in order to make particularly bleak arguments and prophecies about the detrimental power of numbers in institutional and societal life. 'The Wire' is set in the grimly depicted working environment of Baltimore policemen, who find themselves pressurised to chase crime statistics. The actual internal debates entered into by higher ranked policemen about the efficacy of performance measurement systems, as well as the stark variation in the importance of research output indicators across different academic environments, were hardly addressed or of interest in these conversations.

My ethnographic study of how the NPA's performance measurement systems shape South African prosecutors' understandings of accountability and their prosecutorial practices is an attempt to contextualise and historicise people's use of quantitative forms of accountability within specific power relationships and institutional configurations. The NPA provides an interesting case study because South Africa's distrusted, detested and to a large extent unaccountable prosecution authority came under immense pressure after the country's democratic transition to democracy in 1994. It had to legitimise itself in the eyes of those it had, until very recently, suppressed. To turn prosecutors into accountable 'lawyers of the people' became one of the central objectives for the leaders of the newly established National Prosecuting Authority in 1998. The introduction of a performance measurement system around the turn of the new millennium formed an important part of the NPA's rigorous transformation strategy.

In summary, my book, a product of that ethnographic study seeks to make five points. Firstly, the meaning, use and effect of quantitative accountability are context-dependent and time-specific. That knowledge is situational and relational is something which social anthropologists stress in most research settings. It is a key analytical concept in the methodology of the discipline (Emerson, Fretz and Shaw 1995: 169ff.). This professional invocation of context somehow seems to be applied less often when it comes to numerical representations. This is no doubt connected to the reason why numbers were (or are) propagated and used in many contexts in the first place: namely, that they seemingly provide actors with a more objective, precise and impartial way of knowing, which is supposed to eliminate the importance of the contextual knowledge that is often associated with subjectivity, favouritism or more generally with equivocality (Porter 1995).

My research has shown that performance statistics, rates, indicators, targets and rankings were a common feature in the working world of most South African prosecutors I observed, shadowed and interviewed in state courts and NPA head offices between 2008 and 2012. These numbers were central to how lower court prosecutors talked about their work and accounted for it to their seniors; and further, for how managerial prosecutors managed their staff and the NPA on a regional, provincial and national level; and lastly for how members of the NPA upper management accounted for the organisations' work to the public, namely to parliament and the media. The commonly raised concern, however, that quantitative forms of accountability supersede other non-quantitative and deliberative forms of accountability, that they narrow actors' understanding of their work and options to account for their work and limit their professional discretion, cannot be confirmed for this setting. I showed in Chapter 3 that concepts like professionalism, legal accountability/liability and personal ideas and ideals of justice and public service were strong alternatives for how court prosecutors understood and practised their accountability. In other words, they had some control and flexibility over how their reputations were defined and what good prosecutorial performance should entail.

I have provided, for example, descriptions which demonstrate that court prosecutors were indeed aware of cases where guilty pleas, mediations or diversions were 'good for the stats' because they took less time to finalise and would consequently count positively towards their finalisation rate performance indicator. However, this did not mean that prosecutors perceived other more complicated cases as 'bad for the stats'. In contrast, I argued that a trial, the most time-consuming way to finalise a case for a prosecutor, was what the majority favoured since their professional identity was closely linked to being a litigator and not to being a case administrator. I also showed that prosecutors' interest in speedy alternative dispute resolution mechanism could not only be explained by their pressure to reach a certain target of finalised cases each month, but also by an awareness that not all complainants can afford and/or enjoy adversarial legal court battles as much as they do. For example, mediation gave prosecutors, especially those whose understanding of professional accountability also included the desire to ensure high levels of courtesy for their clients, the opportunity to accommodate complainants who demanded the informal involvement of an official criminal justice employee for their dispute management but not the formality and infinity of a trial or a criminal conviction.

That these prosecutors did not feel torn between making decisions which were 'good for the stats' and ones which were 'good for justice' was also evident when I discussed their approach to the NPA performance indicator conviction rates. While convictions mattered to most prosecutors, to which phrases such as 'no one likes to lose a case' attest, it was not the number of convictions that counted most when prosecutors talked with their colleagues about 'their trials'. The focus in these conversations was predominantly on *how* they obtained the convictions: in which types of cases and in spite of which obstacles. Harshness towards the accused and/or clever cross-examination tactics, the sophistication of a case strategy or the style of legal argumentation and case law used to 'take apart' the 'smart private defence lawyer', as well as the intricacies of the specific case, were what made them visibly proud or portrayed them as well-performing prosecutors in their own and in their colleagues' eyes.

In a second step, I showed in Chapters 5 and 6 that managerial prosecutors' understanding and practice of accountability are also wider than having 'good stats'. While they use the quantitative performance information for internal management purposes to create economic awareness and for adhering to external accountability demands, I provided examples which demonstrate that they were clearly aware of its limits and shortcomings. The managers in the observed meetings I described did not treat the quantified performance information as completely objective, precise and accurate. In other words, they did not perceive the information as containing simple and straightforward facts. Despite emphasising the way that quantitative performance information can enable oversight by assisting them to know 'all things relevant to our work [. . .] will know exactly each court in each province', when prosecutorial managers made sense of the stats in front of them, they always relied on their own and other trusted people's judgement, discretion and interpretation. It was clear to them that numerical representations are selective, often more ambiguous than they might first appear and that they did not tell them everything they needed to know to manage a situation or make a decision.

Therefore I would suggest, and this is my second point, that the dominance of quantitative forms of accountability depends upon how much power, faith and credibility powerful actors in organisational setting place on numerical representations. As Vormbusch (2007: 61) writes, 'the power of numbers, to a large extent, relies on the social construction of calculations remaining hidden' (own translation). Being aware of this, is 'the basis for a new, in a sense, clarified instead of enlightened handling' of numerical information (Vormbusch 2007: 61); and a sign for a more 'reflexive approach to numbers' in certain societal domains (2007: 61). Prosecutors' awareness of the limits and shortcomings of the constructedness and constructiveness of the quantified performance information, and their insistence and reliance on other forms of knowledge and accountability when assessing a situation or making a decision are more clear signs, I argue, that professionals in this setting were not so easily disciplined into 'auditable selves'. Through their daily involvement with numbers, they gained, as I would call it, *numerical reflexivity*.

For most of the observed prosecutors there was no inherent contradiction between being concerned about quality and quantity; there was more of an assumption that one is helpful, or needed, to preserve the other and that they are capable of having simultaneous but differing thoughts. Prosecutors' notion of the relationship between quantity and quality is important because when one always presumes there is a contradiction between the two, it becomes difficult to evaluate the adequacy of the relationship more closely in different settings and at different times. There is always the underlying feeling that one exists at the cost of the other (Stinchcombe 2001). This hinders the establishment of a set of factors (e.g. institutional, historical, economic, political or metric specific) by which one can make normative judgements about quantification and accountability.

My third point offers some guidance for building such a framework. The individual numerical reflexivity of relevant actors is essential when trying to understand the meaning, use and effect of quantitative accountability in specific settings. I suggest that the institutional setup of an organisational field, and how entrenched quantification is historically therein, are equally important factors in this scholarly endeavour. Espeland and Sauder (2007) showed in their law school ranking study that professionals can be clearly aware of the constructedness and constructiveness of numerical representations, but can nevertheless still fail to protect their professional discretion and lose the authority to define the central parameters within which their work is evaluated. Although the law school leaders depicted deeply resented the methodology of the public law school ranking, they felt forced to take them seriously. This was because external audiences relied on them to make far-reaching decisions which effected the law school's status and resources, both human and financial, in such a tangible way that they could not any longer be ignored.

I emphasized in Chapter 4 that the professionals in my research setting had conciliatory attitudes towards their organisation's performance measurement system. Most prosecutors were not afraid of them and felt that their professional discretion remained intact despite being required by the PFMA of 1998 to account quantitatively. I suggest that this is the case because the allocation of resources in the NPA and the Department of Justice and Constitutional Development are not tightly coupled to the NPA's performance measurement system. I argue that the authority of specific legal principles like 'equality before the law', 'due process' or 'jurisdiction', which are enshrined in the country's criminal procedure act and its constitution, slow down or even prevent active competition between courts for clients, cases and funds. The rules of law require that each court in the country functions in the same manner; that the accused and complainants are treated equally; and that cases are heard where the court has the jurisdiction to hear that case. As a result, resources are allocated on a needs basis and not on merit in this setting. In other words, a well-performing court does not get more resources than a poorly performing court. Furthermore, I show that the rules of law also limit the choice of all involved legal actors as prosecutors cannot cherry-pick their cases, nor can complainants or their attorneys/advocates take their case to the best-ranked court of the province or country.

Alongside the authority of certain legal principles, which temper resource competition via performance measurement figures in this setting, I argued that the lack of (sophisticated) quantification chains slows down the proliferation of such painful and unproductive effects in this organisational field. Cases are classified in a limited fashion; according to district, regional or High Court matters; and as serious or less serious crimes. There are currently no further attempts to classify and quantify the complexity of these cases. This means that there is no clear score or parameter on which prosecutors can easily choose a case which is 'good for the stats' over one which is 'bad for the stats'. That most NPA performance numbers do not travel far means that they are not made public and do not leave the organisation. This prevents images such as 'best-ranked court' or 'prosecution cluster' from emerging and circulating in the public realm, which in turn means that poorly performing courts and clusters are not subject to immense pressure.

I argued lastly on the point of resource allocation. Indeed, the NPA intended to introduce performance-related pay mechanisms for their employees in order to create a more competitive work environment, but this plan never quite materialised. Promotions, demotions, praises and sanctions were not clearly coupled to prosecutors' quantitative performance information. This was firstly due to there being insufficient funds to pay out such bonuses or increases, and, secondly, due to a twenty-year-old struggle for a raise in salary for all prosecutors. Since the occupational group of prosecutors achieved professional status in the 1990s, their claim for better remuneration became un-ignorable. Furthermore, over the last years, the objective of transforming the profession of prosecutors into one that is attractive to talented and skilled lawyers seemed more important for the NPAs than singling out underperformers.

My fourth point is simply that empirical research about the 'doing of numbers' is important. It provides knowledge that can shift discussions pertaining to the social studies of numbers beyond the point where numerical representations' reality-obscuring-capacity is repetitively emphasised. While a critical stance towards the quantification of complex social phenomena and quantitative accountability is no doubt essential, I argue that the 'taken-for-granted mistrust' in numbers, which is particularly prevalent among anthropologists, can be as damaging as the 'taken-for-granted validity of numbers' many scholars are rightly concerned about. The aim of my study is not to advocate for a disregard of these concerns entirely – not at all – but to say that if one focuses too narrowly on these poles when analysing people's interactions with numbers, then it becomes possible to miss the larger spectrum of locally relevant ways of working with numbers in various settings.

In Chapter 6 I described a professional work environment in which some of the numerical representations the organisation produces are called 'creative' and 'inflated' by some external audiences. The NPA is accused of misleading the public with its conviction rate instead of informing it of the 'real' workings of the organisation. I showed that one could certainly interpret prosecutorial managers' insistence on their own conviction rate counting standard as straightforward numerical interest politics. I argued, however, that this form of analysis neglects how these actors use these numbers as valid sensemaking and rationalising tools. They carved out, with these numerical representations which they call 'not perfect' and 'not 100% correct', a specific narrow area of the wider working landscape of the criminal justice system that would not be visible otherwise. In doing so, important aspects and subtleties become apparent that are not visible from the perspective of other used or proposed conviction rate standards. While it is suggested that the NPA uses its good conviction rate to avoid criticism and reject responsibility for the country's overall conviction rates, I argued that the different rates allow for important debates and negotiations – about the division of labour and accountability attributions between the different state criminal justice actors – to emerge.

In that sense, the conviction rates contribute to public accountability and do not obscure it. These types of nuances can assist us in engaging seriously and trying to understand the context-specific meanings, uses and purposes of numerical representations. This is essential when living in a world surrounded by ever-increasing amounts of numbers and at a time when increasing demands for quantitative accountability coincide with scarcities of public resources, both in South Africa and elsewhere.

My last point provides an outlook. This book describes how accountability is made in practice; which methods and tools people and organisations use in that process; and how they reflect upon it. It does not explain what accountability is (see Reckwitz 2002a; 2002b; 2003). I discussed the most prominent accountability concepts for the NPA, namely accountability as the separation of powers, representation and professionalism and as a performance measurement. I made clear that accountability has more logical, visible, tangible and technological aspects to it (e.g. performance statistics, annual reports, legal acts, legal reviews, meetings, architecture or skin colour). It also has more implicit, bodily, informal and invisible aspects (e.g. trust, gut feeling, ethics, courtesy, gender, informal conversations). The different forms of accountability I presented herein are not equally important at all times for all parts of the prosecuting authority, since different constituencies can have different accountability demands and these can have dissimilar effects on disparate parts of the NPA, on the people who work in these units and on the cases they handle.

Performance measurement systems play an important role to hold lower court prosecutors accountable for the court resources they spend on the several hundreds of cases they often have to deal with per month. The prosecutors are faced with the difficult job of having to do the right thing and be fair, but also to ensure that all of this is being done in a reasonable amount of time. Owing to the fact that law works incredibly slowly, even if it is not slowed down as a result of mistakes, negligence or through the intentions of actors, it requires time to operate effectively and therefore, large amounts of public money. The fear that critics of performance measurement systems hold is that when a measurement is put on justice, there is the risk that justice falls by the wayside. Justice should not have a price like any other commodity since it is considered a right, a human right that everyone is entitled to. The South African prosecutors, as well as the magistrates and judges I worked with, would confirm that statement wholeheartedly. Currently there is no price on justice and for good reasons.

Nevertheless, justice has a price. Where does the money come from to pay for this human right/for justice? How is it raised and from which part of society? Where and how are the public finances for redistribution and collective action negotiated? And lastly, who decides how much a country's justice system receives from public (tax) money and which justice issues will be addressed with it? These are basic questions relating to the economic side of justice, which my research has not answered – they do not form part of the going concerns of most of the prosecutors I worked with – but somehow, they raised themselves strongly while writing this book. Despite the fear that there should not be a price put on justice, paying attention to the economic side of justice is crucial for future in-depth anthropological understandings of justice, public accountability and the working of state apparatuses – this is my last point.

BIBLIOGRAPHY

Abel, Richard (1995). *Politics by Other Means: Law in the Struggle against Apartheid, 1980-1994*. New York: Routledge.

Abraham, Andrea (2012). Framing Quality. Constructions of Medical Quality in Swiss Family Medicine. Dr. phil. dissertation, Department for Social Anthropology, University of Bern.

AGSA (2014). 'Auditor General South Africa. 100 Years of Legacy and Legends'. Available at: www.agsa.co.za/Portals/0/AG/AGSA%20Legacy%20Book.pdf [6 July 2018]

Anders, Gerhard (2008). 'The Normativity of Numbers: World Bank and IMF Conditionality'. *PoLAR: Political and Legal Anthropology Review* 31(2): 187–202.

Arndt, Christiane (2008). 'The Politics of Governance Ratings'. *International Public Management Journal* 11(3): 275–297.

Arndt, Christiane and Charles Oman (2006). *Uses and Abuses of Governance Indicators*. Paris: Development Centre of the Organisation for Economic Co-operation and Development.

Artz, Lilian and Dee Smythe (2007a). 'Case Attrition in Rape Cases. A Comparative Analysis'. *South African Journal of Criminal Justice* 20 (2): 158–181.

Artz, Lilian and Dee Smythe (2007b). 'Losing Ground? Making Sense of Attrition in Rape Cases'. *SA Crime Quarterly* 22: 13–20.

'Assets worth R24 m seized from ANC MP'. (26 October 2012). Available at: www.iol.co.za/news/crime-courts/assets-worth-r24 m-seized-from-anc-mp-1.1412184#.U-JIARY8hd0 [26 October 2012]

Barrell, Howard and Mungo Soggott (17 June 1998). 'Nice guy, but can he do the job?' *Mail & Guardian*.

Basson, Adrian (11 February 2012). 'How the NPA lost its way'. *City Press*. Available at: www.citypress.co.za/columnists/how-the-npa-lost-its-way-20120211/ [13 March 2012]

Bateman, Barry (21 May 2010). 'Criminals our best allies in war on crime'. *IOL*. Available at: www.iol.co.za/news/south-africa/criminals-our-best-allies-in-war-on-crime-484691 / [13 March 2012]

Beek, Jan (2012). 'There Should Be No Open Doors in the Police: Criminal Investigations in Northern Ghana as Boundary Work'. *The Journal of Modern African Studies* 50(4): 551–572.

Beek, Jan and Mirko Göpfert (2011). '"Ground work" and "Paper Work": Feldzugang bei Polizeiorganisationen in Westafrika'. *Zeitschrift Fur Ethnologie* 136: 189–214.

Bezuidenhout, Jessica (16 January 2018). 'Asset Forfeiture Unit eyes R50 Billion in state capture loot'. *Daily Maverick*. Available at: www.dailymaverick.co.za/article/2018-01-16-newsflash-asset-forfeiture-unit-eyes-r50-billion-in-state-capture-loot/#.Wz969q35xMM [5 July 2018]

Bierschenk, Thomas (2010). 'States at Work in West Africa: Sedimentation, Fragmentation and Normative Double-Binds'. Working Paper of the Department of Anthropology and African Studies, Johannes Gutenberg University. No. 113. Mainz: Ifeas.

(2008). 'The Everyday Functioning of Benin's Legal System'. *The Journal of Legal Pluralism and Unofficial Law* 57: 101–140.

Bierschenk, Thomas and Jean-Piere Olivier de Sardan (eds.) (2014). *States at Work: Dynamics of African Bureaucracies*. Leiden: Brill Academic Publishing.

(2014). Ethnographies of Public Services in Africa: An Emerging Research Paradigm. In Bierschenk, Thomas and Jean-Piere Olivier de Sardan (eds.) *States at Work. Dynamics of African Bureaucracies*. Leiden: Brill Academic Publishing, 35–65.

Blundo, Giorgio, Jean-Pierre Olivier de Sardan, N. B. Arifari, and M. T. Alou. (2006). *Everyday Corruption and the State. Citizens and Public Officials in Africa*. London: Zed Books.

Boström, Magnus and Christina Garsten (eds.) (2008). *Organizing Transnational Accountability*. Cheltenham: Edward Elgar.

Bourgoin, France (2012). On Being Cosmopolitan: Lifestyle and Identity of African Finance Professionals in Johannesburg. In Abbink, Jon and Tijo Salverda (eds.) *The Anthropology of Elites. Power, Culture, and the Complexities of Distinction*. New York: Palgrave Macmillan, 227–248.

Bowker, Geoffrey and Susan Leigh Star (2000). *Sorting Things Out: Classification and Its Consequences*. Cambridge, MA: MIT Press.

Boyer, Dominic (2008). 'Thinking through the Anthropology of Experts'. *Anthropology in Action* 15(2): 38–46.

Breidenstein, Georg, Stefan Hirschauer, Herbert Kalthoff and Boris Nieswand (2013). *Ethnografie. Die Praxis der Feldforschung*. Konstanz UVK Verlagsgesellschaft.

Broughton, Tania (10 December 2002). 'Shocking: SA's conviction rate for rape'. *IOL*. Available at: www.iol.co.za/news/south-africa/shocking-sa-s-conviction-rate-for-rape-1.98486?ot=inmsa.ArticlePrintPageLayout.ot [6 August 2013]

(7 November 2001). '"Drug baron" to pay for fight against crime'. *IOL*. Available at: www.iol.co.za/news/south-africa/drug-baron-to-pay-for-fight-against-crime-1.76538?ot=inmsa.ArticlePrintPageLayout.ot [5 May 2011]

(3 November 1999). 'Elite unit flooded by potential recruits'. *IOL*. Available at: www.iol.co.za/news/south-africa/elite-unit-flooded-by-potential-recruits-1.18365?ot=inmsa.ArticlePrintPageLayout.ot [5 May 2011]

Bruce, David (2005). 'Interpreting the Body Count. South African Statistics on Lethal Police Violence'. *South African Review of Sociology* 36(2): 141–159.

Budniok, Jan (2012). The Politics of Integrity. Becoming and Being a Judge in Ghana. Dr. phil. dissertation, Department of Anthropology and African Studies, Mainz, Johannes Gutenberg University.

Burman, Sandra and Wilfried Schaerf (1990). 'Creating People's Justice: Street Committees and People's Courts in a South African City'. *Law and Society Review* 24: 693–745.

Büscher, Monika and John Urry (2009). 'Mobile Methods and the Empirical'. *European Journal of Social Theory* 12(1): 99–116.

Buur, Lars (2003). 'Crime and Punishment on the Margins of the Postapartheid State'. *Anthropology and Humanism* 28(1): 23–42.

Challenor, Martin (18 October 1999). 'Smith has 11 days to appeal asset swoop'. *IOL*. Available at: www.iol.co.za/news/south-africa/smith-has-11-days-to-appeal-asset-swoop-1.16511?ot=inmsa.ArticlePrintPageLayout.ot [21 March 2012]

Chipkin, Ivor. (2011). 'Transcending Bureaucracy: State Transformation in the Age of the Manager'. *Transformation* 77: 31–51.

CIETafrica (1998). *Prevention of Sexual Violence: A Social Audit of the Role of the Police in the Jurisdiction of Johannesburg's Southern Metropolitan Local Council*. Johannesburg: CIETafrica.

Comaroff, Jean and John Comaroff (2006). 'Figuring Crime: Quantifacts and the Production of the Un/Real'. *Public Culture* 18(1): 209–246.

Comaroff, John and Jean Comaroff (2004). 'Criminal Justice, Cultural Justice: The Limits of Liberalism and the Pragmatics of Difference in the New South Africa'. *American Ethnologist* 31(2): 188–204.

Czarniawska, Barbara (2008). 'Organizing: How to Study It and How to Write about It'. *Qualitative Research in Organizations and Management: An International Journal* 3(1): 4–20.

(2007). *Shadowing: And Other Techniques for Doing Fieldwork in Modern Societies*. Copenhagen: Copenhagen Business School Press.

Das, Veena and Deborah Poole (2004). *Anthropology in the Margins of the State*. Santa Fe, NM, Oxford, UK: School of American Research Press.

Daston, Lorraine (1995). 'The Moral Economy of Science'. *Osiris* 10: 3–24.

Davis, Angela J. (2007). *Arbitrary Justice: The Power of the American Prosecutor*. New York: Oxford University Press.

Davis, Dennis and Michelle le Roux (2009). *Precedent and Possibility: The (Ab) Use of Law in South Africa*. Johannesburg: Double Story Publishers.

Davis, Kevin E., Benedict Kingsbury and Sally Engle Merry (2010). 'Indicators as a Technology of Global Governance'. *ILJ Working Paper* 2010/2. New York: New York University School of Law.

Davis, Kevin E., Angelina Fisher, Benedict Kingsbury, and Sally Engle Merry (eds.) (2015). *Governance by Indicators: Global Power through Classification and Ranking*. Oxford: Oxford University Press.

Davis, Rebecca (29 May 2018). 'Why the latest Gupta court victory bodes badly for the NPA- and South Africa'. *Daily Maverick*. Available at: www.dailymaverick.co.za/article/2018-05-29-why-the-latest-gupta-court-victory-bodes-badly-for-the-npa-and-south-africa/#.WzzZEq35yjQ [30 May 2018]

De Lange, Ilse (10 October 2013). 'Clean audit for NPA – elusive targets remain'. *The Citizen*. Available at: citizen.co.za/65399/sex-crime-convictions-fall-short/ [10 October 2013]

Desrosières, Alain (2015). Retroaction: How indicators Feed Back onto Quantified Actors and the Effects, Intended or Not. In Rottenburg, Richard, Sally Engle Merry, Sung-Joon Park and Johanna Mugler (eds.) A *World of Indicators*. Cambridge: Cambridge University Press.

(2009). 'How to Be Real and Conventional: A Discussion of the Quality Criteria of Official Statistics'. *Minerva* 47(3): 307–322.

(2001). 'How Real Are Statistics? Four Possible Attitudes'. *Social Research* 68(2): 339–355.

(1998). *The politics of Large Numbers: A History of Statistical Reasoning*. Cambridge, MA: Harvard University Press.

De Vos, Pierre (11 April 2018). 'How credible are the racketeering corruption money laundering and fraud charges against Jacob Zuma'. *Constitutionally Speaking. This Blog Deals with Political and Social Issues in South Africa, Mostly from the Perspective of Constitutional Law. Written by Pierre de Vos*. Available at: constitutionallyspeaking.co.za/how-credible-are-the-racketeering-corruption-money-laundering-and-fraud-charges-against-jacob-zuma/ [5 July 2018]

(1 September 2016). 'Why Legal Safeguards Alone Cannot Protect Independence of the Hawks'. *Constitutionally Speaking Blog*. Available at: constitutionallyspeaking.co.za/why-legal-safeguards-alone-cannot-protect-independence-of-the-hawks/ [20 May 2018]

(27 May 2013). 'Breytenbach: Too Little Fear, Favour and Prejudice?' *Constitutionally Speaking Blog*. Available at: https://constitutionallyspeaking.co.za/breytenbach-too-little-fear-favour-and-prejudice/ [5 July 2018]

(7 March 2012). 'Thoughts on Scape Goating and Endemic Corruption'. *Constitutionally Speaking Blog*. Available at: http://constitutionallyspeaking.co.za/category/scorpions/ [18 August 2012]

De Wee, K. (2009). Presentation to the Selected Committee on Security and Constitutional Development. NPA Acting CEO NPA. 1 September 2009.

De Wet, Phillip (12 September 2016). 'The NPA's Annual Report figures show a troubled criminal justice system'. *Mail & Guardian*. Available at: mg.co.za/article/2016-09-12-the-npas-annual-report-figures-show-a troubled-criminal-justice-system [5 July 2018]

Dixon, Bill (2004). Cosmetic Crime Prevention. In Dixon Bill and Elrena van der Spuy (eds.) *Justice Gained? Crime and Crime Control in South Africa's Transition*. Cape Town: UCT Press, 163–192.

DOJCD (2013). Report on the Re-establishment of Sexual Offences Courts. Ministerial Advisory Task Team on the Adjudication of Sexual Offences Matters. August. Available at: www.justice.gov.za/vg/sxo/2013-sxo-courts-report-aug2013.pdf [5 July 2018]

Dowdle, Michael W. (2006). *Public Accountability: Designs, Dilemmas and Experiences*. Cambridge: Cambridge University Press

Du Toi, Pieter (29 May 2018). 'Gupta judgment shows how deep in crisis the NPA finds itself'. *Huffpost*. Available at: https://www.huffingtonpost.co.za/2018/05/29/gupta-judgment-shows-how-deep-in-crisis-the-npa-finds-itself_a_23445772/ [25 June 2018]

Ehlers, Louise (2008). Frustrated Potential: The Short and Long Term Impact of Pretrial Services in South Africa. In Berry David (ed) *Pretrial Detention*. New York, Budapest: Open Society Justice Initiative, 121–140.

Eisner, Marc A. (1991). *Antitrust and the Triumph of Economics: Institutions, Expertise, and Policy Change*. Chapel Hill: University of North Carolina Press.

Emerson, Robert M., Rachel Fretz and Linda Shaw (1995). *Writing Ethnographic Fieldnotes*. Chicago: University of Chicago Press.

Espeland, Wendy Nelson (1997). 'Authority by the Numbers: Porter on Quantification, Discretion, and the Legitimation of Expertise. Trust in Numbers: The Pursuit of Objectivity in Sciences and Public Life by Theodore M. Porter'. *Law & Social Inquiry* 22(4): 1107–1133.

Espeland, Wendy Nelson and Michael Sauder (2016). *Engines of Anxiety: Academic Rankings, Reputations, and Accountability*. New York: Russell Sage Foundation.

(2009). 'Rankings and Diversity'. *Southern California Review of Law and Social Justice* 18(3): 587–608.

(2007). 'Rankings and Reactivity: How Public Measures Recreate Social Worlds'. *The American Journal of Sociology* 113(1): 1–40.

Espeland, Wendy Nelson and Mitchell L. Stevens (2008). 'A Sociology of Quantification'. *Archives Europeennes De Sociologie* 49(3): 397–432.

(1998). 'Commensuration as a Social Process'. *Annual Review of Sociology* 24 (1): 313–343.

Espeland, Wendy Nelson and Berit I. Vannebo (2007). 'Accountability, Quantification, and Law'. *Annual Review of Law and Social Science* 3(1): 21–43.

Evans, Tony (2011). 'Professionals, Managers and Discretion: Critiquing Street-Level Bureaucracy'. *British Journal of Social Work* 41(2): 368–386.

Fagan, Hannes (2005). 'Our Bursting Prisons'. *The Advocate*. Available at: www.csvr.org.za/wits/confpaps/fagan.htm. [5 August 2009]

Faull, Andrew (2010). 'Missing the Target. When Measuring Performance Undermines Police Effectiveness'. *SA Crime Quarterly* 31: 19–25.

Fernandez, Lovell (1993). 'Profile of a Vague Figure: The South African Public Prosecutor'. *South African Law Journal* 110(1): 115–126.

Fionda, Julia (1995). *Public Prosecutors and Discretion: A Comparative Study*. Oxford: Clarendon Press.

Flick, Uwe (20 February 2001). 'Triangulation. Eine Einführung. *Wiesbaden Verlag für Sozialwissenschaften*. Forfeiture Unit goes after the big fish'. Available at: www.iol.co.za/news/south-africa/forfeiture-unit-goes-after-the-big-fish-1.60078#.U-JGvhY8hd0 [21 March 2012]

Garfinkel, Harold (1967). *Studies in Ethnomethodology*. Englewood Cliffs, NJ: Prentice-Hall.

Geissler, Wenzel, Richard Rottenburg and Julia Zenker (2012). *Rethinking Biomedicine and Governance in Africa. Contributions from Anthropology*. Bielefeld: Transcript.

Gifford, Gill and Peta Krost (13 August 1999). 'Supercops hit their fifth hijack jackpot'. *IOL*. Available at: www.iol.co.za/news/south-africa/supercops-hit-their-fifth-hijack-jackpot-1.9110#.U-JEOxY8hd0. [5 May 2011]

Göpfert, Mirko (2012). 'Security in Niamey. An Anthropological Perspective on Policing and an Act of Terrorism in Niamey'. *Journal of Modern African Studies* 50 (1): 53–74.

Gordon, Sanford C. and Gregory A. Huber (2009). 'The Political Economy of Prosecution'. *Annual Review of Law and Social Science* 5: 135–156.

(2007). 'The Effect of Electoral Competitiveness on Incumbent Behavior'. *Quarterly Journal of Political Science* 2: 107–138.

Hacking, Ian (1990). *The Taming of Chance*. Cambridge England, New York: Cambridge University Press.

Haggerty, Kevin D. (2001a). *Making Crime Count*. Toronto, Buffalo: University of Toronto Press.

(2001b). 'Negotiated Measures: The Institutional Micropolitics of Official Criminal Justice Statistics'. *Studies in History and Philosophy of Science* 32 (4): 705–722.

Hannerz, Ulf (2003). 'Being There ... and There ... and There!: Reflections on Multi-Site Ethnography'. *Ethnography* 4(2): 201–216.

Hartley, Wynham (16 September 2013). 'NPA misses over half its targets: auditor-general'. *Business Day*. Available at: www.bdlive.co.za/national/

law/2013/09/16/npa-misses-over-half-its-targets-auditor-general [1 March 2014]

Heintz, Bettina (2010). 'Numerische Differenz. Überlegungen zu einer Soziologie des (quantitativen) Vergleichs'. *Zeitschrift für Soziologie* 39 (3): 162–181.

Herselman, Ivan (19 April 2017). 'Op-Ed: Personal legal cost orders against rogue public officials are the frontline in the war against impunity'. *Daily Maverick*. Available at: www.dailymaverick.co.za/article/2017-04-19-op-ed-personal-legal-cost-orders-against-rogue-public-officials-are-the-front line-in-the-war-against-impunity/#.WzzU_K35yjQ [4 July 2018]

'High conviction rate for Cape courts: NPA' (29 June 2012). Available at: www.iol.co.za/news/crime-courts/high-conviction-rate-for-cape-court s-npa-1.1331318#.U-NL5RY8hd1 [15 August 2012]

Ho, Karen Z. (2009). *Liquidated: An Ethnography of Wall Street*. Durham: Duke University Press.

Hofmeyer, Willie (2007). *The Role of Specialists Units. Power Point Presentation at The National Prosecuting Authority of South Africa Stake Holder Conference*. Gallagher Estate, Johannesburg. 28–30 March 2007.

Hood, Christopher C. (2007). 'Public Service Management by Numbers: Why Does It Vary? Where Has It Come from? What are the Gaps and the Puzzles?' *Public Money & Management* 27(2): 95–102.

Hood, Christopher, Ruth Dixon and Craig Beeston (2008). 'Rating the Rankings: Assessing International Rankings of Public Service Performance'. *International Public Management Journal* 11(3): 298–358.

Hornberger, Julia (2009). Translating Human Rights: A Police-Migrant Encounter in Johannesburg. In Jefferson, Andrew and Steffen Jensen (eds.) *State Violence and Human Rights: State Officials in the South*. New York: Routlegde-Cavendish, 79–101.

Hosken, Graeme (30 October 2017). 'The 8% percent conviction rate is disturbing'. *Sowetan Live*. Available at: www.sowetanlive.co.za/news/201 7-10-30-the-8-conviction-rate-is-disturbing-how-the-justice-system-fail s-rape-victims/ [5 July 2018]

'Households under siege by armed robbers' (19 July 2009). Available at: www .iol.co.za/news/south-africa/households-under-siege-by-armed-robbers-1.450156?ot=inmsa.ArticlePrintPageLayout.ot [19 July 2009]

Huber, Gregory A. and Sanford C. Gordon (2004). 'Accountability and Coercion: Is Justice Blind When It Runs for Office?' *American Journal of Political Science* 48: 247–263.

Hunter, Quaanitah (4 July 2018). 'Analysis: Ramaphosa's legal strategy may backfire'. *First Thing / Daily Maverick*. Available at: firstthing .dailymaverick.co.za/article?id=109611#.WzzTs635yjR [4 July 2018]

Jefferson, Andrew and Steffen Jensen (2009). *State Violence and Human Rights: State Officials in the South*. New York: Routledge-Cavendish.

Jehle, Jörg-Martin, Marianne Wade and Beatrix Elsner (2008). 'Prosecution and Diversion within Criminal Justice Systems in Europe. Aims and Design of a Comparative Study'. *European Journal on Criminal Policy and Research* 14(2–3): 93-99.

Jensen, Steffen (2009). The Vision of the State: Audiences, Enchantments and Policing in South Africa. In Jefferson, Andrew and Steffen Jensen (eds.) *State Violence and Human Rights: State Officials in the South.* New York: Routlegde-Cavendish, 60–78.

Johnson, David T. (2012). 'Japan's Prosecution System'. *Crime and Justice* 41 (1): 35–74.

'Judgement day for Tony Yengeni' (11 November 2005). Available at: mg.co.za/article/2005-11-11-judgement-day-for-tony-yengeni [26 October 2012]

Kalthoff, Herbert (2000). 'Entscheiden unter Ungewissheit: Bankwirtschaftliche Standortsuche in Mittel- und Osteuropa'. *Zeitschrift für Soziologie* 29(2): 103–120.

Kalthoff, Herbert, Richard Rottenburg and Hans-Jürgen Wegener (eds.) (2000). *Facts and Figures – Economic Representations and Practices.* Jahrbuch Ökonomie und Gesellschaft Band16. Marburg: Metropolis-Verlag.

Kinnes, Irvin and Gareth Newham (2012). 'Why an Anti-corruption Agency Should Not Be in the SAPA'. *SA Crime Quarterly* 39: 33–40.

Kipnis, Andrew B. (2008). 'Audit Cultures: Neoliberal Governmentality, Socialist Legacy, or Technologies of Governing?' *American Ethnologist* 35(2): 275–289.

Klug, Heinz (1988). 'The South African Judicial Order and the Future: A Comparative Analysis of the South African Judicial System and Judicial Transitions in Zimbabwe, Mozambique, and Nicaragua'. *Hastings International and Comparative Law Review* 12: 173–234.

Koppell, Jonathan G. S. (2005). 'Pathologies of Accountability: ICANN and the Challenge of "Multiple Accountabilities Disorder"'. *Public Administration Review* 65(1): 94–108.

Krajewski, Krzysztof (2012). 'Prosecution and Prosecutors in Poland: In Quest of Independence'. *Crime and Justice* 41(1): 75–116.

Lampland, Martha (2010). 'False Numbers as Formalizing Practices'. *Social Studies of Science* 40(3): 377–404.

Lampland, Martha and Susan Leigh Star (2009). *Standards and Their Stories: How Quantifying, Classifying, and Formalizing Practices Shape Everyday Life.* Ithaca, NY: Cornell University Press.

Latour, Bruno (1987). *Science in Action: How to Follow Scientists and Engineers through Society.* Cambridge, MA: Harvard University Press.

Lau, Thomas and Stephan Wolff (1983). 'Der Einstieg in das Untersuchungsfeld als soziologischer Lernprozeß'. *Kölner Zeitschrift für Soziologie und Sozialpsychologie* 35(3): 417–437.

Law, John (1996). 'The Manager and His Powers Mediaset Convention'. Venice Mediaset Convention, Venice, 12 November.

Leggett, Ted (2003). 'What Do the Police Do? Performance Measurement and the SAPS'. Paper 66. Pretoria: Institute for Security Studies.

(18 August 2000). 'South Africa: Crime statistics moratorium is no solution'. *Mail & Guardian*. Available at: allafrica.com/stories/200008180068.html [11 April 2011]

Leggett, Ted, Antoinette Louw, Martin Schönteich and Makubetse Sekhonyane (2003). *Criminal Justice in Review 2001/2002*. Monograph 88. Pretoria: Institute for Security Studies.

Le May, Jean (2 September 2000). 'Chasm grows between Scorpions and cops'. *IOL*. Available at: iol.co.za/news/south-africa/chasm-grows-between-scorpions-and-cops-1.46339#.U-JL5xY8hd0 [5 May 2011]

Lenart, Severin (2013). Chiefs and Witches in a Gendered World. Legitimacy and The Disputing Process in the South African Low Veld. Dr. phil. dissertation, Max Planck Institute for Social Anthropology, Halle, Martin-Luther-University.

Lewin, Julius (1944). 'Native Courts and British Justice in Africa'. *Africa: Journal of the International African Institute* 14(8): 448–453.

Lindwert, Jessica (2008). The Political Logics of Accountability: From 'Doing the Right Thing' to 'Doing the Thing Right'. In Boström, Magnus and Christina Garsten (eds.) *Organizing Transnational Accountability*. Cheltenham: Edward Elgar, 147–159.

Lipsky, Michael (1980). *Street – Level Bureaucracy. Dilemmas of the Individual in Public Services*. New York: Russell Sage Foundation.

Lobban, Michael (1996). *White Man's Justice: South African Political Trials in the Black Consciousness Era*. Oxford, New York: Clarendon Press, Oxford University Press.

Luna, Erik and Marianne Wade (2012). *The Prosecutor in Transnational Perspective*. New York: Oxford University Press.

Madibogo, Julia (14 October 2016). 'NPA's Willie Hofmeyr publicly backs Pravin Gordhan'. *Business Live*. Available at: www.businesslive.co.za/news/latest-news/2016-10-14-npas-willie-hofmeyr-publicly-backs-pravin-gordhan/ [5 July 2018]

Marais, Hein (2011). *South Africa Pushed to the Limit. The Political Economy of Change*. Claremont: University of Cape Town Press.

Marcus, George (1995). 'Ethnography in/of the World System: The Emergence of Multi-sited Ethnography'. *Annual Review of Anthropology* 24: 95–117.

Marks, Monique (2004). 'Researching Police Transformation: The Ethnographic Imperative'. *British Journal for Criminology* 44(6): 866–888.

(2000). 'Transforming Police Organizations from Within'. *British Journal of Criminology* 40(4): 557–573.

Marks, Monique and Clifford Shearing (2005). 'Reconceptualising Reform Practice in South African Policing'. *South African Review of Sociology* 36 (2): 131–140.

Masemola, Lesego and Otto Hanti (4 September 2008). 'Prosecutors to get pay rise, a year late'. *IOL*. Available at: iol.co.za/news/south-africa/prosecutors-to-get-pay-rise-a-year-late-1.415048?ot=inmsa.ArticlePrintPageLayout.ot [5 May 2011]

Mashaw, Jerry L. (2006). Accountability and Institutional Design: Some Thoughts on the Grammar on Governance. In Dowdle, Michael W. (ed) *Public Accountability: Designs, Dilemmas and Experiences*. Cambridge: Cambridge University Press, 115–156.

Matisonn, John (5 October 2001). 'Yengeni hits out at "all-white" Scorpions'. *IOL*. Available at: iol.co.za/news/politics/yengeni-hits-out-at-all-white-scorpions-1.74762#.U-JK9RY8hd0 [5 May 2011]

Maughan, Karyn (31 May 2018). 'Ramaphosa leaves Zuma to fly solo in his legal fees battle'. *Times Live*. Available at: www.timeslive.co.za/politics/2018-05-31-ramaphosa-leaves-zuma-to-fly-solo-in-his-legal-fees-battle/ [4 July 2018]

(2008a). 'Prosecutors set to receive salary increase'. *IOL*. 11 September. Available at: www.iol.co.za/news/south-africa/prosecutors-set-to-receive-salary-increase-1.416048#.U-I9-hY8hd0. [5 May 2011]

(2008b). 'We'll see you in court'. *IOL*. 2 October. Available at: www.iol.co.za/news/south-africa/we-ll-see-you-in-court-1.418568#.U-JAGBY8hd0. [5 May 2011]

(2008c). 'Prosecutors scrap for pay'. *IOL*. 18 August. Available at: iol.co.za/news/south-africa/prosecutors-scrap-for-pay-1.412788#.U-I-dRY8hd0. [5 May 2011]

Maylam, Paul (1990). 'The Rise and Decline of Urban Apartheid in South Africa'. *African Affairs* 89(354): 57–84.

Mennicken, Andrea and Hendrik Vollmer (2007). *Zahlenwerk: Kalkulation, Organisation und Gesellschaft*. Wiesbaden: VS Verlag für Sozialwissenschaften.

Merry, Sally Engle (2016). *The Seductions of Quantification. Measuring Human Rights, Gender Violence, and Sex Trafficking*. Chicago: Chicago University Press.

(2011). 'Measuring the World: Indicators, Human Rights, and Global Governance: With CA comment by John M. Conley'. *Current Anthropology* 52 (Supplementary Issue 3): S83–S95.

(2006). 'New Legal Realism and the Ethnography of Transnational Law'. *Law & Social Inquiry* 31(4): 975–995.

(1979). 'Going to Court. Strategies of Dispute Management in an American Urban Neighborhood'. *Law & Society Review* 13(4): 891–925.

Merton, Richard K. (1959). Notes on Problem-Finding in Sociology. In Merton, Robert K., Leonard Broom and Leonard S. Cottrell Jr. (eds.) *Sociology Today: Problems and Prospects*. New York: Basic Books.

Messner, Martin (2009). 'The Limits of Accountability'. *Accounting, Organizations and Society* 34(8): 918–938.

Migdal, Joel S. and Klaus Schlichte (2005). Rethinking the State. In Schlichte, Klaus (ed) *The Dynamics of States. The Formation and Crises of State Domination*. Aldershot, Hants, England, Burlington: Ashgate, 1–40.

Momberg, Eleanor (14 June 2009). 'Date set for OSD to take effect'. *IOL*. Available at: www.iol.co.za/news/south-africa/date-set-for-osd-to-take-effect-1.446351. [5 May 2011]

Mosse, David (2006). 'Anti-social Anthropology? Objectivity, Objection, and the Ethnography of Public Policy and Professional Communities'. *Journal of the Royal Anthropological Institute* 12(4): 935–956.

Mposo, Nontando (23 October 2012). 'Alarm over rape conviction rate'. *IOL*. Available at: www.iol.co.za/news/crime-courts/alarm-over-rape-conviction-rate-1.1409314#.U-OBwxY8hd0 [23 October 2012]

Mugler, Johanna (2006). Life behind the Walls. Crime Prevention and a Sense of Security in Hout Bay, South Africa. Unpublished MA Thesis, Institut für Ethnologie, Ludwig-Maximilians-Universität München.

(2005). 'To Live and Move in Safety: Fear of Crime, Crime and the Social Consequences of Spatial Security Strategies'. *Postamble* 1(2): 19–33.

Münch, Richard (2011). *Akademischer Kapitalismus: zur politischen Ökonomie der Hochschulreform*. Berlin: Suhrkamp.

Munro, Rolland and Jan Mouritsen (1996). *Accountability: Power, Ethos and the Technologies of Managing*. London, Boston, MA: International Thomson Business Press.

Mvoko (1 March 1996). 'What's the use of justice when there is no one to run it'. *Mail & Guardian*. Available at: www.mg.co.za/article/1996-03-01-whats-the-use-of-justice-when-theres-no-one-to-run-it [18 Jul 2018]

Newham, Gareth (2013). 'The Tatane case raises hard questions for South Africa's National Prosecuting Authority'. Available at: issafrica.org/crimehub/news/the-tatane-case-raises-hard-questions-for-south-africas-national-prosecuting-authority [11 April 2013]

Ngalwa, Sibusiso (4 May 2007). 'NPA faced with crippling situation'. *IOL*. Available at: www.iol.co.za/news/south-africa/npa-faced-with-crippling-situation-1.351495?ot=inmsa.ArticlePrintPageLayout.ot [5 May 2011]

Ngqiyaza, Bonile (19 August 2008). 'Prosecutors stage "silent" pay protest'. *IOL*. Available at: www.iol.co.za/news/south-africa/prosecutors-stage-silent-pay-protest-1.412966#.U-I9gRY8hd0 [5 May 2011]

'NPA defends reshuffling of prosecutors' (30 March 2010). *Mail & Guardian*. Available at: mg.co.za/article/2010-03-30-npa-defends-reshuffling-of-prosecutors [5 August 2013]

'NPA haemorrhages key staff' (28 January 2005). *Mail & Guardian*. Available at: mg.co.za/article/2005-01-28-npa-haemorrhages-key-staff [5 August 2013]

'NPA records 93.8 conviction rate' (13 November 2016). *SA NEWS*. Available at: www.sanews.gov.za/south-africa/npa-records-938-conviction-rate [5 July 2018]

'NPA secures 88% conviction rate in High Courts' (1 March 2013). *SA NEWS*. Available at: www.sanews.gov.za/south-africa/npa-secures-88-conviction-rate-high-courts [5 August 2013]

'NPA's AFU sets eyes on Gupta linked companies' (1 January 2018). Available at: www.enca.com/south-africa/npas-afu-sets-eyes-on-gupta-linked-companies [5 July 2018]

The National Prosecuting Authority of South Africa.

Annual Report 2002 / 2003.

Annual Report 2003 / 2004.

Annual Report 2004 / 2005.

Annual Report 2005 / 2006.

Annual Report 2006 / 2007.

Annual Report 2007 / 2008.

Annual Report 2008 / 2009.

Annual Report 2009 / 2010.

Annual Report 2010 / 2011.

Annual Report 2011 / 2012.

Annual Report 2012 / 2013.

Annual Report 2013 / 2014.

Annual Report 2014 / 2015.

Annual Report 2015 / 2016.

Annual Report 2016 / 2017.

Performance Plan 2012 / 2013.

Performance Plan 2011 / 2012.

Quarterly Performance Overview.

Report of Public Prosecutions. Quarter 2. 2011 / 2012.

HR Oversight Report 2010 / 2011.

HR Oversight Report 2009 / 2010.

HR Oversight Report 2008 / 2009.

Crime and Criminal Justice Survey. *Survey Findings Report*. *Final Report April 2009*.

(2007a). Stake Holder Conference Programme. Gallagher Estate, Johannesburg. 28–30 March 2007.

(2007b). *Executive Summary*. *Strategy 2020*.

(2004). *Ethics. A Practical Guide to the Ethical Code of Conduct for Members of the National Prosecuting Authority*.

(undated). *Aspirant Prosecutor Programme*.

(undated). *Code of Ethics*.

OSF (2006). 'Guidelines for the Establishment and Functioning of Hatfield-type Community Courts, December 2006'. Pretoria: Open Society Foundation for South Africa and the Department of Justice and Constitutional Development.

Otto, Hanti (27 August 2008). 'Meeting sought to avert lawyers strike'. *IOL*. File with the author. Retrieved from internet on 5 May 2011.

Peters, Katharina (2001). 'When Reform Comes into Play: Budgeting as Negotiations between Administrations'. *Accounting, Organizations and Society* 26(6): 521–539.

(2000). 'Die Doppelkonstruktion budgetärer Wirklichkeit. Repräsentationen und Praktiken der Finanzverwaltung'. *Zeitschrift für Soziologie* 29(2): 121–137.

Porter, Theodore M. (1995). *Trust in Numbers: The Pursuit of Objectivity in Science and Public Life*. Princeton, NJ: Princeton University Press.

(1986). *The Rise of Statistical Thinking, 1820–1900*. Princeton, NJ: Princeton University Press.

Posel, Deborah (1997). *The Making of Apartheid, 1948-1961: Conflict and Compromise*. Oxford, New York: Clarendon Press, Oxford University Press.

Power, Michael (2008). Foreword. In Boström, Magnus and Christina Garsten (eds.) *Organizing Transnational Accountability*. Cheltenham: Edward Elgar, xv–xvii.

(2004). 'Counting, Control and Calculation: Reflections on Measuring and Management'. *Human Relations* 57(6): 765–783.

(2003). 'Evaluating the Audit Explosion'. *Law & Policy* 25(3): 185–202.

(1997). *The Audit Society: Rituals of Verification*. Oxford, England, New York: Oxford University Press.

'Prosecutors courting pay row' (6 April 2005). *NEWS 24*. Available at: www.news24.com/SouthAfrica/News/Prosecutors-courting-pay-row-20050406 [5 August 2013]

'Prosecutors to get back pay' (3 September 2008). *IOL*. Available at: iol.co.za/news/south-africa/prosecutors-to-get-back-pay-1.414978#.U-I9FBY8hd0 [5 April 2012]

Public Protector (2016). *State of Capture. Report on an Investigation into Alleged Improper and Unethical Conduct by the President and Other State Functionaries Relating to Alleged Improper Relationships and Involvement of the Gupta Family in the Removal and Appointment of Ministers and Directors of State-Owned Enterprises Resulting in Improper and Possibly Corrupt Award of State Contracts and Benefits to the Gupta Family's Businesses – Report*

No 6 of 2016/17. 14 October. Available at: www.pprotect.org/sites/default/files/legislation_report/State_Capture_14October2016.pdf [1 May 2018]

'Radebe puts on hold plans on AFU' (20 April 2010). *Polity Org*. Available at: www.polity.org.za/print-version/radebe-puts-on-hold-plans-on-afu-2010-04-30 [25 May 2018]

Reckwitz, Andreas (2003). 'Grundelemente einer Theorie sozialer Praktiken. Eine sozialtheoretische Persepktive'. *Zeitschrift für Soziologie* 32(4): 282–301.

(2002a). 'The Status of the "Material" in Theories of Culture: From "Social Structure" to "Artefacts"'. *Journal for the Theory of Social Behaviour* 32(2): 195–217.

(2002b). 'Toward a Theory of Social Practices'. *European Journal of Social Theory* 5(2): 243–263.

Redpath, Jean (2012). *Failing to Prosecute? Assessing the State of the National Prosecuting Authority in South Africa*. Monograph 186. Pretoria: Institute for Security Studies.

Roitman, Janet. L. (2005). *Fiscal Disobedience: An Anthropology of Economic Regulation in Central Africa*. Princeton, NJ: Princeton University Press.

Ross, Robert J. (1999). *A Concise History of South Africa*. Cambridge: Cambridge University Press.

Ross, Robert J. and Alicia F. Schrikker (2012). The VOC Official Elite. In Worden, Nigel (ed) *Cape Town between East and West. Social Identities in a Dutch Colonial Town*. Johannesburg: Jacana, 26–45.

Rottenburg, Richard (2009). *Far-fetched Facts: A Parable of Development Aid*. Cambridge, MA: MIT Press.

(2002). *Weit hergeholte Fakten: eine Parabel der Entwicklungshilfe*. Stuttgart: Lucius & Lucius.

(2000). Accountability for Development Aid. In Herbert Kalthoff, Richard Rottenburg and Hans-Jürgen Wagener (eds.) *Facts and Figures; Economic Representations and Practices*. Ökonomie und Gesellschaft: Jahrbuch 16. Marburg: Metropolis-Verlag, 143–173.

Rottenburg, Richard, Sally Engle Merry, Sung-Joon Park and Johanna Mugler (2015). *A World of Indicators. The Making of Governmental Knowledge Through Quantification*. Cambridge: Cambridge University Press.

Sauder, Michael and Wendy Nelson Espeland (2009). 'The Discipline of Rankings: Tight Coupling and Organizational Change'. *American Sociological Review* 74(1): 63–82.

(2007). Fear of Falling: The Effects of U.S. News & World Report Rankings on U.S. Law Schools. Law School Admission Council Research Report Series.

(2006). 'Strength in Numbers? The Advantages of Multiple Rankings'. *Indiana Law Journal* 81(1): 205–227.

Savage, Michael (1986). 'The Imposition of Pass Laws on the African Population in South Africa 1916–1984'. *African Affairs* 85(339): 181–205.

Schafer, Debbie (2012a). 'Conviction rate is not 90%'. Available at: www.politicsweb.co.za/politicsweb/view/politicsweb/en/page71619?oid=303568&sn=Detail&pid=71619 [4 June 2012]

(2012b). 'NPA still missing the plot on conviction rate'. Available at: www.politicsweb.co.za/politicsweb/view/politicsweb/en/page71619?oid=304570&sn=Detail&pid=71619. [8 June 2012]

(2013). 'Statement by Debbie Schafer, DA Shadow Deputy Minister of Justice and Constitutional Development, asserts that the Sexual Offences Courts must be an urgent priority following rape incident in Bredasdorp'. Available at: www.polity.org.za/article/da-statement-by-debbie-schafer-da-shadow-deputy-minister-of-justice-and-constitutional-development-asserts-that-the-sexual-offences-courts-must-be-an-urgent-priority-following-rape-incident-in-bredasdorp-10022013-2013-02-11 [10 February 2013]

Schlichte, Klaus (2005). *The Dynamics of States: The Formation and Crises of State Domination*. Aldershot, Hants, England, Burlington: Ashgate.

Schönteich, Martin (2001). *Lawyers for the People. The South African Prosecution Service*. Monograph 53. Pretoria: Institute for Security Studies.

(2002). 'Court Room Warriors for Justice: History of the South African Prosecution Service'. *Journal for Contemporary History* 27(3): 82–104.

(2009). 'Moratorium on Crime Figures'. Available at: hsf.org.za/resource-centre/focus/issue-19-third-quarter-2000/moratorium-on-crime-figures [12 April 2011]

Shaw, Mark (2002). *Crime and Policing in Post-apartheid South Africa: Transforming under Fire*. Bloomington, IN: Indiana University Press.

Shore, Chris (2008). 'Audit Culture and Illiberal Governance: Universities and the Politics of Accountability'. *Anthropological Theory* 8(3): 278–298.

(2010). 'Beyond the Multiversity: Neoliberalism and the Rise of the Schizophrenic University'. *Social Anthropology* 18(1): 15–29.

Shore, Chris and Susan Wright (1999). 'Audit Culture and Anthropology: Neo-Liberalism in British Higher Education'. *The Journal of the Royal Anthropological Institute* 5(4): 557–575.

(1997). *Anthropology of Policy: Critical Perspectives on Governance and Power*. London, New York: Routledge.

Shore, Chris, Susan Wright and Davide Pero (2011). *Policy Worlds: Anthropology and the Analysis of Contemporary Power*. New York: Berghahn Books.

'Simelane backs down on prosecutor demotions' (6 April 2010). *Mail & Guardian*. Available at: mg.co.za/article/2010-04-06-simelane-backs-down-on-prosecutor-demotions [5 August 2013]

Simelane, Menzi (2010). *Presentation of the NPA Strategic Plan 2016 and Annual Plan 2011*. Director of Public Prosecution. Justice Portfolio Committee.

Sinclair, Amanda (1995). 'The Chameleon of Accountability – Forms and Discourses'. *Accounting Organizations and Society* 20(2–3): 219–237.

Smillie, Shaun (17 August 2008). 'Inside the mind of a robber'. *IOL*. Available at: www.iol.co.za/news/south-africa/inside-the-mind-of-a-robber-1.408670?ot=inmsa.ArticlePrintPageLayout.ot [1 September 2008]

South African Law Commission (2000). *Conviction Rates and Other Outcomes of Crime Reported in Eight South Africa Police Areas*. Project 82. Research Paper 18: 1–29.

Star, Susan Leigh (1999). 'The Ethnography of Infrastructure'. *American Behavioral Scientist* 43(3): 377–391.

Steinberg, Jonny (2001). *Crime Wave: The South African Underworld and Its Foes*. Johannesburg: Wits University Press.

Stinchcombe, Arthur (2001). *When Formality Works: Authority and Abstraction in Law and Organizations*. Chicago: Chicago University Press.

Strannegård, Lars and Maria Friberg (2001). *Already Elsewhere. Play, Identity, and Speed in the Business World*. Stockholm: Raster Förlag.

Strathern, Marilyn (2000a). *Audit Cultures: Anthropological Studies in Accountability, Ethics, and the Academy*. London, New York: Routledge.

(2000b). 'The Tyranny of Transparency'. *British Educational Research Journal* 26(3): 309–321.

Thamm, Marianne (14 July 2016). 'Op-Ed: Time for Specialised Sexual Offences Courts to become a reality'. *Daily Maverick*. Available at: www.dailymaverick.co.za/article/2016-07-14-op-ed-time-for-specialised-sexual-offences-courts-to-become-a-reality/#.Wz87mq35xMN [5 July 2018]

'The case for police reform' (21 March 1987). Available at: 152.111.1.87/argief/berigte/dieburger/1987/03/21/5/1.html [21 March 2012]

Thomas, Robert J. (1993). 'Interviewing Important People in Big Companies'. *Journal of Contemporary Ethnography* 22(1): 80–96.

'Three unions shelve strike for talks' (2 August 1999). *IOL*. Available at: www.iol.co.za/news/south-africa/three-unions-shelve-strike-for-talks-1.7888#.U-I7DBY8hd0 [21 March 2012]

Timmermans, Stefan and Marc Berg (2003). *The Gold Standard: The Challenge of Evidence-Based Medicine and Standardization in Health Care*. Philadelphia, PA: Temple University Press.

Timmermans, Stefan and Steven Epstein (2010). 'A World of Standards but Not a Standard World: Toward a Sociology of Standards and Standardization'. *Annual Review of Sociology* 36(1): 69–89.

Tonry, Michael H. (2012a). *Prosecutors and Politics: A Comparative Perspective*. Chicago, London: The University of Chicago Press.

(2012b). 'Preface'. *Crime and Justice* 41(1): iii–vi.

Truth and Reconciliation Commission (2003). *Holding the State Accountable* 6, Section 5, Chapter 2. Available at: www.justice.gov.za/trc/report/index .htm [5 August 2012]

Tshehla, Boyathe J. (2001). Non-state Ordering in the Post-Apartheid South Africa – A Study of Some Structures of Non-State Ordering in the Western Cape Province. Master of Laws, Thesis, Law Department, University of Cape Town.

Tsoukas, Haridimos (1997). 'The Tyranny of Light: The temptations and the Paradoxes of the Information Society'. *Futures* 29(9): 827–843.

UN (1990). *Guidelines on the Role of Prosecutors Adopted by the Eighth United Nations Congress on the Prevention of Crime and the Treatment of Offenders, Havana, Cuba.*

UN (2007). *Accountability and the United Nations System, Policy Brief No. 8.* Written by Michael Fowler and Sumihiro Kuyama, United Nations University.

Underhill, Glynnis (20 August 2015). 'NPA realigment, step 2: Willie Hofmeyr out of Asset Forfeiture Unit'. *Daily Maverick*. Available at: www .dailymaverick.co.za/article/2015-08-20-npa-realignment-step-2-willie-hofmeyr-out-of-asset-forfeiture-unit/#.WzzcxK35yjQ [25 May 2018]

Van de Walle, Steven (2008). 'What Services Are Public? What Aspects of Performance Are to Be Ranked? The Case of "Services of General Interest"'. *International Public Management Journal* 11(3):256–274.

Von Benda-Beckmann, Franz, Keebet von Benda-Beckmann and Anne Griffiths (2005). *Mobile People, Mobile Law. Expanding Legal Relations in a Contracting World.* Aldershot: Ashgate.

Von Benda-Beckmann, Keebet (1981). 'Forum Shopping and Shopping Forums: Dispute Processing in a Minangkabau Village in West Summatra'. *Journal of Legal Pluralism and Unofficial Law* 19: 117–159.

Von der Spuy, Elrena (2005). 'International Assistance and Focal Pressures in the Reform of Policing: The Case of the Eastern Cape'. *South African Review of Sociology* 36(2): 191–207.

Von Dornum, Deirdre (1997). 'The Straight and the Crooked: Legal Accountability in Ancient Greece'. *Columbia Law Review* 97(5): 1483–1518.

Vormbusch, Uwe (2007). 'Stichwort: Die Herrschaft der Zahlen (1)'. *WestEnd Neue Zeitschrift für Sozialforschung* 4. Jg (Heft 2): 57–63.

(2008). 'Von der Buchhaltung der Dinge zur Kalkulation des Immateriellen. Zahlenbasierte Steuerung im Wissenskapitalismus'. *WestEnd Neue Zeitschrift für Sozialforschung* 5 Jg. (Heft 1): 87–101.

Weick, Karl E., Kathleen M. Sutcliffe and David Obstfeld (2005). 'Organizing and the Process of Sensemaking'. *Organization Science* 16(4): 409–421.

West, Martin (1982). 'From Pass Courts to Deportation: Changing Patterns of Influx Control in Cape Town'. *African Affairs* 81(325): 463–477.

Whyte, William F. (1993). *Street Corner Society: The Social Structure of an Italian Slum*. Chicago: University of Chicago Press.

Wilson, Richard A. (2000). 'Reconciliation and Revenge in Post-Apartheid South Africa: Rethinking Legal Pluralism and Human Rights'. *Current Anthropology* 41(1): 75–98.

Witten, Jade (24 July 2009). 'State prosecutors in peaceful pickets'. *IOL*. Available at: www.iol.co.za/news/south-africa/state-prosecutors-in-peaceful-pickets-1.450872#.U-I8JhY8hd0 [5 May 2011]

Wolpe, Harold (1972). 'Capitalism and Cheap Labour-power in South Africa: From Segregation to Apartheid'. *Economy and Society* 1(4): 425–456.

Worden, Nigel (2012). *The Making of Modern South Africa: Conquest, Apartheid, Democracy*. Chichester, West Sussex, Malden, MA: Wiley-Blackwell.

Zinn, Rudolph (2010). *Home Invasion: Robbers Disclose What You Should Know*. Cape Town, Pretoria: Tafelberg.

INDEX

Abrahams, Shaun, 19, 41, 48, 141
access *See* ethnography
accountability
  alternative expressions of, 16, 77–91, 117
  and South African public, 17, 138, 140–142
  attribution of, 163
  avoidance of, 48, 172
  constituencies, 15, 46, 140–142
  def. of concept, 2, 46, 117
  demand for and demonstration of, 1, 11, 140
  increase in quantitative *See* quantitative accountability
  internal and external, 17, 76, 118–127, 149, 151, 161–164, 168
  lack of, 19, 31, 46, 141
  management accounting, 76, 127
  public, 17, 51, 141–142
  understanding of, 2, 90, 117, 127, 138, 140–142, 164, 167
  web of, 46
affirmative action policies, 34, 112
African jurisprudence, 52
alternative dispute resolution, 42, 63, 74, 86, 124, 167
  effect on performance, 142
Anders, Gerhard, 9
ANDPP v DA, 48
ANDPP v DA (1170/2016), 19, 48
anthropology of the state
  criminal justice actors, 9
  ethnographies of disciplinary, regulatory and enforcement practices, 6
  ethnographies of public bureaucracies / African state apparatuses, 6, 9, 71–72, 172–173
  margins of the state, 6
Apartheid
  abuse of law and state power, 6–7, 25–31
  classification, 12
  criminalisation of everyday life, 25–28
  criminalisation of political life, 28–31
Asset Forfeiture Unit, 38
Attorney-General, 24–25, 29, 32, 34
audit culture, 2
audit mentality, 3–4, 17, 86–90, 115
audit society, 2, 151
auditable self, 3, 5, 17, 91
Auditor-General, 44
authority of law, 90, 114

backlog, 74, 95, 99, 103, 124–125
bail, 21, 110, 162
Bantustan, 26
Batho Pele, 86
Bierschenk, Thomas, 5–6, 9, 52
Biko, Steve, 30
Boström, Magnus, 46
Bowker, Geoffrey, 11–12
Breytenbach, Glynnis, 18, 126
budget, 38, 40, 42, 110–111, 154, 172–173
Buur, Lars, 8

case load, 19, 49, 72, 108, 119, 124, 135, 156, 172
cases
  cherry-picking, 78, 104
  classification of, 104, 170
  complexity of, 19, 137, 160
  high-profile, 18, 38, 49, 126
  petty, 36, 47, 104, 128–129
  postponement of, 51, 74, 78–79, 89, 99, 103, 120, 137
  resource allocation, 49, 172
  type of offences, 19
categories of similarities, 11
Certification of the Constitution of the Republic of South Africa, 33
classification, 11–12
clerks, 36
Comaroff, Jean, 9, 52
Comaroff, John, x, 9, 52
commensurability, 11–12
Commissioners' Courts, 27
compensation orders, 89
confiscation orders, 19
Constitution of the Republic of South Africa 1996, 16, 21, 32
Constitutional Court, 33, 37, 40, 48

conviction rate
  alternative calculation method, 144–145
  and media, 77, 142
  Crime Information Analysis Centre (CIAC), 44
  critic on NPA calculation method, 97, 141, 142–145, 147, 151
  managers' reflection on NPA, 17, 152
  role in prosecutors' work life, 134, 142, 168
  South African Police Service (SAPS), 142
corruption, 18, 38, 52, 125, 126
court hours, 42, 103, 109, 129, 135–136
court management statistics, 42, 108
court management unit, 42, 108
court proceedings
  control of, 135
courtesy, 85–86, 98
courts
  infrastructure, 102
  jurisdiction, 104
  under-performing, 109
crime
  economic, 38, 46
  perceived growth of, 41
  political violence and, 12
  rates, 57, 58, 82, 153
crime control, 39
Crime Information Analysis Centre (CIAC), 44
crime prevention, viii, 8, 51, 82–83, 128, 131
criminal justice system, viii, 7, 8, 17, 21, 49, 72, 143–146, 162, 170–173
Criminal Procedure Act of 1977, 25, 104

Das, Veena, 6
Davis, Dennis, 7, 29, 30, 141
de Lange, Johnny, 159
de Lille, Patricia, 47
de Sardan, Jean-Pierre, Olivier, 5, 52
de Vos, Pierre, 18, 40
decision-making, 1, 10–14, 19–21, 25, 32–34, 44–47, 87, 103, 118, 127, 137, 148–151, 168–170
Democratic Alliance (DA), 48, 141, 144
Democratic Alliance v The President of the RSA & Others, 48
Department of Justice and Constitutional Development, 34, 102, 111, 144
Desrosières, Alain, 4
Director of Public Prosecution (DPP), 19
Directorate for Priority Crime Investigation (DPCI), 40
Directorate of Special Operations (DSO), 38–41, 46–48, 56, 72
  disbandment, 40, 48
discretion, 10–16, 92, 98, 114, 160, 164–167
distrust in experts, 10
diversion rate, 129
domestic violence, 21, 58, 82–88, 113, 153
due process, 28, 97, 102, 170
Dutch East India Company, 22, 36

Eckert, Julia, x
economic control, 17, 122
Economic Freedom Fighters (EFF), 48
Employment Equity Act of 1998, 34
Espeland, Wendy, x, 4, 13, 14, 93, 163
ethnography
  access to lower courts, viii, 59–65
  access to NPA management, 67–70
  access to prosecutors, viii
  confidentiality agreement, 53
  distributed knowledge, 64
  field sites, 15, 51, 53
  gaining credibility, 70
  gaining trust, 65, 69
  mobility and simultaneity, 71
  NPA organogram, 68
  research participants, 54
  stationary fieldwork and mobile methods, 54, 71
  studying experts, 65–67, 70
evidence based governance, 43

fear of numbers, 4, 92, 101, 114–115, 165
feeling of safety, 148
Fernandez, Lovell, 31, 37
fiskaal, 22–23, 36
formalizing practices, 14, 157
forum-shopping, 88

gaming, 14, 90, 103, 104, 141, 146, 165
Garsten, Christina, 46
Ginwala inquiry, 48
Glenister v President of the Republic of South Africa and Others, 40
Gordhan, Pravin, 18
Group Areas Act of 1950, 25

Haggerty, Kevin, 141, 152–155
Hannerz, Ulf, 69
Hawks, 41 *See* Directorate for Policy Crime Investigation (DCPI)
Heintz, Bettina, 11
Helen Suzman Foundation v President of the Republic of South Africa and Others, 41
history of prosecution services in South Africa
  between 1948 and 1994, 25–31
  prior 1948, 22–23, 25
Hoexter commission, 37
Hofmeyr, Willie, 39

Immorality Act of 1950, 26
influx control, 25–26

Jensen, Steffen, 8
justice
 access to, 24, 82–85
 cluster and division of labour, 41, 130, 137, 150, 172
 community, 131
 cost of / price of, 49, 86, 87, 173
 delivery of, 97–98
 doing and ensuring, 85–90
 ethics of, 130, 172–173
 ideals of, ix, 81, 91
 lack of, viii, 24, 51, 140, 144, 162
 legal costs, 48–49, 173
 measuring, 97, 132, 173
 notions of, 6
 proxy for, 16
 quantification of, 3, 95–97, 136, 173
 time, 98, 100
 time pressure, 52, 172

Kalthoff, Herbert, 14
Klug, Heinz, 27

Lampland, Martha, 4, 14, 157–158
Law School Admission Test (LSAT), 94, 104
Law, John, 14
Law, Organization, Science and Technology (LOST), ix
Le, Roux, Michelle, 7, 29, 30, 141
legal accountability, 31, 48, 81, 141, 162, 167
legal assistants, 36
legal equality, 12, 18, 24, 102
legal review, 18, 48, 49, 141
legitimacy, 97, 132, 141, 153
liability *See* legal accountability
litigator, 85, 167
lower courts, 49, 72

magistrate, 36–37, 83
magistrate court, 19
maintenance disputes, 83
managers
 def. of NPA, 118
Mandela, Nelson, 28
Mandonsela, Thuli, 49
Marks, Monique, 8
Max-Planck Institute for Foreign and International Criminal Law, 69
Max-Planck Institute for Social Anthropology, ix, x
Mbeki, Thabo, 49, 159
Mdluli, Richard, 18, 64, 126
mechanical objectivity, 10, 108, 167
media, 18, 39, 41, 49, 65, 72, 77, 123, 142, 167
mediation, 74, 85–90
Medium Term Expenditure Framework (MTEF), 42
meetings, 55, 75, 78, 82, 100, 118, 127, 168
Merry, Sally Engle, x, 4, 13, 43, 50, 71, 92
Minister of Police, 41
Mpshe, Mokotedi, 18, 47–48
multi-site ethnography *See* ethnography
multi-sited fieldwork *See* ethnography
multi-local organisation, 50

National Director of Public Prosecution (NDPP), 18, 24, 48, 65, 109, 110, 118, 124, 126, 141
 appointment procedure, 32, 48
 independence and political interference, 17–20, 33, 46–49, 141
National Prosecuting Authority
 concern over accountability and independence, 17
 establishment, 7, 32–33
 responsibility, 147
 working morale, 72
National Prosecuting Authority Act of 1998, 21, 32, 38
Nationalist Party, 25–26
neoliberalism, 151
new public management, 43, 151
Ngcuka, Bulelani, 18, 34
NPA Aspirant Prosecutor Programme, 36
number of decision dockets, 42
number of finalised cases, 42, 74, 123–126
number of outstanding cases, 42, 74, 79, 108, 123–126
number of protection orders, 83–84
number of received dockets, 42
numbers
 accuracy, 141, 155
 aggregated data, 75
 as thinking device, 155–161
 constructedness and constructiveness, 118, 132, 146, 163, 169
 cost of, 12, 43, 133
 counts, ratios and composites, 43
 discipline, 3–4, 17, 101, 169
 doing of, 1, 13, 17, 157, 171
 expert systems, 3
 false and provisional, 158
 information reductionism, 3
 infrastructure, 12
 limits and shortcomings, 114, 138, 168
 list of / technical specification, 12
 managing with, 75, 127–138
 misleading and creative, 17, 144–145, 161, 171
 misrepresentation and simplification through, 3, 92–97, 133–138, 164

mistrust in, 171
politics of, 141, 152–154, 171
power of, 4, 10–11, 77, 114, 117, 153, 163, 168–171
pressure of, 16, 95–96
production of, 11
public and non-public, 105, 170
purpose of, 1, 4, 11, 152–161, 172
technologies of distance and persuasion, 10
trust in, 10, 171
numeracy, 118, 162–163
numerical reflexivity, 17, 114, 127–138, 161, 168–169

objectivity, 10, 138
Occupation specific dispensation for legally qualified professionals (OSD), 111
occupational classification system, 36
Office of Race Classification, 25
Orr, Wendy, 31

Parliamentary Committee on Justice and Correctional Services, 36, 124, 126, 150
Pass laws, 7, 24–28
performance
agreement, 109, 136
Annual Plan, 42, 144
Annual Report, 39, 143, 147
cluster efficiency rate, 43
establishment of court management unit, 42
history of court management statistics, 42
indicators, 1, 42, 132–133, 142, 147
information, 118, 130, 171
monthly statistical sheet, 74
national aggregate figures, 43, 105
National Prosecuting Services (NPS), 42, 74
rankings, 90, 105–106
rates, 1, 142
statistics, x, 1, 128, 135, 138
targets, 1, 109, 149, 167
performance measurement
and the public, 141
performance measurement system
design of, 135, 147
effects on academia, 92, 166
effects on US higher legal education, 13–14, 93–96, 101, 163
general critique, 3–4
genesis of NPA, 15, 41–45
infrastructure for NPA, 43
lack of statistics, 44, 107
police, 166
prosecutors' reaction and attitude towards NPA, 16, 76, 95–102, 146–151
purpose and use of NPA, 42
resentment towards, 93
role in prosecutors' work life, 73–77
sanctions, 100, 106–107, 115, 133, 171
Pikoli, Vusi, 48
Population Registration Act of 1950, 25
Porter, Theodore, x, 4, 10–11, 146, 167
Power, Michael, 2–3, 44
Prevention of Organised Crime Act of 1998 (POCA), 39
professionalism, 3, 35–41, 81, 90
promotion, 9, 34, 38, 107, 112–115, 133–137
prosecutors
abuse of power during Apartheid, 18, 24–31
as apartheid administrators, 7
career and career pathing, 37–38, 111, 133–138
code of conduct, 36, 79, 90
competition, 36, 107, 114
distrust during Apartheid, 25, 34
independence and accountability, 21–23
independence and political interference, 46–49, 72
occupational identity of the profession and pride, 78, 88, 98, 105, 133, 167
power of, 1, 7, 14, 21–22
prosecution figures during Apartheid, 27
reputational control, 85, 91, 115, 138
staff fluctuation, 37
status and image of, 36–40, 171
tasks and responsibilities, 16–17, 21–22, 24, 76–77, 88, 98, 135, 150, 162
training, qualification and skill, 35–38, 83, 135, 140
work morale, 113
Public Finance Management Act of 1999 (PFMA), 9, 41–43, 90, 132, 170

quality and quantity, 4, 5, 78, 84–90, 96–100, 114, 132–133, 169
quality control, 84–85, 97, 127, 159–160, 167
quantification
formalizing practices, 14
law, 90, 105, 114
tradition, 16, 105, 114, 170
quantification and translation chains *Siehe* quantification / tradition
quantitative accountability
demand for, 1–3, 147, 164, 172
effects on prosecutorial work practices, 1, 16, 76–90, 138, 141, 168, 172
effects on understanding and practices of accountability of professionals, 2–4, 10–13, 169
general critique, 9
professionals' attitude towards, 92–94

race, 26, 46, 102
racial segregation, 25
racism, ix, 46, 57, 85, 107
Ramaphosa, Cyril, 49
rankings
  multiple, 163
rape conviction rate, 142–143, 154
rationalisation, 14
reactivity, 3–4, 92, 105
recidivism rate, 130
Redpath, Jean, 32–33, 140
referral rate, 157
regional court, 19
remuneration
  history of performance based, 107–114
  performance based bonuses, 137, 171
  performance based salaries, 171
  salary negotiations, 102, 109
  strike action, 109, 111
representation, 33–35, 46
Research Assessment Exercise (RAE), 92, 101
resistance movement, 25
resource allocation, 14, 16, 101, 108, 133, 137, 170
  academia, 92
  competition and, 102–106
  NPA and DOJCD, 102–106
Rivonia trials, 28
Rottenburg, Richard, ix, x, 9, 14

S v Shaik and Others, 47
Sauder, Michael, 4, 13–14, 93, 163
Schaefer, Debbie, 144
Schönteich, Martin, 38, 107–110
Science & Technology Studies
  production and communication of numbers, 11
Scorpions *See* Directorate of Special Operations (DSO)
Selebi, Jackie, 46
sensemaking, 119–123, 141, 155–161, 171
separation of powers, 25, 32–33, 38, 45–46, 141
service delivery, 4, 41, 81, 85–90, 108
Sexual Offences Court, 143
shadowing, 54, 82–83
Shaik, Shabir, 18, 47
Shore, Chris, 2–3, 101, 151
Simelane, Menzi, 41, 48, 118
social studies of numbers, 9–14
South Africa's Black Consciousness Movement, 30
South African Criminal Procedure Act of 1998, 16, 79, 85
South African Exchequer and Audit Act of 1975, 44
South African Law Commission, 141, 144, 162
South African Police Service (SAPS), viii
  abuse of police power during Apartheid, 29–31
  brutality, 8
  organisational transformation after 1994, 7–8, 79
South African Students' Organisation (SASO), 30
Special Investigating Units, 38, 40, 46
Specialised Commercial Crime Unit, 18
Star, Susan Leigh, 11–12
state capture, 19
State of Capture' report, 49
Stevens, Mitchell, 13
Strathern, Marylin, 2–3, 92, 165
studying-up *See* ethnography
Supreme Court of Appeal, 19, 28, 48, 141

Terrorism Act of 1967, 30
The General Law Amendment Act of 1963, 30
traditional courts, 97
transparency, 3, 17, 147
trials, 78, 142, 144, 167
Trust in Numbers, 10
Truth and Reconciliation Commission, 7, 12, 30, 190

U.S American Federal Sentencing Guidelines, 105
University of Cape Town, viii
USN Law School Ranking, 13–14, 93, 163
  power of, 93–94
  resource allocation, 101

violence, 8, 57
  police brutality, 8, 31
violence against women, 82, 88, 140, 162
von Benda-Beckmann, Keebet, ix, 88
Vormbusch, Uwe, 105, 169

warrants, 22
Weick, Karl, 155–156
West, Martin, 27–28
Westwood Insurance Brokers (Pty) Ltd v Ethekwini Local Municipality and Others, 49
withdrawal rate, 74, 87, 95
Wright, Susan, 2–3, 101, 151

Yengeni, Toni, 46
Yutar, Percy, 29

Zinn, Rudolph, 142
Zuma v DA (771/2016), 19, 48
Zuma, Jacob, 17–20, 47–49, 126, 141, 172–173

CAMBRIDGE STUDIES IN LAW AND SOCIETY

Books in the Series

Diseases of the Will: Alcohol and the Dilemmas of Freedom
Mariana Valverde

The Politics of Truth and Reconciliation in South Africa: Legitimizing the Post-Apartheid State
Richard A. Wilson

Modernism and the Grounds of Law
Peter Fitzpatrick

Unemployment and Government: Genealogies of the Social
William Walters

Autonomy and Ethnicity: Negotiating Competing Claims in Multi-Ethnic States
Yash Ghai

Constituting Democracy: Law, Globalism and South Africa's Political Reconstruction
Heinz Klug

The Ritual of Rights in Japan: Law, Society, and Health Policy
Eric A. Feldman

Governing Morals: A Social History of Moral Regulation
Alan Hunt

The Colonies of Law: Colonialism, Zionism and Law in Early Mandate Palestine
Ronen Shamir

Law and Nature
David Delaney

Social Citizenship and Workfare in the United States and Western Europe: The Paradox of Inclusion
Joel F. Handler

Law, Anthropology, and the Constitution of the Social: Making Persons and Things
Edited by Alain Pottage and Martha Mundy

Judicial Review and Bureaucratic Impact: International and Interdisciplinary Perspectives
Edited by Marc Hertogh and Simon Halliday

Immigrants at the Margins: Law, Race, and Exclusion in Southern Europe
Kitty Calavita

Lawyers and Regulation: The Politics of the Administrative Process
Patrick Schmidt

Law and Globalization from Below: Toward a Cosmopolitan Legality
Edited by Boaventura de Sousa Santos and Cesar A. Rodriguez-Garavito

Public Accountability: Designs, Dilemmas and Experiences
Edited by Michael W. Dowdle

Law, Violence and Sovereignty among West Bank Palestinians
Tobias Kelly

Legal Reform and Administrative Detention Powers in China
Sarah Biddulph

The Practice of Human Rights: Tracking Law between the Global and the Local
Edited by Mark Goodale and Sally Engle Merry

Judges beyond Politics in Democracy and Dictatorship: Lessons from Chile
Lisa Hilbink

Paths to International Justice: Social and Legal Perspectives
Edited by Marie-Bénédicte Dembour and Tobias Kelly

Law and Society in Vietnam: The Transition from Socialism in Comparative Perspective
Mark Sidel

Constitutionalizing Economic Globalization: Investment Rules and Democracy's Promise
David Schneiderman

The New World Trade Organization Knowledge Agreements: 2nd Edition
Christopher Arup

Justice and Reconciliation in Post-Apartheid South Africa
Edited by François du Bois and Antje du Bois-Pedain

Militarization and Violence against Women in Conflict Zones in the Middle East: A Palestinian Case-Study
Nadera Shalhoub-Kevorkian

Child Pornography and Sexual Grooming: Legal and Societal Responses
Suzanne Ost

Darfur and the Crime of Genocide
John Hagan and Wenona Rymond-Richmond

Fictions of Justice: The International Criminal Court and the Challenge of Legal Pluralism in Sub-Saharan Africa
Kamari Maxine Clarke

Conducting Law and Society Research: Reflections on Methods and Practices
Simon Halliday and Patrick Schmidt

Planted Flags: Trees, Land, and Law in Israel/Palestine
Irus Braverman

Culture under Cross-Examination: International Justice and the Special Court for Sierra Leone
Tim Kelsall

Cultures of Legality: Judicialization and Political Activism in Latin America
Javier Couso, Alexandra Huneeus, and Rachel Sieder

Courting Democracy in Bosnia and Herzegovina: The Hague Tribunal's Impact in a Postwar State
Lara J. Nettelfield

The Gacaca Courts, Post-Genocide Justice and Reconciliation in Rwanda: Justice without Lawyers
Phil Clark

Law, Society, and History: Themes in the Legal Sociology and Legal History of Lawrence M. Friedman
Edited by Robert W. Gordon and Morton J. Horwitz

After Abu Ghraib: Exploring Human Rights in America and the Middle East
Shadi Mokhtari

Adjudication in Religious Family Laws: Cultural Accommodation, Legal Pluralism, and Gender Equality in India
Gopika Solanki

Water on Tap: Rights and Regulation in the Transnational Governance of Urban Water Services
Bronwen Morgan

Elements of Moral Cognition: Rawls' Linguistic Analogy and the Cognitive Science of Moral and Legal Judgment
John Mikhail

Mitigation and Aggravation at Sentencing
Edited by Julian V. Roberts

Institutional Inequality and the Mobilization of the Family and Medical Leave Act: Rights on Leave
Catherine R. Albiston

Authoritarian Rule of Law: Legislation, Discourse and Legitimacy in Singapore
Jothie Rajah

Law and Development and the Global Discourses of Legal Transfers
Edited by John Gillespie and Pip Nicholson

Law against the State: Ethnographic Forays into Law's Transformations
Edited by Julia Eckert, Brian Donahoe, Christian Strümpell and Zerrin Özlem Biner

Transnational Legal Ordering and State Change
Edited by Gregory C. Shaffer

Legal Mobilization under Authoritarianism: The Case of Post-Colonial Hong Kong
Waikeung Tam

Complementarity in the Line of Fire: The Catalysing Effect of the International Criminal Court in Uganda and Sudan
Sarah M. H. Nouwen

Political and Legal Transformations of an Indonesian Polity: The Nagari from Colonisation to Decentralisation
Franz von Benda-Beckmann and Keebet von Benda-Beckmann

Pakistan's Experience with Formal Law: An Alien Justice
Osama Siddique

Human Rights under State-Enforced Religious Family Laws in Israel, Egypt, and India
Yüksel Sezgin

Why Prison?
Edited by David Scott

Law's Fragile State: Colonial, Authoritarian, and Humanitarian Legacies in Sudan
Mark Fathi Massoud

Rights for Others: The Slow Home-Coming of Human Rights in the Netherlands
Barbara Oomen

European States and Their Muslim Citizens: The Impact of Institutions on Perceptions and Boundaries
Edited by John R. Bowen, Christophe Bertossi, Jan Willem Duyvendak, and Mona Lena Krook

Environmental Litigation in China: A Study in Political Ambivalence
Rachel E. Stern

Indigeneity and Legal Pluralism in India: Claims, Histories, Meanings
Pooja Parmar

Paper Tiger: Law, Bureaucracy and the Developmental State in Himalayan India
Nayanika Mathur

Religion, Law and Society
Russell Sandberg

The Experiences of Face Veil Wearers in Europe and the Law
Edited by Eva Brems

The Contentious History of the International Bill of Human Rights
Christopher N. J. Roberts

Transnational Legal Orders
Edited by Terence C. Halliday and Gregory Shaffer

Lost in China? Law, Culture and Society in Post-1997 Hong Kong
Carol A. G. Jones

Security Theology, Surveillance and the Politics of Fear
Nadera Shalhoub-Kevorkian

Opposing the Rule of Law: How Myanmar's Courts Make Law and Order
Nick Cheesman

The Ironies of Colonial Governance: Law, Custom and Justice in Colonial India
James Jaffe

The Clinic and the Court: Law, Medicine and Anthropology
Edited by Ian Harper, Tobias Kelly, and Akshay Khanna

A World of Indicators: The Making of Government Knowledge through Quantification
Edited by Richard Rottenburg, Sally Engle Merry, Sung-Joon Park, and Johanna Mugler

Contesting Immigration Policy in Court: Legal Activism and Its Radiating Effects in the United States and France
Leila Kawar

The Quiet Power of Indicators: Measuring Governance, Corruption, and Rule of Law
Edited by Sally Engle Merry, Kevin Davis, and Benedict Kingsbury

Investing in Authoritarian Rule: Punishment and Patronage in Rwanda's Gacaca Courts for Genocide Crimes
Anuradha Chakravarty

Contractual Knowledge: One Hundred Years of Legal Experimentation in Global Markets
Edited by Grégoire Mallard and Jérôme Sgard

Iraq and the Crimes of Aggressive War: The Legal Cynicism of Criminal Militarism
John Hagan, Joshua Kaiser, and Anna Hanson

Culture in the Domains of Law
Edited by René Provost

China and Islam: The Prophet, the Party, and Law
Matthew S. Erie

Diversity in Practice: Race, Gender, and Class in Legal and Professional Careers
Edited by Spencer Headworth and Robert Nelson

A Sociology of Constitutions: Constitutions and State Legitimacy in Historical-Sociological Perspective
Chris Thornhill

A Sociology of Transnational Constitutions: Social Foundations of the Post-National Legal Structure
Chris Thornhill

Shifting Legal Visions: Judicial Change and Human Rights Trials in Latin America
Ezequiel A. González Ocantos

The Demographic Transformations of Citizenship
Heli Askola

Criminal Defense in China: The Politics of Lawyers at Work
Sida Liu and Terence C. Halliday

Contesting Economic and Social Rights in Ireland: Constitution, State and Society, 1848–2016
Thomas Murray

Buried in the Heart: Women, Complex Victimhood and the War in Northern Uganda
Erin Baines

Palaces of Hope: The Anthropology of Global Organizations
Edited by Ronald Niezen and Maria Sapignoli

The Politics of Bureaucratic Corruption in Post-Transitional Eastern Europe
Marina Zaloznaya

Revisiting the Law and Governance of Trafficking, Forced Labor and Modern Slavery
Edited by Prabha Kotiswaran

Incitement on Trial: Prosecuting International Speech Crimes
Richard Ashby Wilson

Criminalizing Children: Welfare and the State in Australia
David McCallum

Global Lawmakers: International Organizations in the Crafting of World Markets
Susan Block-Lieb and Terence C. Halliday

Duties to Care: Dementia, Relationality and Law
Rosie Harding

Insiders, Outsiders, Injuries, and Law: Revisiting 'The Oven Bird's Song'
Edited by Mary Nell Trautner

Hunting Justice: Displacement, Law, and Activism in the Kalahari
Maria Sapignoli

Injury and Injustice: The Cultural Politics of Harm and Redress
Edited by Anne Bloom, David M. Engel, and Michael McCann

Ruling before the Law: The Politics of Legal Regimes in China and Indonesia
William Hurst

The Powers of Law: A Comparative Analysis of Sociopolitical Legal Studies
Mauricio García-Villegas

A Sociology of Justice in Russia
Edited by Marina Kurkchiyan and Agnieszka Kubal

Constituting Religion: Islam, Liberal Rights, and the Malaysian State
Tamir Moustafa

The Invention of the Passport: Surveillance, Citizenship and the State, Second Edition
John C. Torpey

Law's Trials: The Performance of Legal Institutions in the US 'War on Terror'
Richard L. Abel

Law's Wars: The Fate of the Rule of Law in the US 'War on Terror'
Richard L. Abel

Transforming Gender Citizenship: The Irresistible Rise of Gender Quotas in Europe
Edited by Eléonore Lépinard and Ruth Rubio-Marín

Muslim Women's Quest for Justice: Gender, Law and Activism in India
Mengia Hong Tschalaer

Children as 'Risk': Sexual Exploitation and Abuse by Children and Young People
Anne-Marie McAlinden

The Legal Process and the Promise of Justice: Studies Inspired by the Work of Malcolm Feeley
Jonathan Simon, Rosann Greenspan, Hadar Aviram

Sovereign Exchanges: Gifts, Trusts, Reparations, and Other Fetishes of International Solidarity
Grégoire Mallard

Measuring Justice: Quantitative Accountability and the National Prosecuting Authority in South Africa
Johanna Mugler